Estimating Output-Specific Efficiencies

Applied Optimization

Volume 64

Series Editors:

Panos M. Pardalos
University of Florida, U.S.A.

Donald Hearn
University of Florida, U.S.A.

The titles published in this series are listed at the end of this volume.

Estimating Output-Specific Efficiencies

by

Dieter Gstach

Vienna University of Economics, Austria

SPRINGER-SCIENCE+BUSINESS MEDIA, B.V.

A C.I.P. Catalogue record for this book is available from the Library of Congress.

ISBN 978-1-4613-4883-2   ISBN 978-1-4615-0007-0 (eBook)
DOI 10.1007/978-1-4615-0007-0

Printed on acid-free paper

For Aurelia with love
and gratitude

Contents

Preface

The present book is the offspring of my Habilitation, which is the key to academic tenure in Austria. Legal requirements demand that a Habilitation be published and so only seeing it in print marks the real end of this biographical landmark project. From a scientific perspective I may hope to finally reach a broader audience with this book for a critical appraisal of the research done. Aside from objectives the book is a reflection of many years of research preceding Habilitation proper in the field of efficiency measurement.

Regarding the subject matter the main intention was to fill an important remaining gap in the efficiency analysis literature. Hitherto no technique was available to estimate output-specific efficiencies in a statistically convincing way. This book closes this gap, although some desirable improvements and generalizations of the proposed estimation technique may yet be required, before it will eventually establish as standard tool for efficiency analysis.

The likely audience for this book includes professional researchers, who want to enrich their tool set for applied efficiency analysis, as well as students of economics, management science or operations research, intending to learn more about the potentials of rigorously understood efficiency analysis. But also managers or public officials potentially ordering efficiency studies should benefit from the book by learning about the extended capabilities of efficiency analysis. Just reading the introduction may change their perception of value for money when it comes to comparative performance measurement.

The prerequisites for reading this book are a basic understanding of non-parametric efficiency estimation techniques and intermediate level statistical calculus. But even without these prerequisites it is possible to read the extensive introduction, which develops the main ideas and concepts without the formal apparatus to follow.

I hope that the material presented will find interested readers who appreciate it in substance and style and I look forward to see further developments in the literature along the lines sketched in this book.

Vienna, September 7, 2001

DIETER GSTACH

Acknowledgments

I would have never been able to write this book without the massive support of Aurelia Wusch in every vital respect. She contributed beyond measure to this work and deserves as much credits for it as I do. Sylvia Frühwirth-Schnatter made most valuable suggestions in numerous discussions, which essentially gave the book it's final shape. By reading early versions and commenting critically on it Agha Iqbal Ali and Finn Førsund helped to significantly improve the book in substance. Susanne Warning had the idea for a first application of the technique and surveyed the relevant literature for me. The persistent encouragement of Thomas Grandner and Mikulas Luptacik gave me the confidence, that I could do it and do it well, whenever I doubted it. And the most productive working periods are owed to the hospitality of family Wöls, who offered perfect research conditions for my taste at the Gasthof Hubinger.

To all those mentioned: Thanks a lot!

Remaining errors and omissions are of course my sole responsibility.

I

MOTIVATING THE CONCEPT

Chapter 1

INTRODUCTION

The subject of the present work is a novel type of comparative and quantitative performance analysis of firms producing multiple outputs. Hitherto it was impossible to satisfactorily quantify differences between the efficiency in producing various goods, although modern comparative performance analysis has come a long way. So if indeed an economic sector typically produces some good A more efficiently than some good B, and we are unable to observe this directly, the application of existing estimation techniques would at best result in a suspicion about this fact. The present book attempts to remove this deficiency in the relevant literature. In practical terms the benefit from what I labeled *output-specific efficiency estimation* is thus better informed economic advice about performance improvement potentials to firms and public authorities, who eventually regulate the operating environment of these firms.

Depending on the context, purpose and the information available, various strategies have been proposed in the literature to effect comparative performance analysis. One such strategy will play an important preparatory role within the approach to be developed. But none of these strategies as such provided a statistical basis for performance analysis in a per-product-fashion. So what shall be asked in this book is the following: How much more of *each output specifically* could a firm have produced with the actually used inputs and what is the statistical confidence associated with corresponding claims ? It will be argued that performance analysis focused on these questions must not only look at the actual input/output quantities describing the production processes and compare them across firms. Rather it must also take into account further information contained in the usually poor available data about original *production targets* but so far has been left unexploited. The question of potential input savings for given amounts of outputs will not be considered here, but the logic behind the model would analogously apply to this question.

The notion of production targets plays the key role in the technique to be developed in this book. As considered here production targets are either quantities (or revenues) per product a firm plans to produce (henceforth usually called target outputs) or the ratios between the quantities (or revenues) of any two types of products a firm plans to produce (henceforth called target output ratios). Ultimately the proposed approach will rely on the latter, but it is worthwhile to study the links between these notions to clarify matters.

The probably most commonly encountered notion of production targets in business are revenues per product. It is clear that with given price expectations of a firm (a prerequisite of production and financial planning) their target revenues per product also imply certain target quantities, i.e. target outputs. The latter in turn necessarily imply certain target output ratios. So it can be argued that target output ratios, whether explicitly formulated as such or not, are also amongst common business targets. Note also, that the primary distinction here is not whether targets are formulated in revenue or quantity terms, but rather whether they are formulated in levels per product or ratios between products. It thus is immaterial from an econometric point of view, if the observed outputs with which the analyst has to deal are revenues or quantities per product. For a purely technical (rather than an economic) performance analysis quantities would suffice.

It must be emphasized that target output ratios are less informative than target outputs: Just knowing the target output ratios but not a single target output does tell nothing about the quantities a firm plans to produce (or the expected revenues). Thus the concept of target output ratios clearly is inferior compared to that of target levels in a planning perspective. But it will turn out to be extremely powerful if used in conjunction with the economists concept of *technology* in the estimation perspective of the applied analyst who wants to learn about output specific efficiencies but lacks the firms planning data.

The basic argument underlying the approach to be presented is, that target output ratios (rather than target outputs) should guide us in determining the appropriate reference point for performance comparisons, which would otherwise be either indeterminate, infeasible or inappropriate. In the numerical illustration to follow below I will therefore start off with discussing the potential role of target outputs for the purpose of comparative performance analysis. This will reveal their shortcomings and will show why target output ratios should and how they could be used for that purpose instead.

In performance analysis of non-profit organizations, it is common practice to talk about goals rather than targets, which, at least for the present purpose, is merely a semantic difference. To the extent that non-profit organizations also want to make the best use of given inputs in the sense of producing maximum quantities of outputs (or providing maximum amounts of services) and given that they operate according to goals formulated in quantity or revenue terms (whether in levels or ratios does not matter) the arguments developed here will apply as well.

It is in line with common terminology to characterize a shortfall of produced output quantities versus targeted quantities as some sort of suboptimal performance. But note that this seemingly innocuous terminology carries the implicit assumption, that firms have full control over inputs and outputs, or in other words, that no uncontrollable influences interfere with production. In specific contexts, like in agricultural production, this may be an unrealistic assumption and the use of such performance terminology somewhat ambiguous, in another context it may be well justified. Throughout this book the full-control- assumption will be maintained, but the above qualification about it's plausibility should be kept in mind.

Henceforth I will synonymously use the term *inefficiency* for the just described type of suboptimality. For the reader familiar with the literature on efficiency measurement it will turn out that the meaning of the term *efficiency* as used here is in basic accordance with the meaning in this literature. Stressing the notion of targets should not distract the reader in this regard. The present work will be solely devoted to measure the extent of such inefficiency on a quantity basis. It will neither deal with reasons for choosing specific targets nor with causes of inefficiency.

It seems like a plausible requirement for performance analysis that the analyst should take target outputs into account in one way or the other.

Accordingly serious practical problems arise if these targets are unknown to the analyst as is regularly the case. But even if the targets were known, a carefully designed performance analysis would require first to check the adequacy of these target outputs as potential reference point for comparisons. This condition would need to be checked in addition to the one given above to warrant the label *suboptimal performance* or *inefficiency* for a shortfall of realized versus targeted output quantities.

So whether known or not, the adequacy of targets outputs must be checked against a yardstick which must not be based on these target outputs themselves. Henceforth this required yardstick will be labeled *best production possibilities.* In practice information about best production possibilities is not readily available but must be generated via estimation in a separate step before eventual information about targets can be taken into account properly.

Combining this information about more general best production possibilities with knowledge about targeted output-ratios of a specific DMU yields the unique combination of output quantities which serve as proper reference point for efficiency comparisons for that DMU. This is true regardless of whether or not the targeted quantities were chosen in accordance to these best production possibilities or not. Therefore the target output quantities matter only insofar as they imply certain target output-ratios, because only the latter are needed for efficiency comparisons on a per product basis, i.e. for the determination of output-specific efficiencies. These are the quantities of ultimate interest in this book.

For practical purposes the case for output-specific efficiency estimation can be established for example by observing that the efficiency of a firms division responsible for producing one output may be quite different from the efficiency of a division for another output, while there inputs used are often hard to attribute clearly to one or the other. So in order to address the division specific performance problems one would have to treat the divisions as parts of a bigger DMU (distinguished solely via their outputs) and then describe the output-specific efficiencies of the latter.

In practice the analyst usually has only input/output data available to determine such output-specific efficiencies. Based on input/output data it is possible to generate an estimate of best production possibilities with one of various well established techniques, but as was argued above this does not suffice for determination of output specific efficiencies. So the problem remains to be analyzed how estimation of output-specific efficiencies could be effected when only realized input/output data are known but the target output-ratios of individual DMU's are unknown.

The solution offered in this book to this estimation problem is the assumption, that the analyst has at least vague ideas of how output-specific efficiencies and target output-ratios are distributed across DMU's, albeit he or she is unable to attribute specific values of these variables to each DMU. These vague ideas will be formulated as assumptions about the basic type (form) of distributions involved. The estimation of the few parameters determining these distributions will be the primary theoretical focus of this book.

As such parameters refer to population characteristics (rather than characteristics of individual DMU's) this means that the immediate purpose of applying the proposed technique is to reveal eventually systematic efficiency differences between the production of some output A and that of some other output B within a certain economic sector.[1] Reasons for such systematic differences are abundant, but include in particular differently distributed managerial talents devoted to specific production tasks. The capability of the presented approach to shed light on this issue is the main contribution of this book for practical purposes.

But as a byproduct of this estimation of population characteristics we will also get estimates of expected output specific efficiencies on a per DMU basis, for some readers possibly the most interesting feature of the proposed technique in an empirical perspective.

Numerical illustration

To illustrate the indicated problems involved in choosing a proper reference point for comparative performance analysis consider for example a firm, labeled A, producing only two outputs with various kinds of inputs. The original managerial target of firm A might have been to produce 50 units of the first output and 100 of the second for a given period. This

[1] The notion of an economic sector as used here includes the public sector as well. This is important to note, because it reflects the fact, that we will not rely on price information in any of the subsequently developed estimation models. Thus the proposed technique may as well be used to study sectors producing non-marketable outputs, for which no price information of whatever type may be available.

would imply a target output ratio of the 50:100, i.e. 0.5.[2] As mentioned, we will not deal with reasons for choosing these targets, but it is clear that these reasons will include observations on prevailing and expectations about future market conditions including prices in particular, and including the markets for outputs as well as those for inputs as both will influence overall firm profitability.

Now the actual production of firm A might lead to different quantities than were targeted. Let's say the firm produced only 49 units of the first output and 80 of the second, so it realized an output ratio of 49:80 $\simeq$ 0.61. No attempt will be made here to investigate the possible reasons for not achieving the targeted outputs. All that matters here is how to properly quantify the extent of suboptimal behaviour.

A straightforward way to measure inefficiency of the example firm would be as follows: Because the target quantity of the first output was 50 and the actually produced quantity was 49 the inefficiency in producing the first output could be calculated as the ratio of the shortcoming of 1 relative to the target of 50, i.e. 0.02 or 2%. In the same manner the inefficiency in producing the second output could be calculated, leading to a figure of 0.2 or 20%. Note that for similar prices of both outputs this implies that inefficiency in producing the first output should be of relatively little concern in revenue terms, whereas the inefficiency in producing the second output is really something to worry about.

These inefficiency figures are very informative as long as it can be assumed, that the target outputs themselves represent some sort of best possible practice, in the sense, that with the inputs actually used firm A could not have produced more of any one output without sacrificing some of the other. If on the other hand it turns out that with the same inputs the firm could have produced more of one output without sacrificing some amount of the other output, these figures do not tell much. This would be an instance where the target outputs are inadequate as reference points for performance analysis because the targeted quanti-

---

[2] This is not the only way to define an output-ratio but the most appropriate for the purpose of this illustration. Later such a ratio will be defined as quantity of one output over the sum of the quantities of all outputs or as the logit of this ratio. But it should be clear that these definitions are equivalent to the one used here in terms of information about the production structure. Note also that the number of such output-ratios needed to describe a production structure is always one less than the number of outputs. For the present illustration with two outputs therefore only one output-ratio is needed.

ties themselves do not correspond to best production possibilities, i.e. they should be considered inefficient.

Assume now that we had additional information about a firm B from the same economic sector and producing for the same markets. Assume we observed that B produced 80 units of the first and 100 of the second output with the same input quantities as firm A had used. Nothing will be said about the underlying targets of firm B and eventual discrepancies between firm B's target outputs and its actual achievements, because all that matters for the comparative performance evaluation of firm A outside the realm of speculation is what B actually did achieve.

Given the observed production of firm B the statement of a 2% inefficiency of firm A in producing the first output clearly seems overly optimistic, because firm B produced even more of the first output (and as much of the second) than A targeted to, not to talk about what A actually managed to produce. So instead of using A's targeted outputs one might consider the discrepancies between the actual output quantities of firms A and B as basis for an efficiency comparison of the above ratio type. Then the inefficiency of firm A in producing the first output would be approximately 39% vs. an unchanged 20% in producing the second output. Clearly under these circumstances the management of firm A should be more worried about the shortfall in production of the first output. Note also that the output-ratio of Firm B is 0.8, quite different from the 0.5 targeted by firm A. So whether firm B is a proper reference in evaluating A's performance is questionable, but lacking further comparison possibilities it seems like the only solid choice.

To complicate matters assume two more firms, labeled C and D, would operate in this industry and their inputs consumed and outputs produced were known. Assume that C and D would consume as much of every input as A and B do. But C would produce 50 units of the first output and 130 units of the second output, while D produced 60 of the first and 120 of the second output. So C and D both produce more of at least one output and no less of both outputs than firm A for the same amounts of inputs and thus exhibit clearly superior performance than A. But so did firm B. So the appropriate reference point for performance comparisons in analyzing firm A has become indeterminate.

Comparing the performance of firm A with those of B, C and D by calculating the ratios of quantitative shortcomings of A relative to the outputs of B, C and D on a per product basis would lead to the following pairs of inefficiency figures: 39% and 20% when compared to B, 2% and 38% when compared to C and 18% and 33% when compared to D. So each of these comparisons might lead to quite different strategies in dealing with the overall inefficiency of A, because the potential gains from devoting managerial resources to solve the performance problem are different in each case.

If the prices of the two outputs as charged by the different firms are equal across firms and if at least their ratio was known and if furthermore revenue maximization was known to be the top priority of firm A one would not necessarily have to resort to quantitative comparisons for performance analysis. Instead it would then be appropriate to evaluate the performance of A on a revenue basis by simply determining the firm producing maximum revenues and calculate the relative loss in revenues of A compared to that firm. If the ratio of the two prices were equal to 1 for example, such a comparison would yield an inefficiency of A of approximately 28% compared to each of the other firms.

But this presumption, that all firms would face the same prices for their products might be at odds with the true operating environment of these firms. Different prices for essentially the same product means, that firms, unlike under perfect competition, do have some market power due to geographical market segmentation or brand loyalty of customers or whatever. With market power and associated output price differences across firms, a performance comparison on a revenue basis, as proposed above, would require knowledge of the price levels of all outputs charged by each individual firm. This sort of information usually is not available to the analyst which brings us back to the problem of a proper choice of a reference point for performance comparisons on a quantity rather than a revenue basis.

If on the other hand penetration of the market for the first product was the top priority of firm A (or by the same token, if the price for the first output was significantly higher than for the second product) then the comparison with B would be appropriate, because B in this respect did better than any other of the observed firms with the same inputs. Analogous reasoning would lead to the conclusion, that firm C was the appropriate reference point for performance evaluation of firm A, if its top priority was penetration of the market for the second product. But usually the analyst does not know what this top managerial priority of each firm has been which precludes such potentially helpful reasoning.

Now consider yet another possibility by assuming that the original target outputs of firm A had been 80 units of the first product and 160 of the second, while actual production of firms A, B, C and D had been as described above. The target outputs of A are now more than has been practically achieved by any of the four firms under consideration, despite the fact that all of them were using the same amounts of each input. This is an instance where one should seriously question the feasibility of the targets in the first place. At least it is impossible to verify from the observed production outputs of the various firms that such targets could have possibly be met and therefore is questionable whether they correspond to best production possibilities.

Assume for the moment without further justification that the actual production of firms B,C and D rather than the target production of A is indeed indicative of such best production possibilities, although in different ways as expressed by the different proportions in which the first and the second output are being produced. This necessarily implies hat one should reject the idea of feasibility of the original targets of firm A, in particular since firm D did produce the first and the second output in exactly the proportions that were targeted by firm A.

This leads to the following observation: If the target output ratio of firm A is considered as relevant part of the information implied by A's target outputs, then the actual outputs of firm D would constitute the appropriate reference point in assessing the performance of firm A, because D produced the first and the second output in exactly the proportions firm A targeted to. This logic then clearly does not only apply to the case where the targeted quantities were infeasible but also to the case where these targeted quantities were inefficiently chosen in the first place.

The relevance of the information contained in A's choice of an output ratio can be substantiated by considering it as a reflection of firm A's expectation about the price ratio between the two outputs that would prevail at selling time. Now, irrespective of whether or not these expectations were fulfilled, if at least they led to a choice of target output ratio in accordance with best production possibilities, then the actual production of firm D should serve as reference for performance comparison, because it also exhibited best performance in a revenue perspective amongst all firms observed given this price ratio (actually B and C did equally well as D in this respect but no better).

The implication of the above argument is: Amongst the available reference points (firms B,C and D in our example) to assess the extent of firm A's inefficiency a single appropriate reference point (firm D) can be uniquely identified, when the target outputs of firm A are taken into account and when at least the implied target output ratio is based on some economic rationale. For this identification purpose it suffices to know firm A's target output ratio and it is unimportant whether or not the target outputs themselves were set in accordance with the best production possibilities.

This leaves us with the tiny little problem mentioned above, that usually these target output ratios are not known to the analyst who is supposed to make such performance comparisons.

1. Outline of the book

The following section 2 of **Chapter 1** will describe in detail the various links which relate the present work to the existing literature. In particular the points of departure from existing approaches will be emphasized. To motivate the approach for practitioners two specific settings in which the analysis of output-specific efficiencies may be practically relevant will be described in Section 3. One setting has more of a microeconomic, the other one a rather macroeconomic flavor. Section 4 will geometrically illustrate the general problem of choosing reference points for efficiency comparisons in the presence of output specific efficiencies for a fictitious sample data set. This illustration is meant for the reader familiar with similar illustrations for related approaches and who thus will find it easier to identify the main differences between them and the present approach. Section 5 will further elaborate upon the sample data set from section 4 by looking at specific firms and what the present approach means to their performance assessment as compared to traditional approaches. For proper understanding it requires familiarity with fundamental statistical concepts like conditional densities and as such it also serves as guideline with regard to the type of prior knowledge that will be required for an understanding of the remainder of this book.

Reading this paper one should always keep in mind that the proposed approach is actually a 2-step estimation procedure: Frontier estimation succeeded by output specific efficiency estimation. In **Chapter 2** the peculiarities of frontier estimation in the presence of output-specific efficiencies will be discussed along with the necessary adaptations to DEA to serve the present purpose. By the end of this chapter familiarity of the reader with this necessary first estimation step will be taken for granted and this issue, being of secondary importance here anyway, will not be discussed again.

DEA per se is a non statistical approach and so needs to be augmented by an explicit data generating process (DGP) to put things into statistical perspective. Based on such a DGP it will be possible to tackle for example the question of consistency of the proposed approach. The basic possibilities for such DGP's and their implications will be discussed in section 1. In section 2 the necessary adaptations to a standard DEA program to determine a frontier point for a given output-ratio vector and an input vector will be developed. Section 3 then outlines a recent approach for a bias corrected version of DEA, which is then adapted to the particular case of output specific efficiencies. Section 4 will provide the basic argument for consistency of the whole approach, based on proven consistency of the the two constituent estimation steps.

In **Chapter 3** a tempting conjecture arising from a first shot consideration of the issue of output-specific efficiencies will be investigated. It concerns the relationship between radial and marginal, output-specific efficiency distributions and can be formulated as the following conjecture: Under certain (yet to be specified) conditions the marginal output-specific efficiency distributions are just the limits of the radial efficiency distribution conditional on observed output-ratio vectors as the latter approaches one of the various full specialization cases. If this were indeed true, one could use the DEA-estimated radial efficiency scores to estimate a parametric form of this conditional density and then derive the desired marginal by taking the limit. Unfortunately this simple procedure in general leads to inconsistent estimates as will be shown.

An example with independent efficiencies (across outputs) is analyzed in 2 and shown to conform to the conjecture. Section 3 presents a corresponding formulation of a regression equation, which might be used to estimate the marginal densities. Evidence from simulations tells that (the limits of) such regression equations may in fact lead to good proxies for the marginal output-specific efficiency distributions, but of course do not allow to assess the logical consistency of this approach. By counterexample it will then be shown in 4 that the generalization of the above conjecture does not hold. Despite being theoretically inconsistent it will be argued that the simple type of regression analysis considered in 3 can be useful in providing preliminary evidence of the existence of output specific efficiencies. Along the way Chapter 3 will also offer various opportunities to get a hold on the more concrete formal statistical problems involved here and will provide additional helpful insights into the geometry of output-specific efficiency estimation.

A brief description of the Markov chain Monte Carlo (MC^2) technique is given in **Chapter 4**. MC^2 is widely used nowadays for evaluation of complex and analytically intractable distributions. An instance of the latter in the present context is the posterior joint distribution of density parameters (for output-specific efficiencies and target output-ratios) and the unknown target output-ratios.

The key steps to effect MC^2 estimation, in its most common form known as the *Metropolis-Hastings (MH) algorithm*, are outlined in section 1. A special variant thereof, so called *Gibbs sampling* is sketched in section 2. I will occasionally rely on Gibbs sampling, as it is not only the most easy to implement but also the best understood variant of MH-algorithms in terms of statistical properties. In section 3 the potential of the conjugacy concept (a relationship between distributions) will be explained. Conjugate distributions play a prominent role in Bayesian statistics, because they give rise to posterior distributions which are known to be members of certain parametric families of distributions. Such knowledge is a prerequisite of Gibbs sampling in turn. The present work will also follow a Bayesian approach and so conjugacy may come handy.

Chapter 5 provides the statistical groundwork for output-specific efficiency estimation by formulating a suitable model of the data generating process. This involves choices for the parameterizations of the distributions of target output-ratios (in section 1) and output-specific efficiencies (in section 2) as well as the formal link between these two unobserved quantities and observed outputs. Together this will allow the formal derivation of the conditional (on target output-ratios) likelihood function in section 3, the key function for applying the MC^2 technique later.

The identification issue will be discussed in **Chapter 6** in terms of the unconditional likelihood instead, because we must rely solely on observed input-output quantities for identification. Lacking closed form functionals of the likelihood I will primarily use graphical analysis of the likelihood surface of various parameter combinations to address this issue. The basic, theoretical tradeoffs from changing parameters underlying this likelihood will be analyzed in section 1. Different combinations of parameter values of the involved distributions leading to equal likelihood values would be the classical case of identification failure of these parameters. While this problem in a formal sense vanishes as soon as a certain minimum number of observations is reached, it may continue to adversely affect the estimation process (slow convergence, trapping states in iterations...). So the discussion in section 1 will facilitate the interpretation of the small sample simulation results later.

The question, what sort of information (apart from known parameterizations of density functions) actually drives identification of the parameters of this statistical model, will be analyzed in Section 2. Remember that the key variables in the conditional likelihood function, upon which the whole estimation procedure rests, are the unobserved target output-ratios, so this question is non-trivial. It will be demonstrated how domain restrictions on feasible target output-ratios and the derived feasible output-specific efficiencies will play an identifying role here. From the perspective of efficiency estimation these domain restrictions are considered as observations (although actually being result of an estimation themselves), because they arise from comparing observed outputs with the efficiency frontier, which is estimated separately in advance.

Section 3 aims at identifying potential identification problems by studying the likelihood surfaces associated with different pairs of parameters evaluated for a grid of parameter-combinations. This analysis will be based on a simulated data set with known statistical properties and helps in particular to locate two potentially serious obstacles in MC^2-estimation: multiple likelihood modes (regarded as potential trapping states for numerical optimization routines) and flat likelihood surfaces for certain parameter combinations (regarded as cause of slow convergence of estimation routines and high variance of the estimator distribution). With a proper understanding of these issues it will be possible to design an update mechanism to effect MC^2-estimation, which is appropriate for the very task of output-specific efficiency estimation.

One such obstacle with regard to the distribution of target output-ratios is found and a solution via reparameterization is proposed. It is shown how this leads to a much more pronounced mode of the likelihood thus giving hope for a more stable MC^2 scanning process. But reparameterization may offer additional benefits with regard to eventual availability of prior information as is shown. Clearly, the more such prior information we have, the easier estimation should be. For certain parameterizations it is hard to come up plausibly with such prior information, while for others such information emerges rather straightforward from the data. Finally Section 3 also deals with problems related to the estimation of variance components of output specific-efficiencies, in particular with correlation amongst such efficiencies.

In **Chapter 7** the posterior distributions of the estimation model are derived. Section 1 first motivates potential choices of prior distributions for the parameters which will then lead to the joint posterior distribution. Some of these choices are motivated by conjugacy arguments and in this sense appear as consequence of the data generating process, while others lack such rationale and must be based on different arguments. In Section 2 the full conditional distributions are derived from the joint posterior by splitting up the vector of unknowns (including the parameters and the unknown target output-ratios) into pairwise disjoint sets of parameters resp. latent variables. The MH-algorithm will consist in sampling new random variates from these full conditional distributions iteratively, each time updating one block of unknowns conditional on the old values of all remaining unknown variates. The full sequence of steps is given in detail for the general case which does not require direct sampling from the conditional posteriors to be possible. The issue of scale invariance is addressed in Section 3. It will proven for known distributions that the proposed technique is indeed scale invariant conceptually, which is not quite obvious, because output-ratios clearly do depend on the scaling of outputs.

Chapter 8 investigates the small sample properties of the proposed type of estimator for a specific choice of prior distributions by Monte Carlo simulations. Monte Carlo here means that I will draw a random sample of observations from a known statistical model and then try to estimate the parameters of this model based on these data via MC^2 technique. This process will be repeated hundreds of times and thus will yield hundreds of estimates for each parameter. The resulting distribution of estimates of one particular parameter is labeled Monte Carlo distribution of the estimator. Based on such distributions the small sample properties of the various estimators will be analyzed in terms of bias (compared to the true models) and variance.

Section 1 details the various settings that will be assessed in this manner. They will differ by the degree of substitutability of the underlying technology because the associated frontier curvature may have an impact on estimator performance. The settings will also differ by sample size considered to get a rough idea of the convergence properties of the estimators and of expectable results in applied efficiency analysis based on the proposed technique.

Section 2 provides a discussion of the findings for the practically relevant case, where the technology is estimated in a first step by DEA, where the latter will be of the bias corrected type as proposed in Section 3 of Chapter 2. The findings from 2 will then be compared in section 3 to those resulting from applying the same technique for efficiency estimation, but being based on a known technology (frontier). This comparison should enable to properly attribute the correct proportions of bias resp. variance to the first (frontier estimation) or the second (efficiency estimation) of the necessary estimation steps.

In **Chapter 9** I turn to an application of the proposed procedure. This application will deal with the quality vs. quantity question in UK secondary schooling. Using the methodology developed and investigated in the preceding chapters we will find a significant difference in achieving the quantity goal as opposed to the quality goal. Such a finding is unavailable from standard efficiency estimation procedures and highlights the potential of the approach presented. Dealing with a particular dataset will furthermore give the opportunity to discuss convergence issues in more detail, a neglected topic due to time constraints in the large scale simulations of Chapter 8. Along the way also an alternative parameterization based on logit output-ratios will be introduced and a block updating step, indicating the potential of the approach to be fitted to any particular application with great flexibility. In this sense Chapter 9 can also be regarded as an extension of the material presented until Chapter 8. In section 1 of the final **Chapter 10** the proposed technique and the performance findings from the Monte Carlo simulations will be summarized and section 2 will pinpoint potentially fertile areas for future research.

2. Brief review of related literature

Basically there are three specific strands of literature which are linked in one or the other way to the presented approach and thus will be reviewed. One covers non-parametric techniques for comparative performance evaluations and usually comes under the label of *Data Envelop-*

ment Analysis (DEA). Another deals with parametric techniques for the same purpose and has been labeled *Stochastic Frontier Analysis* (SFA). Then there is the statistical literature using *Markov Chain Monte Carlo* (MC^2) techniques to estimate parameters from complex distributions, one of the key issues of this book. In the sequel it will be explained how each of these strands of literature relate to the present approach. Furthermore this work will frequently refer to standard concepts from microeconomic theory, which are explained in every intermediate level textbook on microeconomics and so no specific literature references are given in this respect. For more rigorous treatments of production theory in particular see for example in Beattie and Taylor, 1985 and Färe and Primont, 1995.

In the DEA and SFA literature the problem of quantifying eventual performance shortcomings of one firm as compared to others (although not as compared to targets) usually is labeled efficiency measurement, efficiency evaluation or efficiency estimation. Furthermore the more general term of *decision making units* (DMU's) is often used there rather than *firms* to denote producing entities, because efficiency evaluation for all types of non-profit institutions is as much a topic there as the efficiency analysis of firms producing for profit. This terminology will also be used in the present work.

The common theoretical background for DEA and SFA are the works of Vilfredo Pareto (in particular Pareto, 1971, the English translation of the 1906 published Italian original *Manuale di economia politica*), who laid the foundations for the notion of efficiency in a social welfare context in the 1890ies, and the axiomatic production analysis of Koopmans, 1951 and Debreu, 1951. In these works today's widely used notion of Pareto-efficiency (also referred to as *Pareto-optimality* or *Pareto-Koopmans efficiency* in the DEA context) in economics was established. With regard to related estimation issues the pioneering works in the literature are Farrell, 1957, who proposed the envelopment idea for efficiency estimation (later taken up in DEA) and Leibenstein, 1966. He summarizes empirical evidence to conclude, that in practice technical inefficiency (using the term *X-efficiency*) clearly dominates allocative inefficiency, which until then was a much more disputed topic in economics.

The seminal papers introducing DEA with proportional reduction of all inputs for given outputs are Charnes et al., 1978 for constant returns to scale technologies and Banker et al., 1984 for variable returns to scale technologies. The analogous case of possible proportional expansion of all outputs for given inputs is easily dealt with but was not described in Charnes et al., 1978. Both of the cited papers present what has become known as *orientated models*, where either input reduction (for given outputs) or output augmentation (for given inputs) is aimed at, but not both at the same time.

In Charnes et al., 1981, Charnes et al., 1985 and Charnes et al., 1987 the so called *additive DEA* models were presented, which identify improvement possibilities on the input and output side simultaneously and find more general, eventually non-proportional input reduction and output augmentation possibilities. In Ali and Seiford, 1993 a handsome two-stage formulation of the basic idea underlying additive models (maximizing sums of slacks rather than some proportionality factor) was presented for orientated models. Additive models in their original formulations compared to orientated models lack the desirable property of *scale invariance* (see below) but on the other hand are *translation invariant* (see below) as proven in Ali and Seiford, 1990 and Pastor, 1996. But with some modifications, leading to what has been labeled a *slack-based measure of efficiency*, additive models may be made scale invariant as shown in Tone, 2001.

DEA was basically designed for deterministic environments, where it may be assumed that production is under full control of management and where potential measurement errors can be safely ruled out (or at least assumed insignificant). But even when these conditions are violated DEA may be used for frontier and efficiency estimation if the analyst is willing to add some more parametric structure as shown in Kneip and Simar, 1996 for panel data or Gstach, 1998 for cross-section data. An alternative way of dealing with noisy data, albeit without explicit statistical foundation (unlike the two aforementioned approaches) is to use chance-constraint programming, as has been proposed for example in Sengupta, 1987, Olesen and Petersen, 1989 or Land et al., 1993. But the usefulness of this approach was questioned in Desai et al., 1994, who found very poor performance of corresponding efficiency estimators from their Monte-Carlo simulations.

SFA was originally developed in Aigner et al., 1977 and Meeusen and van den Broeck, 1977, but it has long been restricted to the single output case. But as long as efficiencies may be assumed to be proportional (the very restriction this book attempts to surmount), also multiple outputs can be accommodated with SFA. For such SFA the reader is referred to Grosskopf and Hayes, 1993, Coelli and Perelman, 1996, Löthgren, 1997 and Read and Thanassoulis, 1996 or Gstach, 1999b for a comparison with DEA.

Apart from the seminal papers in the two fields there are numerous textbooks available today covering DEA and/or SFA at various levels of technicality. At the general introductory level these include Färe et al., 1985, Sengupta, 1989, Fried et al., 1993, Charnes et al., 1994, Coelli et al., 1998, Kumbhakar and Lovell, 2000, and Cooper et al., 2000. Examples of books with specific focus include Färe and Primont, 1995 (axiomatic, duality, various projections), Sengupta, 1995, Färe and Grosskopf, 1996 (dynamic DEA), Dogramaci and Färe, 1988, Ganley and Cubbin, 1992 (several applications). Two comprehensive bibliographies about DEA are Beck, 1991 (for applications only) and Seiford, 1994. Försund and Sarafoglou, 2000 give a brilliant account from an economist's viewpoint of the development of DEA and in particular the route leading from Farrell's 1957 paper to the "official" seminal DEA paper of Charnes et al., 1978.

In standard DEA or SFA an eventual shortfall of realized outputs from the maximum possible quantities is expressed by a scalar efficiency measure. Clearly this allows a direct, performance based ranking of the analyzed production units. But if we are to measure efficiencies in an output-specific manner, as proposed here, this will no longer be possible. On the other hand output-specific measures should yield insights into performance problems unavailable from a traditional scalar efficiency measure. So it also will depend upon whether or not a ranking of the units under investigation has top priority, that the applied researcher will find the proposed technique useful or not. Output-specific efficiency measures based on statistical reasoning are in any case a novelty in the relevant literature.

The logical prerequisite of performance evaluation, whether output-specific like in the present work or not, is knowledge of what was labeled *best production possibilities* above. In production theory the label for the latter would be *technology*, whereas it is often denoted as *efficiency frontier* or *best practice* in the DEA and SFA literature. As an aside note that the term best practice indicates that usually such best production possibilities are estimated based on observed production, i.e. the very observations whose eventual inefficiencies the analyst will evaluate are typically also used to estimate the best production possibilities.

DEA as well as SFA can basically be applied for the purpose of technology estimation, although it will be argued below, that for a particular reason DEA is the proper choice of technique to estimate an efficiency frontier when dealing with output-specific efficiencies. So generally speaking, the DEA literature is more relevant for the approach presented here, than the SFA literature. Nevertheless both approaches share one common aspect which distinguishes them from the present approach: They both estimate technology and specific types of efficiency simultaneously. The present approach instead will decouple the task of technology estimation to a large extent from the task of efficiency estimation.

The prevailing practice in the DEA literature is to evaluate efficiencies relative to some more or less arbitrary chosen reference point from the estimated and often huge set of best production possibilities. Arguments for choosing particular reference points, for example based on their proximity in mix proportions (inputs as well as outputs) to the DMU to be evaluated, as in Coelli, 1998, are an exception. In this book instead the argument for the choice of a reference point will be based on information about the distribution of target output ratios for the reasons given above. It remains to be shown how this choice of a reference point will command statistical plausibility in a specific sense, unlike the particular choice in standard DEA but also unlike the one in Coelli, 1998.

Some readers may strictly oppose to the above claim that DEA chooses arbitrary reference points for efficiency comparisons. They will instead point out that the DEA choice of a reference point is always based on an optimal projection (maximizing a specific type of distance function) of observed outputs upon the efficiency frontier and as such is not arbitrary. This is not to be questioned here. But this choice does not relate in whatever manner to target output ratios of firms and is completely avoid of statistical underpinning and in this sense it is considered as arbitrary here.

Regarding the relationship between standard DEA and the present approach it should be noted first that *output-ratios* and *production targets*, although sometimes under different labels, are common topics in the DEA literature. In Halme et al., 1999 for example target outputs are used to establish the notion of *value efficiency*, although the authors admit, that target outputs usually are not observed and thus the concept may be hard to implement. A different use of target outputs is made for example Lovell and Pastor, 1997 or Thanassoulis, 1999, where targets are derived as ex post quantities from a prior, standard type of efficiency analysis.

The concept of output-ratios, sometimes synonymously labeled *output-mix* in the literature, has been used for example to establish a distinction between the outcome of oriented DEA models (where estimation of proportional output expansion preempts possible additional output improvements and possible input savings) and the outcome of additive DEA models (with no such preemption), as in Cooper et al., 2000. Yet another use of the concept of output-ratios (although under a different label) has been made in Fox and Hill, 2000, where output-ratios (along with input-ratios) are instrumentalized for outlier detection.

So both of these concepts have been used before for various purposes before, but never in the way they are employed here, namely as cornerstone for describing a statistical model which drives the observed input/output data and thus allows to find statistically plausible target output-ratios and corresponding output-specific efficiencies (for example as averages of the resp. conditional posterior distributions).

It must also be noted, that in a non-statistical sense, particularly the so called additive DEA models have implicitly been dealing with output specific efficiencies from the very beginning. This is because the reference point used for efficiency evaluation of a DMU in an additive DEA model (unlike in oriented DEA models) regularly has different output-ratios than the DMU to be analyzed. So relating observed outputs of the DMU to the corresponding outputs of the reference DMU on a per product basis along the lines of the numerical illustration above would of course lead to output-specific efficiency scores.

But the tempting interpretation of the implicit output-specific efficiencies associated with reference points from additive DEA models is at odds not only with the different primary aim of these models (to provide scalar performance scores and identify truly Pareto-Koopmans efficient points only) but also with their conceptual framework: In DEA of whatever type the choice of a reference point is always based upon the maximization of a particular type of distance function (the L_1 norm of slacks in the case of additive models) rather than upon the notion of target output-ratios as variables which determine the data generating process as proposed here. So despite superficial similarity, the introduction of the concept of target output-ratios makes a big difference when it comes to output-specific efficiencies and as such probably marks the crucial departure point of the present approach from the existing literature.

With regard to the relationship between SFA and the present approach matters are different, because SFA effects frontier estimation quite differently then DEA. Unlike DEA it basically stipulates a parametric form of the efficiency frontier and explicitly takes the possibility of measurement errors and of uncontrollable production influences (of paramount importance for example in agricultural production) into account. But the crucial feature with regard to the approach presented in this book is the fact, that frontier estimation in SFA is inextricably linked to efficiency estimation (unlike in DEA).

This last feature makes a big difference when it comes to output-specific efficiency estimation, because SFA ultimately relies upon the very specific concept of radial efficiencies. In a setting with DMU's producing multiple-outputs this concept implies that eventual inefficiency has a proportional impact on all outputs, but this is not the case I am interested in. If this radiality assumption underlying SFA were to be replaced with an output-specific efficiency concept, one would have to reconstruct the core statistical model of SFA, even if it were only to be used as frontier estimation rather than efficiency estimation technique. This challenging possibility will not be pursued here.

The technique of DEA on the other hand used for frontier estimation is independent of the specific type of efficiency that may actually have generated the observed output data. Therefore in principal DEA may be used for frontier estimation in the presence of output specific efficiencies as well without any modifications, which is the main reason for only considering DEA in this book as technique for frontier estimation. But in any case, frontier estimation is just a first step, upon which a separate efficiency estimation step will be based. So it is ultimately irrelevant, which technique is used to effect frontier estimation, as long as it can accommodate output-specific efficiencies. Despite some superficial similarity it must be noted though, that the approach to be presented here is very distinct from existing two-step procedures (surveyed in Grosskopf, 1996): There DEA is used for estimating frontier AND efficiency scores simultaneously in a first step, and then the efficiency scores are subjected in a second step to further analysis, for example regressing them on some explanatory variables, not considered in the first step DEA.

Consistency of DEA frontier point estimates have been proven in (Banker, 1993, Korostelev et al., 1995a or Kneip et al., 1998) under rather weak conditions and for general statistical structures. To handle the case of output-specific efficiencies a more specific statistical structure is needed, but one, which will still allow to invoke the consistency results mentioned above. So consistency of DEA will be a maintained feature within the present setting too and will play a crucial role in the claim, that the more elaborate technique (including a second estimation step) presented here will again be consistent. In any case it should be noted, that modifications of the statistical structure do not affect DEA as such.

But not only the favorable feature of consistency of DEA, also the discomforting fact of inherent bias of standard DEA frontier point estimates is well known (for a formal account see Wilson, 1994). Therefore rather than using standard DEA, bias corrected DEA based on bootstrapping will be promoted here as technique for frontier estimation, as proposed in various forms in Simar and Wilson, 1995, Gstach, 1995, Ferrier and Hirschberg, 1997 or Ferrier and Hirschberg, 1999. Yet it should be recalled again, that the problem of frontier estimation is not the main concern of this paper and thus whether standard or bias corrected DEA is used for frontier estimation is only of secondary importance. The problem of estimating output-specific efficiencies in either case remains the very same.

The main reference for bootstrapping is the seminal paper of Efron, 1979. Since then bootstrapping has found widespread acceptance in statistics as technique to investigate small sample distributions of estimators when asymptotic results can not be invoked meaningfully or when closed form solutions of such distributions are unavailable, the very case in this book. The relevant theory along with many applications and the general usage of bootstrapping for bias correction is described in Efron and Tibshirani, 1993.

The closest links to the present work to be found in the SFA literature are to be found in approaches that were recently presented to estimate the efficiency specific to one of several inputs. See Reinhard et al., 1999 and as Bayesian adaptation thereof Kurkalova and Carriquiry, 2000. These approaches also deviate from the idea of proportional inefficiency, albeit in a very particular sense. They deal only with a limiting case where the whole observed excessive input usage (relative to the efficiency frontier) is attributed to one particular input only. This limiting case arises naturally from the applied context of the cited papers, but plays only a negligible role in the present work. Here I deal more generally with the distribution of all the possibilities for efficiency comparisons which arise between such limiting cases.

In order to estimate output-specific efficiencies, the central issue of this book, the proposed approach will invoke the assumption, that the distributions of target-output ratios and of output-specific efficiencies can be described by parametric densities. That is, the principal form of these distributions will be assumed known. Without this assumption the identification of the underlying structural quantities will in general be impossible. But even with this assumption such an identification potential needs to be established.

While invoking this assumption of known distributional forms means a loss of generality from the DEA point of view, it is the standard way to proceed in statistical approaches like SFA, where it allows to distinguish (in an expectational sense) between noise and efficiency effects upon observed output data. In this sense the parameterization of the efficiency distribution clearly is a step towards SFA. On the other hand the nonparametric representation of technology and the assumption of noise-free data will be maintained as in DEA. Thus the present work is located on boundary terrain in the perspective of traditional efficiency estimation.

Let's look for a moment at the problems discussed so far from the viewpoint of microeconomic theory. There the question of the proper reference point for efficiency evaluation comes down to the question of what the expected price ratios are. Once the latter are known, the target outputs can at least in principal be simply calculated and used as reference points for efficiency calculations of any desired kind. So there is no need for example to question which other firm to choose for an appropriate performance comparison. Furthermore the possibility of target outputs not in accordance with the efficiency frontier must not be considered as the technology is usually assumed to be known.

For the present purpose of efficiency estimation it clearly can not be assumed a priori as in microeconomic textbooks, that all firms do in fact produce efficiently. As already mentioned, Leibenstein, 1966 found sufficient evidence for rejecting this assumption on empirical grounds.

On the other hand the textbook idea of target output ratios of firms being uniquely related to output price ratios can be easily reconciled with the present approach. All this requires is to assume that firms may have market power, an assumption which necessarily must be accompanied by consideration of possibly different target output-ratios of the individual firms (a key feature of the approach to be presented). So in the microeconomic textbook sense the present approach simply reflects the idea of potential market power and actually is a way to quantify it as the variance of the estimated target output-ratio distribution.

It is illuminating to consider for a moment the opposite assumption, namely to rule out possible market power of firms. In the case of homothetic production functions (no such restriction will be invoked actually) this would imply unique (output-) price-ratios for all firms. This theoretical consequence combined with the empirical observation of actually different output-mix of individual firms then immediately leads to the distinction of technical vs. allocative inefficiencies as proposed in Banker and Maindiratta, 1988. In this particular sense the here maintained assumption of a distribution of target output-ratios substitutes for the assumption of a distribution of allocative inefficiencies used elsewhere.

Returning to the estimation issue it should be noted, that even with the additional assumption of a parametric distribution of target output-ratios the problem of estimating output-specific efficiencies remains out of reach of analytical econometric solutions. An important factor contributing to this problem is that DEA (unlike SFA) does not lead to a closed form functional description of the set of best production possibilities, a set which in one way or the other must necessarily be part of the description of the data generating mechanism for statistical evaluation. As a consequence the likelihood of observing specific output quantities for given distribution parameters can not be represented in a closed form either.

As a way to surmount these difficulties the use of data-augmented Markov Chain Monte Carlo (MC^2) will be proposed. MC^2 methodology, on top of other useful properties, will allow to deal with the issue of non functional representations of technology in a straightforward manner. Data-augmentation on the other hand will be the statistical technique to deal with the unknown target output-ratios. It will treat them as unobserved (latent) variables which will be estimated just like the unknown distributional parameters. Once the technology is estimated via DEA and the target output-ratios are estimated via MC^2 (thereby relying on the technology estimate) the output-specific efficiencies will already be estimated by the same token, because they uniquely correspond to output-ratios for a given technology.

MC^2 was pioneered by Tanner and Wong, 1987 and Gelfand and Smith, 1990. Usage of MC^2 methodology in the field of efficiency estimation is not new. It has been successfully applied to solve other tricky problems in this area for example in van den Broeck et al., 1997, Koop et al., 1994, Koop et al., 1995, Fernández et al., 1997 or Koop et al., 1997.

But so far the very issue of output-specific efficiencies in a statistical perspective has not been tackled. The recent paper of Fernández et al., 2000 also presents an MC^2 approach for efficiency estimation and also contains an implicit notion of target output-ratios, but still treats deviations of observed outputs from the frontier as proportional across outputs.

3. Motivation

A principal-agent perspective

Suppose a comparative efficiency study, ordered by the management of one of the involved firms, would have been conducted for an industry comprising of many firms, all producing the same set of outputs, although possibly in very different proportions. The results from this study would include an estimate of the efficiency frontier. So the managers of the involved firms would learn what the most efficient of their competitors did achieve and could set next periods target outputs accordingly. Whether a firms management will actually pursue such a strategy is a different question! But if the owners of the involved firms also get to know the results from this study (they might have ordered it themselves) they can exercise some control over management to the effect of output targeting more in accordance with the findings about best practice.

But possibly managers will be reluctant in formulating targets outputs in full accordance with the findings. They could for example point towards various sorts of idiosyncracies in the operating environment or the long term strategic goals of the firm under their control and thus question the validity of the benchmark findings from the study. Arguments like these leave some room for managerial discretion in formulating output targets to the discomfort of owners. Achieving target outputs under these circumstances may thus tell more about manager capabilities in defending salaries than about the capabilities of owners to exercise control over management.

In the light of this information deficit owners might after all be satisfied by learning from the study that in terms of an overall efficiency measure (a radial DEA efficiency score for example) their management displayed average performance while overall receiving average pay. But it is rather unlikely that owners would still be satisfied if learning additionally that in producing output A their firms performance by far exceeded average performance within this industry while in producing output B it performed poorly compared to industry average. So estimating this industry average performance on a per-product-basis will be beneficial for owners in their attempt to control management more effectively.

Note that it is irrelevant for the conclusion drawn above whether formulated target outputs for the period under investigation fell short of frontier outputs. As long as the output-ratios implied by the formulated target outputs are considered as target output-ratios owners will learn from the frontier estimate what their firms output-specific efficiencies are compared to best practice. So a better informed judgement about management performance on a per-product-basis is possible whenever average industry performance is also available on a per-product-basis.

An economic-policy perspective

Whenever economic policy is targeting the performance of a private or public sector of a nations economy efficiency measurement issues come into play. Whether the reasons for an investigation are conjectured deficiencies in competitiveness of a domestic industry in comparison with the relevant foreign industry or in comparison with more developed sectors of the domestic economy: Numerous examples of efficiency studies directed by public administrative bodies proof the perceived relevance of efficiency estimation in the macro-economic context.

But according to a commonly entertained viewpoint in economics policy officials usually are poorly informed about the operating characteristics of the decision making units and the relevant variables on which their micro-decisions are based. So a cautious guess in this regard is that policy officials only observe input and output quantities of DMU's within the sector whose economic performance is to be evaluated.

So differing from the discussion in the previous section, the ones who ordered the study, policy officials in this case, will most likely have no information about the target outputs of any individual DMU's. Nevertheless these officials would learn from the study about best practice (frontier technology) within the sector under scrutiny just like firm owners or managers did in the previous example. And they could still make inference about output-specific efficiencies on a per-DMU-basis albeit only in an expectational sense. But presumably this will not the primary aim of policy officials anyway.

Instead they might look for scientific guidance in formulating appropriate policies at the macro level. And such guidance, in a more structured way than is available without the proposed approach, emerges from learning about average performance on a per-product-basis. It is conceivable for example that a study about a countries medical care system (with hospitals being the DMU's) revealed a high average efficiency in emergency care and a low average efficiency in regular care. Such a finding should of course lead officials to search primarily for causes of inefficiency and improvement potentials with regard to regular care.

So the performance improvements envisioned here as result from a study of output-specific efficiencies and corresponding policy measures, do not apply to any DMU in particular, but instead to the average performance of a whole economic sector with regard to the production of a particular output. In other words in this macro perspective one should think of improvement measures, which are not at the discretion of managements. Examples of such measures include labor or anti-collusion legislation, education policy or the organization of public transport. From an econometric perspective it is important to note, that such improvement potentials (or simply: inefficiencies) are not due to DMU-specific exogenous constraints and therefore can not be captured simply by using additional environmental variables in the efficiency estimation process (as in many DEA studies) or by using firm effect models (a principal option with SFA).

4. Geometrical illustration

The following geometrical illustration of the problematic choice of reference points for efficiency comparisons is provided for the reader familiar with standard DEA and basic knowledge of microeconomic concepts. It thus supplements the numerical illustration from section 1 on a slightly higher level of technicality and provides a geometric representation of the problem in a more explicit statistical setting based on fictional data.

For this illustration a random sample (of size $n = 30$) of DMU's was generated, all using 1 input x (kept constant at $x = 1$) to produce 2 different outputs y_1, y_2.[3]The target output-ratios (scalar quantities for two-dimensional outputs!) were drawn randomly from a distribution with mean 0.33. The latter figure means that the average target ratio between output quantity 1 and total output quantity is one third.[4]This expected value of course has no meaning beyond that of being a statistical device to generate the data. In particular it has no economic meaning whatsoever, because arbitrary rescaling of the involved outputs would necessarily be accompanied by changing means while technological information delivered by the sample would remain unaltered. This led to efficient production targets, depicted as pinedges in Figure 1.1, distributed along the input $x = 1$ isoquant. Note that these pinedges in reality are usually unobserved by the analyst.

The output-specific efficiencies of this sample (a 2-dimensional vector for each DMU) were drawn randomly from a bivariate distribution with mean vector (0.70,0.93). So the average efficiency in producing output 1 is 0.70 and 0.93 for output 2 respectively. Multiplying a target output with the corresponding efficiency (both being DMU-specific) led to the fictitious observations (sample outputs) drawn as transparent and solid pinheads in Figure 1.1. Three observations with solid pinheads be analyzed in more detail below.

Based on the so constructed sample of y_1, y_2 vectors (the pinheads) then the radial output-efficiency scores were estimated with a bias corrected (see section 3) version of DEA. In an applied analysis the pinheads would

[3] The framework for this construction was a constant returns to scale technology with a constant elasticity of transformation between the two outputs of 0.5.

[4] Different notions of target output-ratios will be frequently employed later in this book when statistically appropriate. But in terms of information content all of these notions are equivalent.

Figure 1.1. Target outputs and actual outputs in geometrical perspective

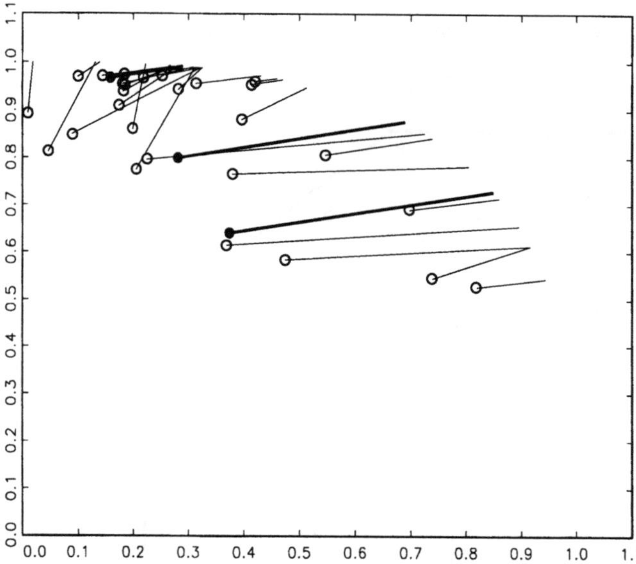

All circles: observed outputs, Solid circles: observed outputs of DMU's described in more Detail in table 1.1. Pinedges: Target outputs, from which observations emanated. Lines connecting pinedges and pinheads: Deviations from targets due to output and DMU specific inefficiencies.

be the only observed data, while the target outputs (the pinedges) on the efficiency frontier (the $x = 1$ input-isoquant here) would, as mentioned above, be unknown. Figure 1.2 shows what will be known beyond observed inputs and outputs after DEA had been applied to the data: A DEA estimated efficiency frontier or what has hitherto been labeled *best production possibilities.* In both graphs the horizontal axis measures the first output y_1 while the vertical axis measures the second output y_2 of the individual DMU's. Table 1.1 gives details about the three sample observations ((solid pinheaded in the graphs), which will be investigated at bit more closely below.

By visual inspection of Figure 1.1 (impossible to draw in empirical analysis) the chosen assumptions are easy to verify: The sample distribution of the output-specific efficiencies shows the expected and very pronounced tendency of low efficiency in producing output 1 and high efficiency in producing output 2. Furthermore the bulk of sample target output-ratios is concentrated significantly below the 0.5 value as assumed above.

Figure 1.2. Output-sample and bias corrected DEA-frontier

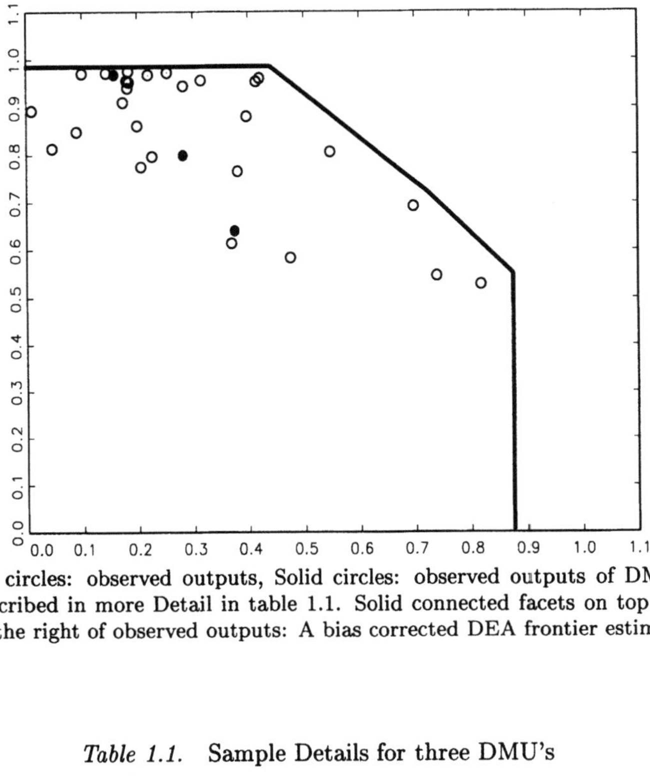

All circles: observed outputs, Solid circles: observed outputs of DMU's described in more Detail in table 1.1. Solid connected facets on top and to the right of observed outputs: A bias corrected DEA frontier estimate.

Table 1.1. Sample Details for three DMU's

		true		observed		estimated
DMU	TOR	EFF1	EFF2	Y1	Y2	R-EFF
A	.23	.55	.98	.16	.97	.99
B	.44	.41	.91	.26	.81	.81
C	.54	.44	.88	.37	.67	.71

TOR= target output-ratio ($m_1 = y_1/[y_1 + y_2]$), EFF1, EFF2 = efficiency in producing output 1 resp. 2, Y1, Y2= observed output quantities, R-EFF=radial efficiencies as estimated via DEA

Figure 1.1 also shows that the low average efficiency in producing output 1 vs. the high average efficiency in producing output 2 leads to a significant difference between observed output ratios and target output-ratios: The lines connecting target outputs and observed outputs clearly tend to be flat rather than radially oriented towards the origin (as would be the case if target and observed output-ratios would coincide). If the observed output-ratios would be taken as indicators of underlying targets the corresponding mean estimate would be 0.27, significantly below the true mean of 0.33. Applying an output oriented DEA with bias correction to the observed data yielded an average radial efficiency score of 0.91. This figure is far beyond the sample mean efficiency in producing output 1 of 0.64, but only slightly below the sample mean efficiency in producing output 2 of 0.94. So these DEA based radial efficiency scores are of doubtful value in describing the underlying problems.

Note however that this result does not primarily reflect a deficiency of DEA, but rather a deficiency in the particular choice of reference DMU's, which in the present example are constructed from radial projections of observed DMU's upon the frontier. Given on the other hand that the true input-isoquant underlying this data set has the form of a quarter circle with radius one, the frontier estimate as provided by DEA on the other hand appears by visual judgement as rather good. So one part of the job, which DEA is supposed to do, is done rather well and the other rather poor. Note also, that other choices of reference points regularly used in DEA would not lead to a better fit with respect to the true underlying efficiency distribution and would suffer from the same arbitrariness in a statistical perspective as the radially chosen reference points.

From visual inspection of Figure 1.2 we are tempted to conclude, that relative radial deviations (inefficiencies) of observed outputs from the DEA estimated frontier will be positively correlated with output-ratios of the corresponding observations (a conclusion which could be substantiated with a simple regression of DEA-estimated efficiency scores on observed output-ratios). Does this imply higher average efficiencies of DMU's with lower target output-ratios (of output 1 relative to output 2) or does this point towards a different underlying population characteristic ? Clearly visual inspection can never be conclusive to diagnose higher output 2 efficiency and lower output 1 efficiency but it points in the right direction and should motivate the analyst to further investigate this finding. In Chapter 9 we will take up this topic in an applied perspective again.

Finally look at the indicated general problem from a DMU-specific perspective: The data for DMU B given in table 1.1 tell that from the ex post DEA-viewpoint DMU B suffers from 19% inefficiency (=81% efficiency) in producing both outputs, while in fact it did rather well (like most others in this example) with regard to output 2 (achieving 91% efficiency) and very poor only with regard to output 1 (achieving only 41% of best practice quantity given the prior target output-ratio). Now the only statement about improvement potentials that can be supported in a statistical sense by standard DEA is, that these potentials for DMU B lie somewhere along the frontier to the right and above the observed outputs. This offers little guidance in assessing the relative importance of the two inefficiencies actually involved. In the light of the idea of production targets therefore such claims about DMU specific improvement potentials should be replaced by proper analysis of potentially systematic efficiency differences across outputs.

5. Interpreting the difference between output-specific and radial efficiencies

This section describes results from output-specific efficiency evaluation for three particular DMU's from the dataset in the previous section. Thus it provides a look ahead, since the methodology applied will only be developed in the following chapters. The example evaluations should help in interpreting the resulting estimates of original target output-ratios and the implied output-specific efficiencies vs. the traditional radial efficiency estimates.

To start with, it should be clearly understood, that changing the reference point along the efficiency frontier for a given observation on outputs of a particular DMU involves two distinct changes with regard to the underlying variables: First and foremost the output specific efficiencies change with the particular choice of the reference point. Secondly at the same time the output-ratios of this frontier point (the possible target output-ratios) change. When both of these variables can be described in statistical terms via parametric densities, this change in projection thus implies a change in the posterior likelihood of observing the given outputs of this DMU. Under this condition it is possible to compare different reference points based on the associated value of the likelihood function (in the sequel often simply labeled *plausibility*).

To illustrate this statement let's look at the three sample observations from table 1.1 from the perspective of the posterior density of target output-ratios as depicted in Figures 1.3-1.5. In the left graphs in each of these Figures the solid curve represents the true (based on true density parameter values) posterior density of the target output-ratio for a particular DMU, given the corresponding observation on output quantities. The dashed function lines in these graphs instead are the posterior densities based on the estimated density parameters These estimates, based on all 30 sample observations, are derived from the very technique to be proposed and investigated in the following sections of this work. The dashed vertical linea are the expected target output-ratios under these estimated posterior densities. The solid half circle and the triangle on the horizontal axis show the observed output ratio and the true target output-ratio respectively of a particular DMU.

In the right hand graphs of the tree figures the location of the respective observation (solid circle) and the frontier point corresponding to the target output-ratio (solid triangle) are shown relative to the efficiency frontier, which is assumed here to be known exactly, not just estimated like in the previous section. The latter assumption is for expositional clarity, because I don't want to mess with the issue of frontier estimation here. But the arguments also apply to a setting with an estimated frontier, albeit with an accuracy yet to be tested.

Figure 1.3. Posterior target output-ratio distribution for A

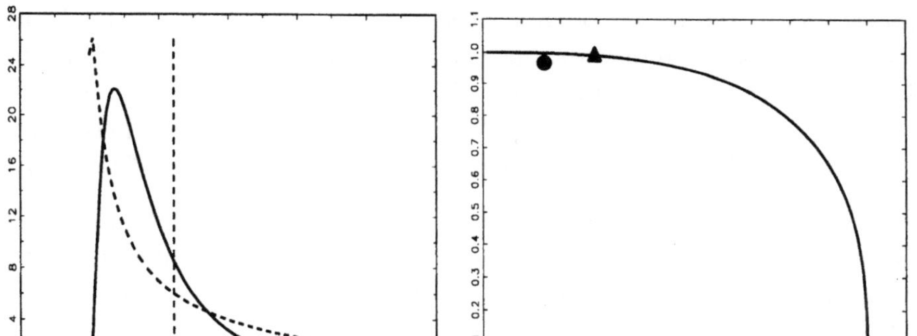

Observe first that in all three cases considered the observed output-ratio lies at the lower end of the possible spectrum of output-ratios as seen from the perspective of the observations, while the true target output-ratios tend to lie at the upper end.[5] This reflects the typical difference between observed and target output-ratios resulting from the underlying efficiency differentials as discussed above. Note also, that in all three cases the posterior expectation of the target output-ratio lies between the respective true value thereof and the output-ratio of the respective observation.

Figure 1.4. Posterior target output-ratio distribution for B

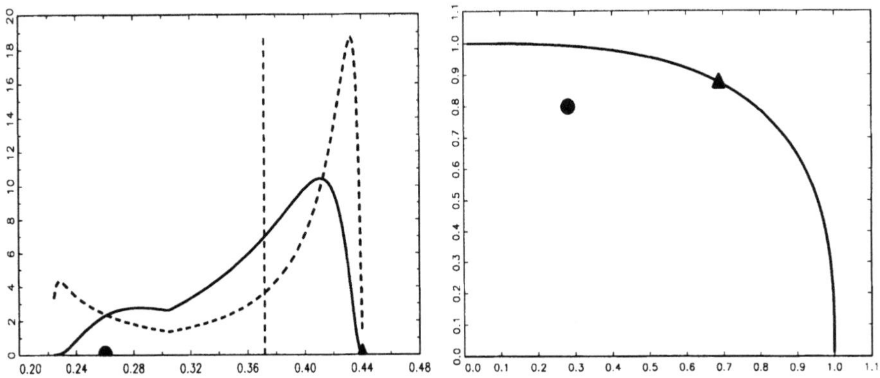

In figure 1.3 the results for DMU A are depicted, which had a radially estimated efficiency score of 0.99 based on the observed output ratio of 0.14. Calculating output-specific efficiencies based on the posterior expectation of the target output-ratio of 0.19 (the vertical dashed line) this picture would change dramatically leading to almost full efficiency with regard to output 2 but only about 70% efficiency with regard to output 1. So while not hitting the target values exactly, these latter figures are much more in line with the actual performance of DMU A.

DMU C had a target output-ratio of 0.54 and ended up producing outputs at a ratio of 0.37. Both of these ratios are higher than the population average of target output-ratios of 0.33. But the posterior density of DMU B's target output-ratios as shown in figure 1.5 is left skewed with concentration on the upper end of feasible output-ratios and thus the posterior mass points further away from the distribution mean of

[5] The careful observer might wonder why some observations lie exactly on the lower boundary of the (posterior) target output-ratio distribution here. This is because the sample data were constructed on the basis of a finite grid of feasible target output-ratios rather than a continuous version of target output-ratios.

Figure 1.5. Posterior target output-ratio distribution for C

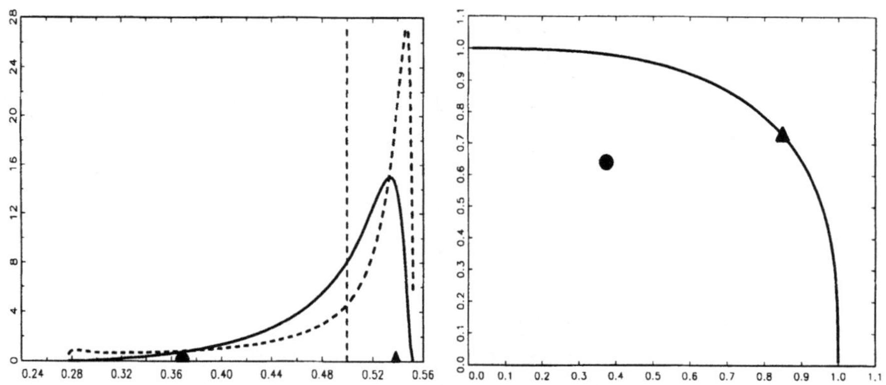

0.33. Note that this holds for the posterior density based on true parameter values as well as the one based on estimated values. Analogous reasoning holds for DMU A with reverse signs.

This indicates that the posterior density estimates of target output-ratios do not exhibit a uniform correcting tendency towards the true population center (in which case the posterior expectations of target output-ratios would lie above or below the observed ratios, depending on whether the latter are below or above the population center) but seem to reflect also additional sample information related to output-specific efficiencies. This statement could also be formulated as follows: There is a systematic bias of radial projections in terms of implied target output-ratios, which can not be simply overcome by narrowing down the feasible posterior range for such projections (i.e. the range of feasible target output-ratios).[6]

So on one hand the typical posterior expectations of target output-ratios in the given setting will be higher than the observed ratios. This corresponds to expected reference units which produce less of output 2 and more of output 1 compared to the reference units constructed by radial projection. On the other hand the DMU-specific posterior densities themselves do not have the homogenous type of shape we would ex-

[6] Such an ostensible improvement vs. radial projections is implicit in the additive model, which indeed restricts feasible projections to some central range. See section 2 of Chapter 2 for further explanations.

pect in a setting, where the only task were to estimate an output-ratio distribution from observed output-ratios (disregarding efficiency issues).

This two-sided nature of the likelihood of the sample observations (being result of an efficiency distribution AND a target output-ratio distribution) conditional on a set of parameters is reflected for example by the doublepeaked (bimodal) posterior output-ratio distribution estimate for DMU B depicted in figure 1.4. Without the additional impact of changing projections points upon the efficiency distribution estimate and given the unimodal parameterization of target output-ratios, it would be hard to find a rationale for such bimodality. The emerging picture with regard to the relation between radially projected reference points and other possible reference points is therefore, that the full posterior distribution of the latter matters and this includes DMU- and output-specific efficiency aspects as well as DMU-specific target output-ratio aspects.

The above type of posterior analysis of DMU-specific reference points is ultimately of the same kind as the one underlying the calculation of expected DMU-specific efficiencies in a composed error framework (SFA). The conceptual difference being that the present analysis considers the target output-ratios as unknown quantities along with output specific efficiencies while in SFA the analogous roles are played by noise, efficiency and the shape of the frontier itself. But in both cases the variables of interest will be derived as expected variables under some posterior distributions. As indicated this is in contrast with DEA, which is not based on a statistical model and where the corresponding efficiency estimates therefore do not have such expectational meaning.

From the above analysis it should have also become clear, that target output-ratios and output-specific efficiencies are merely two sides of the same coin. So in estimating output-specific efficiencies we simultaneously estimate target output-ratios and both of these variables will necessarily enter into the likelihood formulation.

II

OPERATIONALIZING THE CONCEPT

Chapter 2

TECHNOLOGY ESTIMATION

In this chapter different statistical structures, which might be used as statistical foundation of DEA, will first be analyzed and one particular structure will be picked as appropriate for output-specific efficiency estimation. This will be followed by a formal description of how DEA may be utilized for a technology representation based on inputs and output-ratios (rather than outputs themselves) based on a fixed set of Farrell-efficient points, a straightforward extension of DEA ideas. Then a simple procedure for bias correction of DEA frontier point estimates will be sketched, because the standard estimates are known to be biased under any of the potentially underlying statistical structures and because such bias correction will also underly the reported results in Chapter 8.

As already indicated basically two options are available for frontier estimation: DEA and stochastic frontier analysis (SFA). Both lead, based on sample data, in one way or another to a description of best production possibilities and tell in particular, what maximum amounts of outputs can be produced from given inputs. As already indicated the present choice of DEA rather than SFA for this purpose is mainly motivated by DEA's capability of separating frontier from efficiency estimation, whereas these two tasks, from a statistical perspective, are inextricably linked under SFA. But the reader should keep in mind that ultimately the type of frontier estimation technique employed is irrelevant for estimation of output-specific efficiencies, which basically requires a representation of the efficiency frontier in terms of inputs and output-ratios.

So the following exposition of frontier point estimation will be restricted to DEA, of which only one particular variant will be considered: Output-oriented DEA for variable returns to scale as introduced in Banker et al., 1984. For the purpose of output specific efficiency estimation any other DEA variant would do as well, in particular one could work with constant returns to scale instead or use an additive DEA model for determination of the efficiency frontier. All these models readily support a representation of this frontier in terms of inputs and output-ratios.

1. Statistical structures underlying DEA

In the exposition of this section I will identify distinguishing statistical assumptions, formulated as Data Generating Processes (DGP's), which may be entertained in the process of estimating deterministic production frontiers and output-technical efficiencies of firms via DEA.[1] Common to DEA estimation approaches is the supposed existence of an attainable technology set $\Psi = \{(x, y) \in \mathbb{R}_+^{R+S} : x \text{ can produce } y\}$, a related output correspondence set $\mathrm{Y}(x) = \{y \in \mathbb{R}_+^S | (x, y) \in \Psi\}$ and a Farrell output-efficient boundary $\mathrm{Y}^F(x) = \{y | y \in \mathrm{Y}(x), \lambda y \notin \mathrm{Y}(x)\ \forall\ \lambda > 1\}$. The latter would be identical to the input isoquant of Ψ under the assumption of strong disposability of outputs. The set of Pareto-Koopmans efficient output combinations $\mathrm{Y}^{PK}(x) = \{y | y \in \mathrm{Y}(x),\ \forall\ y' \geq y : y' \notin \mathrm{Y}(x)\}$ may be only a subset of $\mathrm{Y}^F(x)$.

Depending on the task at hand additional assumptions with regard to the distributions of key variables may eventually enter the stage. In particular it may or may not be assumed, that the efficiencies $\varepsilon_r, \varepsilon_s$ of producing various outputs are equal and that the correlations ρ_{rs} amongst eventual output specific efficiencies are equal to one. The following table summarizes three distinct possibilities, which cover two typical cases encountered in the literature plus a novel one, appropriate for estimation of output specific efficiencies.

[1] The notion of *deterministic frontiers* as opposed to *stochastic frontiers* (the subject of SFA) is used in DEA to indicate, that one considers the data to be free from measurement errors and the production to be under full control of management.

Table 2.1. Statistical structures for DEA

	DGP 1	**DGP 2**	**DGP 3**
Input/Output distribution on Ψ	yes	implicit	implicit
Efficiency distribution	no	yes ($\rho_{rs}=1$, $\varepsilon_r = \varepsilon_s$, $\forall\, r \neq s$)	yes
Target output-ratio distribution	no	implicit	yes

DGP 1 is the most general statistical underpinning of frontier estimation via DEA and suffices to investigate consistency and convergence of this technique as in the papers by Banker, 1993, Korostelev et al., 1995a, Korostelev et al., 1995b or Kneip et al., 1998. In this most parsimoniously described context the efficiency of some observed (x_i, y_i) production could basically be evaluated against any reference point $y \in \mathrm{Y}^F(x_i)$ which satisfies $y_i \leq y$. But no statistical discrimination amongst the plethora of these reference points and associated efficiency scores is possible, because target output-ratios are not accounted for in this setting.

But for given technology a distribution of target output-ratios and a distribution of output-specific efficiencies (plus eventually a distribution of inputs) clearly implies a certain distribution of inputs and outputs, because the latter distributions are based upon the former. So DGP 1 is actually more general than data generating processes formulated in terms of target output-ratios and output-specific efficiencies. On the other hand it is impossible to infer anything about the shape of the distributions of these variates from mere knowledge of the input/output distribution on Φ. But with regard to statistical properties of DEA frontier point estimators DGP 1 is of great help, since all we need to check to establish these properties for such estimators under different data generating processes is whether or not they imply input/output distributions which satisfy the necessary conditions formulated in terms of DGP 1.

DGP 2 is the structure implicitly underlying many applied DEA studies, which routinely estimate radial efficiency scores and draw conclusions about performance improvement potentials based on these scores. Strictly speaking such conclusions are warranted only if perfectly correlated efficiencies across all outputs with equal means can plausibly be assumed (i.e. $\mu_r = \mu_s$ and $\rho_{rs} = 1 \; \forall \; r \neq s$). But such an assumption implies that observed output ratios are equal to target output-ratios which justifies the corresponding entry *implicit* in row three of column DGP 2.

It should also be noted, that the above assumptions underlying DGP 2 with regard to frontier estimation itself (as distinguished from efficiency estimation) are not restrictive: Efficiency measurement means to evaluate a certain type of distance function, but whatever that function, the Farrell-efficient frontier as determined via DEA remains the same for a given data set. The particular choice of a distance function only affects the choice of a reference point from the efficiency frontier for comparison purposes. Furthermore all other possible reference points mentioned under DGP 1 can basically be calculated under DGP 2 as well, a feature of standard DEA which will be exploited for frontier point estimation below. The only difference is that under DGP 2 such non-radial efficiency scores don't make sense any longer from a statistical perspective. Surveys about statistical inference based on DGP 1 resp. DGP 2 include Grosskopf, 1996 and Gstach, 1999a.

DGP 3 adds the idea of target output-ratios to DGP 2 and is appropriate, if these ratios can plausibly be described as random variates from some distribution. This additional feature of DGP 3 is necessary for estimation of output-specific efficiencies and enables statistical discrimination amongst possible reference points without the restrictive $\rho_{sk} = 1$ assumption of DGP 2.

2. Using output-ratios for technology characterization via DEA

As already mentioned, a prerequisite of efficiency estimation is knowledge of the production frontier. In the present context restricted to output-technical efficiencies this requirement can be stated more precisely: Without knowing the Farrell output-efficient frontier $\mathrm{y}^F(x)$ corresponding to a given input vector x, no comparison between an observed output vector y (always observed along with an input vector x!) and some frontier output vector $y^F \in \mathrm{y}^F(x)$ is possible. Usually this frontier has to be estimated and this estimation logically (not necessarily computationally!) preempts the efficiency estimation step.

DEA is a tool to effect frontier estimation and at the same time also provides efficiency estimates of various sorts. The proposed output specific efficiency estimation technique relies on DEA only with regard to the provision of frontier estimates. In this paper the output-oriented variable returns to scale DEA due to Banker et al., 1984 will be used. This linear programming problem can be characterized as constrained search for maximum proportional expansion of an observed output vector $y_j \in \mathbb{R}^S$ relative to a sample of observed input/output vectors $\{x_i, y_i\}_{i=1}^n$, when the underlying technology satisfies convexity, strong disposability and exhibits variable returns to scale.

So we deal here generally with a sample of size n of observations on R-dimensional input vectors and S-dimensional output vectors, each observation corresponding to a particular DMU. Formally the corresponding programming problem may be stated as:

$$\begin{aligned} \max_{\lambda_1 \ldots \lambda_n, \theta_j} \quad & \theta_j \\ \text{s.t.:} \quad & \theta_j y_{js} \leq \sum_{i=1}^{n} \lambda_i y_{is} \quad \forall\, s \\ & x_{jr} \geq \sum_{i=1}^{n} \lambda_i x_{ir} \quad \forall\, r, \\ & \sum_{i=1}^{n} \lambda_i = 1 \end{aligned} \tag{2.1}$$

Denote the solution to (2.1) as $\lambda_1^* \ldots \lambda_n^*, \theta_j^*$. The Farrell output-efficiency score of DMU j associated with this solution is then defined as $\varepsilon_j = 1/\theta_j^*$. If $\varepsilon_j = 1$ then DMU j is called Farrell efficient and simply inefficient if $\varepsilon_j < 1$. For the 2-output example represented in Figure 2.1 (based on the assumption of all DMU's using equal amounts of inputs) the efficient DMU's are DMU 1, DMU 2 and DMU4, while only DMU 3 is inefficient with $\varepsilon_3 \simeq 0.67$. The latter figure as usual means that DMU 3 could have produced about 33% more of each output (a proportional rather than output specific expansion!) given its inputs and the actual achievements of the other DMU's from the sample.

It must be added that due to possible remaining slacks this solution may entail $\theta_j^* y_{js} < \sum_{i=1}^n \lambda_i^* y_{is}$ for some s and/or $x_{jr} > \sum_{i=1}^n \lambda_i^* x_{ir}$ for some r. This is the case for DMU 3 in the graphical example, where

Figure 2.1. DEA-estimated frontier for a 2-output technology

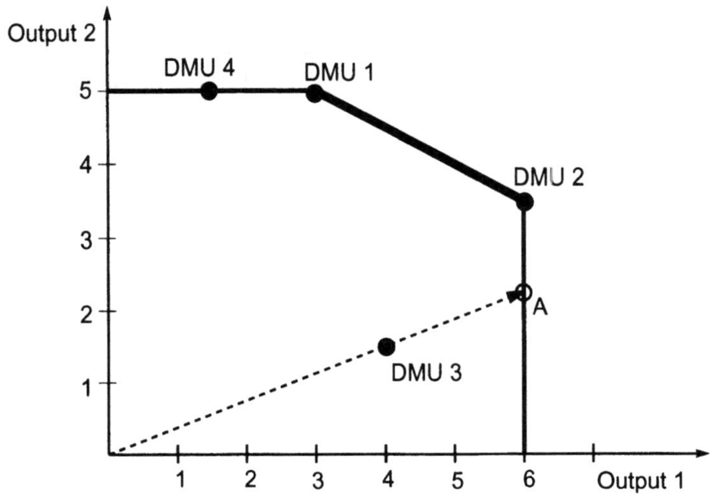

Solid facets: DEA estimated frontier; fat solid facet: Pareto-Koopman efficient frontier, solid circles: observed outputs; transparent circle: radial projection reference point to determine Farrell-efficiency of DMU 3.

$\theta_j^* y_{js}$ corresponds to the outputs of the radial projection point A and $\sum_{i=1}^{n} \lambda_i^* y_{is}$ to outputs of the reference unit DMU 2.

In the sense of Pareto or Koopmans, 1951 production plans like A in the figure should be considered inefficient because they still exhibit improvement potential: Fictitious production A clearly is inferior to actual production of DMU 2 in the example. So the Pareto-Koopmans efficient frontier would only be the fat solid facet connecting DMU 1 with DMU 2 in Figure 2.1. In Cooper et al., 2000, p. 10f the inefficiency remaining after any possible proportional output-expansion and thus not reflected in an efficiency measure like ε_j is labeled (output) mix-inefficiency. From a programming point of view this conceptual distinction between efficiency associated with proportional output expansion (irritatingly called technical efficiency in the cited book) and mix efficiency makes sense, because it directly relates to two different types of programming problems. In the statistical perspective to be employed in this book the only distinguishing feature between any two potential reference points is their posterior likelihood and inferiority of one reference point against another is irrelevant.

To find remaining improvement potentials in addition to radial output expansion in other than this simple example (which can be solved graphically) one would have to do a second stage additive DEA as described for example in Ali and Seiford, 1993. This would then proof for example, that points like DMU 4 in Figure 2.1 are not Pareto-Koopmans efficient. But, as already indicated, this approach will not be followed here because for the task at hand we may indeed consider the set of Farrell-efficient points, i.e. the fat PLUS the thin frontier facets together in Figure 2.1, as proper frontier estimate.

The reason for considering the set of Farrell-efficient points as proper efficiency frontier for the present task of output specific efficiency estimation will become clear from analyzing Figure 2.2, which adds important conceptual pieces of information to the example details already given in Figure 2.1: the true frontier and the true target output ratio of DMU 3.[2]

Figure 2.2. True and DEA-estimated frontier for a 2-output technology

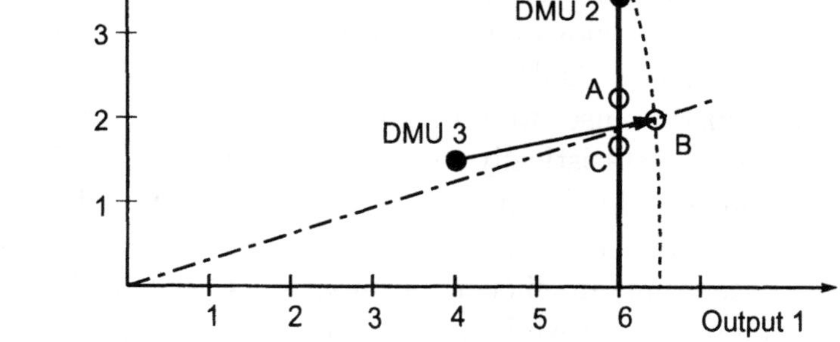

Dashed line: true frontier; solid facets: DEA estimated frontier; solid circles: observed outputs; transparent circles: reference points.

[2] Also outside the context of the present model the emphasis on non-radial slack may be questioned, because, as stated on page 176 of Coelli et al., 1998, "such slacks may be viewed as being an artefact of the frontier construction method chosen (DEA)".

Note first the trivial fact that for any of the statistical structures described above the DEA frontier based on observed data (the three connected facets passing through DMU4, DMU1 and DMU2 in Figure 2.2) is merely an estimate of the true production frontier (the dashed line in Figure 2.2) and a systematically biased one (overestimating true efficiencies). If we assume more specifically that the involved inefficiencies are continuous output-specific random variables following some multivariate distribution, the probability of any single observation lying exactly on the true frontier is zero as is the probability of any realized production to exhibit an output-ratio which is exactly equal to the target output-ratio. I mention this trivial fact because it is sometimes ignored in discussions about the proper choice of reference points for efficiency evaluations with DEA, which led to confusion between the statistical problem of estimating production relationships (Farrell's agenda) and the axiomatic considerations regarding production (Pareto's or Koopmans's agenda).

Now assume that the true target output ratio of DMU 3 is the one depicted as the dash-dotted line passing through point B in Figure 2.2 (the slope of such a line is one way to identify the common output-ratio of points along this line), such that point B is the proper reference point for the purpose of output specific efficiency evaluation. Clearly point B (unlike point A) is no longer inferior to observed production of DMU 2. But, it is true, point B is not observed and therefore cannot be used for efficiency comparison. On the other hand point A (resulting from radial projection of DMU 3 upon the DEA estimated frontier) or point C (resulting from a particular non-radial projection upon the DEA estimated frontier) both come obviously much closer in any meaningful metric to targeted output B than DMU 2. So while A or C are inferior to DMU 2 in a deterministic sense, we still want to consider them as potential reference units for a statistically sound type of output-specific efficiency evaluation. This should rationalize the use of all Farrell-efficient points (rather than the smaller set of Pareto-Koopmans efficient points) as potential reference points in efficiency comparisons henceforth and clearly induces a larger set of feasible output-ratios than would result from a restriction of attention to the Pareto-Koopmans efficient frontier.

In terms of the present example the technique to be developed subsequently will scan the whole array of possible projections of DMU 3 upon the DEA estimated frontier.[3] Therefore frontier points DMU 1 ($= \sum_{i=1}^{n} \lambda_i^* y_j$) or A ($= \theta^* y_j$) or C will be only three amongst the plethora of possible comparison points considered for measuring the output-specific efficiency of DMU 3.

Based on the above discussion we now proceed to the issue of describing the efficiency frontier in terms of output-ratios. Assume for this purpose that (2.1) would have been solved one by one for all DMU's $j = 1 \ldots n$ leading to a vector $\{\theta_1^*, \ldots, \theta_n^*\}$ of maximum proportional expansion values for output vectors of each DMU relative to the sample of observations. The vector $\{\theta_1^*, \ldots, \theta_n^*\}$ leads to a set of frontier points $\{x_i, \theta_i^* y_i\}_{i=1}^n$, which fully describes the frontier of technology under the maintained convexity assumption and by the argument above, we do not care whether these points are efficient in the Pareto-Koopman sense or not, as long as they are Farrell-efficient. Given this we want to characterize a point along this frontier in terms of an input vector x and an output-ratio vector m, where, for the present purpose

$$m = \{m_1 \ldots m_S\} \text{ with } m_s = y_s \Big/ \sum_{k=1}^{S} y_k \quad \forall\, s \in \{0, \ldots, S\}, \tag{2.2}$$

and clearly $\sum_{s=1\ldots S} m_s = 1$.[4] I will henceforth use the shorthand notation $\mathrm{y}^F(x_j, m)$ to describe the relationship between an input vector x and an output-ratio vector m, i.e.

$$\mathrm{y}^F(x_j, m) = \{\mathrm{y}_1^F(x_j, m), \ldots, \mathrm{y}_S^F(x_j, m)\}. \tag{2.3}$$

Now we want to construct an input/output-tuple $(\tilde{x}, \tilde{y})$, which is part of the production possibility set described via frontier points $\{x_i, \theta_i^* y_i\}_{i=1}^n$. So point $(\tilde{x}, \tilde{y})$ should lie on or below the frontier which was estimated from sample $\{x_i, y_i\}_{i=1}^n$ such that reestimating the frontier based on the enlarged sample $(\tilde{x}, \tilde{y}) \cup \{x_i, \theta_i^* y_i\}_{i=1}^n$ would not alter the original frontier

---

[3] Note that possible projections y_i^F under any circumstances must satisfy $y_{is} \leq y_{is}^F$ for all s, in the present example $4 \leq y_{31}^F$ and $1.5 \leq y_{32}^F$. These posterior domain restrictions will be discussed in more detail further below in this section and their role played in identification in Section 2 of Chapter 6 below.

[4] In the course of estimating output specific efficiencies below we will eventually make use of alternative characterizations of output-ratios other than (2.2). But this is immaterial with regard to the present derivation of the relationship between some input vector x, an output-ratio vector m and the corresponding output-vector on the efficiency frontier, as long as the alternative characterization can be transformed uniquely into form (2.2).

estimate. This construction will be based on the definition

$$\kappa = \min_s \{ \min_j \{ y_{j1} : y_{j1} > 0 \}, \ldots, \min_j \{ y_{jS} : y_{jS} > 0 \} \}, \qquad (2.4)$$

which together with any prespecified output-ratio m according to definition (2.2) leads to an output tuple $\tilde{y} = m\kappa$. Coupled with any of the observed input vectors the input/output tuple $(x_i, m\kappa)$ will then constitute a production plan within (or exactly at) the boundaries of the original technology. Let me illustrate this graphically in Figure 2.3.

Figure 2.3. Constructing fictitious inefficient outputs for given output-ratio vectors m in a 2-output model

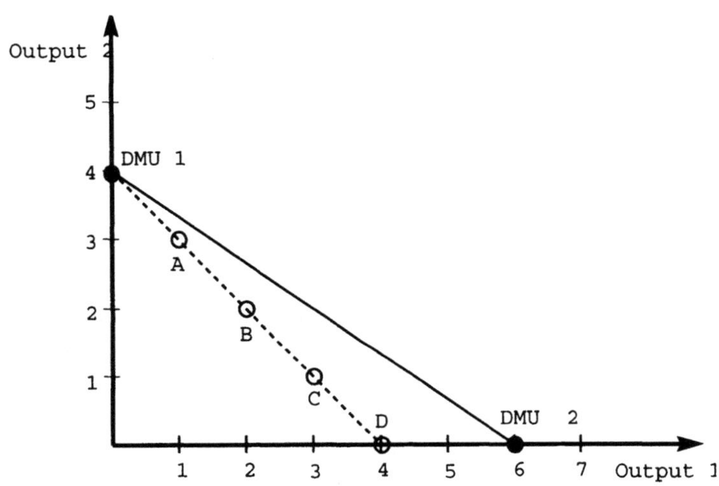

Solid circles: observed outputs; Solid line: DEA estimated frontier; Dashed line: all points constructed via $m\kappa$; Circles A,B,C resp. D: inefficient points corresponding to (m_1, m_2)= (0.25,0.75), (0.5,0.5), (0.75,0.25) resp. (1,0).

This graph depicts a simple case with only two observed DMU's, both using the same amounts of inputs, both being fully specialized in producing one of the two outputs involved and both being efficient in a DEA perspective. So the DEA estimated frontier corresponding to this sample is simply the line connecting DMU 1 with DMU 2 and the associated κ determined via (2.4) is 4. Now set $m = (0.25, 0.75)$ for example to get the output-vector $(\tilde{y}_1, \tilde{y}_2) = (1, 3)$, which is labeled A in the graph. Likewise setting $m = (1, 0)$ would lead to output vector $(4, 0)$. So as is easily verified, any output vector so constructed and coupled with an input vector from the sample observations will lead to production plans within the confines of the originally estimated technology.

Finally solve the linear program

$$\max_{\gamma_1 \cdots \gamma_n, \zeta} \zeta \quad \text{s.t.:} \quad \zeta m_s \kappa_j \leq \sum_{i=1}^{n} \gamma_i \theta_i^* y_{is} \quad \forall\, s \tag{2.5}$$
$$x_{jr} \geq \sum_{i=1}^{n} \gamma_i x_{ir} \quad \forall\, r$$
$$\sum_{i=1}^{n} \gamma_i = 1.$$

and denote the optimal solution of (2.5) as ζ^*. This then leads to the desired description of the technology in terms of input vectors and output-ratio vectors defined as

$$\hat{\mathrm{y}}^F(x_j, m) = \zeta^* m\kappa, \tag{2.6}$$

where the hat is used to indicate that $\hat{\mathrm{y}}^F(x_j, m)$ in fact is only an estimator of the unknown relationship $\mathrm{y}^F(x_j, m)$.

So the simple strategy proposed here to estimate output-ratio dependent frontier points in the non-parametric spirit of DEA is to apply the same DEA-variant as used in (2.1) to the first observation of the enlarged sample $(x_j, m\kappa) \cup \{x_1, \theta_1^* y_1 \ldots x_n, \theta_n^* y_n\}$, where the first (fictitious) observation just has the desired output-ratio.

Note that the input-vectors considered as feasible arguments for $\mathrm{y}^F(\cdot)$ are restricted to the sample input-vectors because all I want is to evaluate the possible output-efficient points corresponding to the original input observations. But frontier points for any convex combination of observed inputs $\{x_i\}$ could be estimated along the lines of program (2.5) in the same manner. Only if one were to consider input vectors smaller in one or more components than the respective minimum of the observed inputs this would require some modification of the definition of κ. I will not deal with this more general case here.

In line with the arguments above no domain restrictions for output-mix vectors m were invoked in the derivation of formula (2.6). So m might take on limiting values such that only one output s will be produced. In this case $m_s = 1$ and $m_r = 0$ for all $r \neq s$. For the subsequent output-specific efficiency estimation purpose this is more than is usually needed, because the set of feasible output ratios corresponding to a given observation (x_j, y_j) and a frontier estimate based on sample $\{x_i, y_i\}$ is necessarily a real subset of the S-dimensional unit simplex on which m is defined.[5]

This sample based domain restriction is an important factor contributing to the very possibility of estimating output specific efficiencies and thus is worth some more elaboration. To illustrate the geometry of this issue look at Figure (2.4), where the estimated frontier (the fat solid line) corresponding to a given input vector x for a two-output example is depicted once again as input-isoquant. From DEA applied to this three observations sample (where it is assumed that all DMU's use equal amounts of inputs) and the resulting frontier estimate we first conclude that DMU 3 operates inefficient, while DMU 1 and DMU 2 constitute the frontier.

Figure 2.4. A simple two-output technology represented via Input-Isoquant

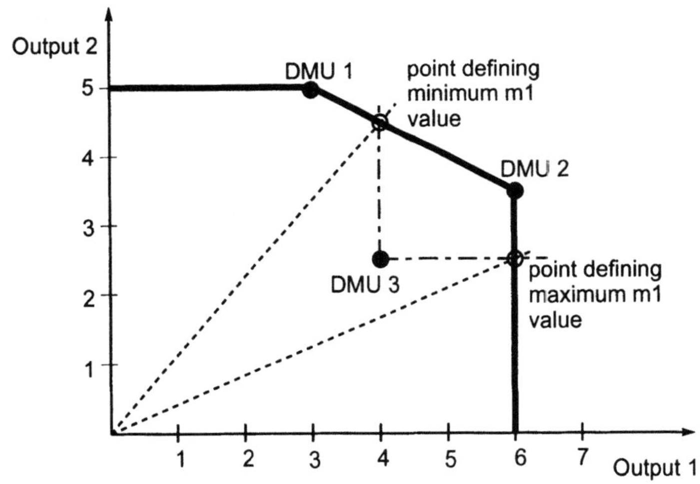

But DEA has more to tell immediately, namely the feasible range of unobserved target output-ratios of DMU 3, bounded by the dashed

[5] This subset must not be confused with the output-ratio subset implied by restricting attention to Pareto-Koopmans efficient points, as was discussed above!

lines in the figure (2.4). To calculate this feasible range numerically in this simple case note that any possible reference (frontier) point $(\mathrm{y}_1^F(x,m), \mathrm{y}_2^F(x,m))$ for DMU 3 must satisfy

$$y_s \leq \mathrm{y}_s^F(x,m) \quad \forall\, s = 1,2. \tag{2.7}$$

So the corresponding minimum and maximum m_1-values can be derived as

$$m_1^{\min} = \min\{\alpha : \mathrm{y}_1^F(x,(\alpha,1-\alpha)) \geq y_1\} \tag{2.8}$$
$$m_1^{\max} = \max\{\alpha : \mathrm{y}_2^F(x,(\alpha,1-\alpha)) \geq y_2\} \tag{2.9}$$

Note that we must not separately consider the m_2-domains in a two-output setting, as output-ratio vectors m defined via (2.2) in this case are fully determined by a single figure (I have arbitrarily chosen m_1 for this purpose, but clearly a representation in terms of m_2 instead would be just as fine). So an m_1-range already determines the feasible m_2-range. Definitions (2.8) and (2.9) lead to a feasible set $\Omega(x,y) \subset [0,1]^S$ of output-mix vectors m for given (x,y) defined as

$$\Omega(x,y) \equiv \left\{\beta\begin{bmatrix} m_1^{\min} \\ 1-m_1^{\min}\end{bmatrix} + (1-\beta)\begin{bmatrix} m_1^{\max} \\ 1-m_1^{\max}\end{bmatrix},\ \beta \in [0,1]\right\} \tag{2.10}$$

$\Omega(x,y)$ will play an important role in estimation below, because the posterior density of m (given (x,y) and a frontier estimate) is defined on this domain. The better we are able to define this domain, the more efficient will estimation of output-specific efficiencies be. As was illustrated, the domain definition is very simple for the 2-output case and allows easy scanning of possible values of m by simply varying β in $[0,1]$.

This nice representation of the feasible set $\Omega(x,y)$ in terms of convex combinations of minimum and maximum m-values is in general not possible in higher dimensional output-spaces ($S > 2$), despite the fact, that analogous definitions for minimum and maximum feasible output-ratio vector components m_s for $1 \leq s \leq S-1$ are easily formulated as

$$m_s^{\min}\left(m_{\neg(s,S)}\right) = \min\left\{m_s : y_k \leq \mathrm{y}_k^F\left(x, m_1, ...m_{S-1}, 1-\textstyle\sum_{k=1}^{S-1} m_k\right)\ \forall\, k\right\} \tag{2.11}$$

$$m_s^{\max}\left(m_{\neg(s,S)}\right) = \max\left\{m_s : y_k \leq \mathrm{y}_k^F\left(x, m_1, ...m_{S-1}, 1-\textstyle\sum_{k=1}^{S-1} m_k\right)\ \forall\, k\right\}, \tag{2.12}$$

where $m_{\neg(s,S)}$ is the output-ratio vector excluding m_s and m_S. Note again that there is no separate restriction on feasible m_S values, since their range is already determined via (2.11) and (2.12). Thus the distinguishing feature of domain restrictions (2.11) and (2.12) for the $S > 2$ case is that they depend on given values of the other components of $m_{\neg S}$. For example in a three-output case the feasible range of m_1-values would depend on a given m_2 value. A change in the latter therefore induces a change in the feasible range of m_1. So in higher-dimensional settings one would have to check feasibility of any particular (x, m)-tuple encountered in the course of randomizing amongst potential (x, m)-tuples (as detailed below in section 2 of chapter 7) against inequalities (2.7). This clearly is computationally more demanding than just varying β in $[0, 1]$ but otherwise straightforward.

3. A bias corrected model with output-specific efficiencies

To motivate bias correction of the original frontier point estimates defined in 2.6 note the following: Standard DEA is an extremal (as opposed to an average) estimator which relies solely on most efficient points to determine a frontier estimate and disregards the underlying distributional characteristics of efficiencies completely. But no matter what this true underlying distribution of efficiencies is, as long as it is continuous, the observed outputs will generically suffer from some inefficiency and thus fall short of the frontier represented as input-isoquant. Therefore the corresponding output oriented DEA estimated frontier will inevitably lie below (in the geometry of input-isoquants as represented for example in Figure 2.2) the true frontier resulting in an overestimation of output-oriented DEA efficiency scores.

Additional motivation for bias correction comes from potentially unbalanced proportions of observations associated with different ranges of output-ratios: Observing many DMU's producing a lot of output 1 compared to output 2 and only a few DMU's producing a lot of output 2 relative to output 1 implies rather accurate DEA frontier point estimates for high output 1 to output 2 ratios, but poor estimates for low output 1 to output 2 ratios. Bias correction should help to mitigate this problem, which is particularly relevant for the estimation of output-specific estimation.

Furthermore standard DEA will always render a certain proportion of observations as efficient. That is, the distribution of DEA-estimated efficiency scores $\{\varepsilon_j\}_{i=1}^{n}$ has a non-vanishing mass point at 1 which is clearly at odds with continuous types of distributions of efficiency scores. To illustrate this problem I calculated the number of DEA-efficient DMU's for a series of independent samples constructed from known technology and known efficiency distributions for a model with one input and two outputs and a model with three inputs and three outputs. The sample size was chosen at random in the range [20,1000]. The resulting numbers of Farrell-output-efficient (as by DEA-estimation) DMU's are displayed in Figures 2.5 and 2.6.

Figure 2.5. Farrell-efficient DMU's with 1 Input, 2 Outputs

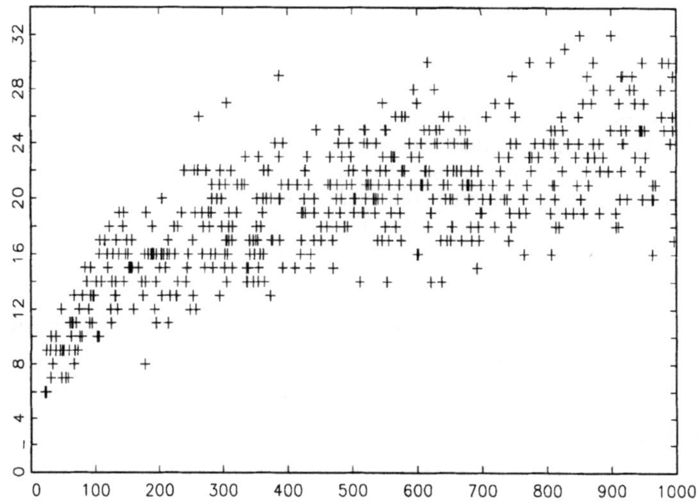

Results from output-oriented BCC-DEA applied to Monte-Carlo samples of size between 25 and 1000. Data generation based on a variable returns to scale, constant-elasticity-of-substitution-technology (elasticity=1) and log-exponentially distributed inefficiency terms (common to all outputs!) with expected efficiency being roughly 0.83.

From a regression of the number of efficient DMU's on the sample size we would thus find that for the lower dimensional model depicted in Figure 2.5 the expected number of efficient DMU's for sample size 1000 is roughly 26. So the prior probability of a randomly drawn DMU to turn out efficient in a standard DEA even for this extremely low-dimensional model is about 2.6%. As can also be seen this probability is monotonically decreasing with sample size. For higher dimensional models like

Figure 2.6. Farrell-efficient DMU's with 3 Inputs, 3 Outputs

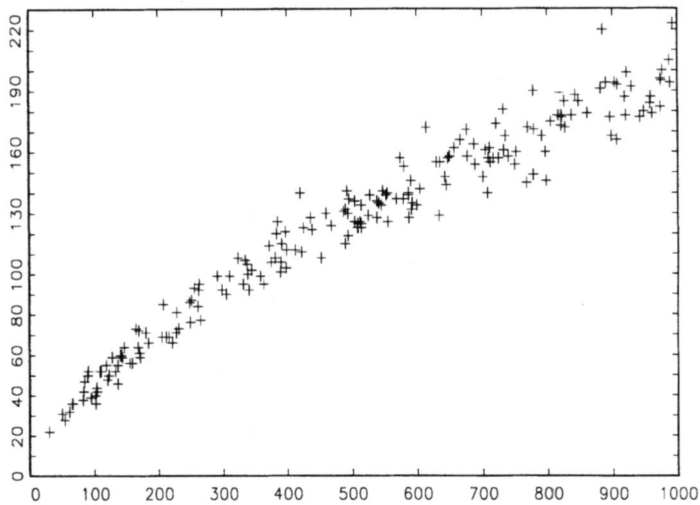

Results from output-oriented BCC-DEA applied to Monte-Carlo samples of size between 25 and 1000. Data generation based on a variable returns to scale, constant elasticity of substitution technology (elasticity=1) and log-exponentially distributed inefficiency terms (common to all outputs!) with expected efficiency being roughly 0.83.

the [3×3] model depicted in Figure 2.6, the corresponding probability figure for sample size 1000 is roughly as large as 20%. But for general, continuous types of multivariate efficiency distributions as will be used below, the probability of observing a sample with one or more such fully efficient DMU's is actually zero. Furthermore, if the value of the underlying density function at full efficiency is zero, no meaningful analysis could be based on such a sample, because the resulting likelihood of such a sample would inevitable be zero.

So for the purpose of output-specific efficiency estimation these apparently fully efficient observations under DEA must either be skipped from the sample or the efficiency estimates must be bias corrected after prior DEA. The latter approach would usually render almost all DMU's inefficient, so that only very few observations would eventually have to be skipped. In the light of the above argument, showing significant proportions of efficient DMU's particularly for smaller samples, I decided to choose the second strategy (i.e. base the output-specific efficiency analysis on a bias corrected version of a DEA frontier) for the simulations to follow, which also cover such small sample sizes. In the application of Chapter 9 instead, the output-specific efficiencies will be estimated for a standard DEA-estimated frontier without bias correction, because there the sample size is comparably large and the potential gain from bias correction small. The relatively small number of efficient DMU's in this application will consequently be skipped from the sample when it comes to output-specific efficiency estimation.

The usual approach to bias correction is to construct a non-parametric Kernel estimator of the density of the original *radial* DEA-efficiency scores and draw bootstrap samples of *radial* efficiency scores from this density to generate bootstrap output samples. For the present purpose of output-specific efficiency estimation this resampling strategy is clearly inconsistent, because the distribution of radial distances of observed outputs will in general depend on the output-mix associated with a specific radial projection. So we should rather base resampling on an output-mix dependent radial efficiency density estimator.

It should be emphasized that the radiallity of projections (underlying the calculation of DEA efficiency scores) per se is *not* the problem here. It is perfectly legitimate to base resampling of efficiency scores on radial efficiency measures even with output specific efficiencies, as long as the distribution of the radial scores is made output-ratio dependent ! So for bias correction of the original DEA-efficiency in the presence of output-specific efficiencies I propose the following bootstrap approach:

Estimate the conditional density $\mathrm{d}(\varepsilon|m)$ of radial efficiency scores for given output-ratio m based on the DEA-estimated scores $\{\varepsilon_j\}_{i=1}^n$, where conditioning is with respect to *observed* output-mixes associated with the individual observations. This could be accomplished for example by defining

$$\varepsilon \equiv 1/(1+e^{-w}) \tag{2.13}$$

$$\text{where } \mathrm{d}(w|m) = \mathcal{N}(\mu_m, \sigma_m^2) \tag{2.14}$$

with

$$\mu_m = \frac{\sum_{i=1}^n \ln\!\left(\frac{\varepsilon_i}{1-\varepsilon_i}\right)(k+\|m_i - m\|)^{-1}}{\sum_{i=1}^n (k+\|m_i - m\|)^{-1}} \tag{2.15}$$

and

$$\sigma_m^2 = \frac{\sum_{i=1}^n \left\{\ln\!\left(\frac{\varepsilon_i}{1-\varepsilon_i}\right) - \mathrm{E}\!\left[\ln\!\left(\frac{\varepsilon_i}{1-\varepsilon_i}\right)\right]\right\}^2 (k+\|m_i - m\|)^{-1}}{\sum_{i=1}^n (k+\|m_i - m\|)^{-1}} \tag{2.16}$$

such that

$$\mathrm{d}(\varepsilon|m) = \frac{1}{\varepsilon(1-\varepsilon)}\,\mathcal{N}\left(\ln\left(\frac{\varepsilon}{1-\varepsilon}\right);\ \mu_m, \sigma_m^2\right) \tag{2.17}$$

This procedure leads to a conditional density estimate for ε based on a logit transformation of efficiencies. These logit transformed variables w are assumed to be normally distributed with mean and variance depending on m, the sample observations m_i and the DEA-estimated efficiency scores ε_i via weights $(k + \|m_i - m\|)^{-1}$. The latter are constructed using the Euclidian distances of m from the observed m_i's and some constant parameter $k > 0$, controlling the relative weights.

Then the following sequence of steps is iterated many times with each iteration superscripted as $^{(b)}$ with $b = 1 \ldots B$:

1 Generate a bootstrap sample of efficiency scores $\{\varepsilon_i^{(b)}\}_{i=1}^n$ where $\varepsilon_i^{(b)}$ is drawn randomly from density $\mathrm{d}(\varepsilon|m_i)$ as defined in (2.17).

2 Define a bootstrap sample of output observations via $y_i^{(b)} = \varepsilon_i^{(b)} y_i / \varepsilon_i$.

3 Use DEA to reestimate the frontier based on the bootstrap sample $\{x_i, y_i^{(b)}\}_{i=1}^n$ yielding corresponding radial efficiency estimates $\{\tilde{\varepsilon}_i^{(b)}\}$.

4 Compare the original y_i observations with the respective frontier point estimates $y_i^{(b)}/\tilde{\varepsilon}_i^{(b)}$ to generate bootstrap estimates of efficiencies $\hat{\varepsilon}_i^{(b)} = y_i \tilde{\varepsilon}_i^{(b)} / y_i^{(b)}$. Thereby note that by construction $\hat{\varepsilon}_i^{(b)} \geq \varepsilon_i$.

After B loops the bias of each individual efficiency score can be calculated as

$$\mathrm{BIAS}(\varepsilon_i) = \mathrm{E}_b(\hat{\varepsilon}_i^{(b)}) - \varepsilon_i, \tag{2.18}$$

which is necessarily positive reflecting overestimation of efficiency by standard DEA. Now bias corrected efficiency scores $\{\varepsilon_i^*\}$ are calculated as

$$\varepsilon_i^* = \varepsilon_i - \mathrm{BIAS}(\varepsilon_i) = 2\varepsilon_i - \mathrm{E}_b(\hat{\varepsilon}_i^{(b)}) \tag{2.19}$$

Definition (2.19) is the general version of a bias corrected estimate based on bootstrapping. In the context of efficiency estimation this correction suffers from a particular deficiency, namely, that the resulting bias corrected efficiency scores not necessarily satisfy $\varepsilon_i^* > 0$ as they should.

This problem can be solved as in the above cited papers of Wilson, 1994 and Simar and Wilson, 1995 by running the bootstrap based on the negative log-efficiencies and, after bias correction, transforming the estimates back onto traditional efficiency scale.

The only remaining problem is the potential non-convexity of the resulting frontier made up by points y_i/ε_i^*. After all DEA is designed as technique to estimate frontiers of convex technologies and the sole purpose of DEA in this paper is to deliver a frontier estimate of such a technology, while the radial DEA-efficiency scores, whether bias-corrected or not, are of no interest per se. But in the course of bias correcting the radial efficiency scores and thus the corresponding efficiency-frontier points this convexity assumption was neglected and most likely lost.

To remedy this I will simply envelope the sample of $\{x_i, y_i/\varepsilon_i^*\}$ points to get the final, bias corrected (subscript $_{BC}$) frontier point estimates $\hat{\mathrm{y}}_{BC}^F(x_i, m)$ as follows:

$$\hat{\mathrm{y}}_{BC}^F(x_j, m) = \zeta^* m\kappa_j \tag{2.20}$$

where ζ^* is the solution to the linear program

$$\max_{\gamma_1 \cdots \gamma_n, \zeta} \zeta \quad \text{s.t.:} \quad \zeta m_s \kappa_j \leq \sum_{i=1}^n \gamma_i y_{is}/\varepsilon_i^* \quad \forall\ s \tag{2.21}$$

$$x_{jr} \leq \sum_{i=1}^n \gamma_i x_{ir} \quad \forall\ r$$

$$\sum_{i=1}^n \gamma_i = 1$$

and where κ_j is defined as in equation (2.4). So the only difference between (2.5) and (2.21) is that in the former the sample outputs are constructed via $\theta_i^* y_i$ and in the latter via y_i/ε_i^*. Apart from this the definitions $\hat{\mathrm{y}}^F(\cdot)$ resp $\hat{\mathrm{y}}_{BC}^F(\cdot)$ for frontier point estimates are equivalent.

Which one of these definitions to use for the subsequent estimation of output-specific efficiencies depends largely on sample size: If n is small, the induced outward shift of the estimated frontier via bias corrected efficiency estimates will be significant and worthwhile, despite the time consuming bootstrapping steps involved and despite the danger of errors related with the necessary specification of a good proxy for the m-dependent radial efficiency densities. If n is large on the other hand, there seems to be little gain in using $\hat{y}^F_{BC}(\cdot)$ rather than the much less demanding $\hat{y}^F(\cdot)$.

4. Estimator consistency

DEA frontier point estimates $\hat{y}^F(\cdot)$ are consistent as has been proven in Banker, 1993 for the single output-case and in Kneip et al., 1998 for the multi-output case. Therefore also deviation estimates (the basis of efficiency scores) from frontier points are consistent, no matter in which direction we are going to evaluate such deviations. On the other hand Markov chain Monte Carlo estimates of quantities describing aspects of posterior efficiency and output-ratio distributions based on true (rather than estimated) deviations are consistent as proven for more general settings than will be considered here for example in Meyn and Tweedie, 1993 or Tierney, 1994. These consistency results combined provide the rational for the central theoretical claim of this book, that the proposed approach, being based on deviations from a DEA-estimated frontier, will yield in turn consistent estimates of output specific efficiencies.

I will not give a formal proof for this claim here, because the heuristics is all too simple: If we have a sequence of two estimation steps, where the output of the first estimation step is input (or quasi-data) to the second and both steps considered separately are consistent (the second step with regard to true data), then small sample deviations of quasi-data to true data will vanish asymptotically allowing to invoke the consistency argument for the second step also for the quasi-data.

But for finite samples the above consistency claim is likely to be of limited use, because it tells nothing about the relative deviations of estimated parameters from their true counterparts in real world, i.e. small sample, applications. So in order to get an idea of how good or bad performance of the proposed estimator for finite samples will typically be, I ran large scale simulations to come up with corresponding evidence reported in Chapter 8. And it is worthwhile in particular, in the light of the merely heuristic argument about consistency of the sequence of estimations steps given above, to study the difference between small sample performance of mean output-specific efficiency estimators obtained from using true frontiers on one hand and DEA-estimated frontiers on the other. So in presenting the Monte Carlo results below I will compare between the performance of estimators for the cases where they are based on a DEA estimated frontier and the case where they are based on the true frontier. This will help to assess the additional small sample error of estimators introduced by relying on consistency arguments twice.

Another issue relating to finite samples is that of correlation amongst frontier point estimates and consequently amongst efficiency estimates of whatever kind. It must be noted, that strictly speaking we don't work with DEA estimated efficiency scores here, but use DEA only for frontier estimation. So if the correlation amongst efficiency scores affects output-specific efficiency estimation it is via the frontier point estimates. But by consistency (see above) this influence vanishes asymptotically, so for consistency of the approach to be proposed this issue is irrelevant. For an approach to bias-correction of standard radial DEA efficiency scores that deals explicitly with this dependency see Xue and Harker, 1999. As an aside note, that Markov chains generated below to derive characteristics of the underlying distribution of output-specific efficiencies and output-ratios will by construction result in serially correlated estimates, so we will have to deal with another type of cross-sample dependency separately.

Chapter 3

STATISTICAL RELATION TO RADIAL EFFICIENCY MEASURES

A consideration arising in the context of output-specific efficiencies is the following: Assume that with positive probability we would observe complete specialization (i.e. $m_s = 1$) of firms with regard to one output (indexed s) and this were true for all outputs. On the other hand we would never observe zero efficiency with regard to any of the outputs (i.e. $\mathrm{d}(\varepsilon_s = 0) = 0$ for all $s = 1 \ldots S$). Neither of the two assumptions seems particularly far fetched.

Shouldn't it be possible under these circumstance to statistically describe observations with full specialization ($m_s = 1, m_{\neg s} = 0$) solely in terms of the ε_s distribution and the frontier point $\mathrm{y}_s^F(x, m_s = 1, m_{\neg s} = 0)$ corresponding to this specialization ? In other words: Shouldn't it be possible to describe efficiencies of fully specialized firms solely by the corresponding marginal density of efficiency for that particular output ? If this were so we could try to estimate an efficiency density conditional on observed output-ratio vector m and then take the limit of this distribution as $m_s \to 1$ to get any desired marginal distribution of output-specific efficiency.

It will be shown in the sequel, that the above question is hard to answer in general. Whether or not output-specific efficiencies are correlated definitely is of importance here, but a distinction of cases according to this criterion is insufficient for a clear-cut answer. An example with uncorrelated efficiencies will be shown to work. But clearly also the trivial case of perfectly correlated efficiencies (with equal means such that radial and marginal efficiency scores are identical) works. On the other hand an example with partial correlation will demonstrate that the above described strategy to derive output-specific efficiencies in general is inconsistent.

1. Output-specific efficiency distributions as limits of radial efficiency distributions ?

First the radial efficiency distribution for a fully specified model with output specific efficiencies will be derived. Output-ratios M are treated as random variables, such that one input vector X a priori gives rise to the full set of possible frontier-output vectors associated with X. The ultimate realization of a specific point along the efficiency frontier thus depends on realization of an output-mix vector $m = \{m_1, \dots m_S\}$, which, for the purpose of this chapter, shall again be defined as in (2.2).

Let $\mathcal{E} = \{\mathcal{E}_1, \dots, \mathcal{E}_S\}$ denote a vector of random output-specific efficiencies that link frontier output quantities y_s^F multiplicatively to observed output quantities y_s for $s = 1, \dots S$. A particular realization of variable $\mathcal{E}$ will be denoted with small letter ε. The data generating process is then fully described via

$$y_s = \mathrm{y}_s^F(m, x)\,\varepsilon_s \quad \forall\ s = 1 \dots S \qquad (3.1)$$
$$\text{where} \quad \varepsilon_s \in [0,1]\ \forall\ s = 1...S$$

and via specifying multivariate densities $\mathrm{d}_{\mathcal{E}}(\varepsilon)$ and $\mathrm{d}_M(m)$ for ε and m respectively, the latter being defined on the S-dimensional unit-simplex. Independence between both variables is assumed, i.e. $\mathrm{COV}(\varepsilon_r, m_s) = 0$ for all $r, s \in \{1 \dots S\}$, so their joint density is simply

$$d_{\mathcal{E},M}(\varepsilon, m) = d_{\mathcal{E}}(\varepsilon)\, d_M(m). \qquad (3.2)$$

We will also assume independence between x and (ε, m) and therefore density (3.2) is identical to the conditional density $d_{\mathcal{E},M|X}(\varepsilon, m)$. The joint distribution (3.2) relates only to unobserved (ε, m)-variates. Ultimately I want to determine the distribution of observed relative radial deviations of y-vectors from the frontier. So this latter distribution captures random elements from the efficiency terms ε as well as from output-mix vectors m. Observability of such radial deviations of course depends on the functions $\mathrm{y}_s^F(.,.)$, which I assume as given at this stage. For the Monte Carlo analysis of the performance of output-specific efficiency estimators in a later chapter we will estimate the frontier via DEA prior to efficiency estimation proper.

The joint distribution of (y, m) (given x) is derived from the joint distribution of (ε, m) via transformation technique. This technique will be frequently used subsequently so it is worthwhile to state the underlying theorem here as formulated in the widely used textbook on mathematical statistics by Mood et al., 1974, p. 211

Theorem: Let $W = \{W_1, \ldots, W_S\}$ be jointly continuous random variables with density function $d_W(w)$. Set $\mathcal{W} = \{w : d_W(w) > 0\}$. Assume that:

a) $y_s = g_s(w)$ for $s = 1 \ldots S$ defines a one-to-one transformation $g(\cdot)$: $\mathcal{W} \mapsto \mathcal{Y}$ and denote $y = \{y_1, \ldots, y_S\}$.
b) The first derivatives of $w_s = g_s^{-1}(y)$ for $s = 1 \ldots S$ are continuous over $\mathcal{W}$.
c) The Jacobian $\left|J_{Y \mapsto W}\right|$ of the transformation $g^{-1}(\cdot)$: $\mathcal{Y} \mapsto \mathcal{W}$ is nonzero $\forall\, w \in \mathcal{W}$.

Then the joint density of $y = \{y_1, \ldots, y_S\}$ is given by

$$d_Y(y) = \left|J_{Y \mapsto W}\right| \, d_W\left(g_1^{-1}(y), \ldots, g_S^{-1}(y)\right) I_{\mathcal{Y}}(y) \tag{3.3}$$

Definitions (3.1) and (3.2) together allow derivation of the joint distribution of (y, m) via theorem (3.3), as the mapping $(\varepsilon, m) \mapsto (y, m)$ has continuous first partial derivatives and a non-vanishing Jacobian $|J| = \prod_{s=1}^{S} (y_s^F(m, x))^{-1}$. The desired density is

$$d_{Y,M|X}(y, m) = \left(\prod_{s=1}^{S} \frac{1}{y_s^F(m,x)} \right)$$

$$\times \, d_{\mathcal{E}}\left(\frac{y_1}{\mathrm{y}_1^F(m,x)}, \ldots, \frac{y_S}{\mathrm{y}_s^F(m,x)} \right) d_M(m_1 \ldots m_S) \tag{3.4}$$

The density of y proper is then derived by integrating over the unobserved variables m_s to yield

$$d_{Y|X}(y) = \int_{m \in \Omega(x,y)} d_{Y,M\,|\,X}(y, m)\, dm \tag{3.5}$$

where the set of feasible output-mix vectors m that are compatible with observed vectors x and y is denoted $\Omega(x,y) = \{m : y_s \leq \mathrm{y}_s^F(m,x),\ \forall\, s = 1 \ldots S\}$. This restriction of feasible m for given (x,y) is a reflection of the domain restriction upon the efficiencies ε_s from (3.1) and of the curvature of $\mathrm{y}^F(\cdot)$ as has been explained above.

Density (3.5) determines the probability of observing a specific output vector y for some given (and observed) input vector x, when mappings $\mathrm{y}_s^F(\cdot)$ are known, but the realization m of the output-mix vector is not.

Now I shall approach the distribution of observed y from another viewpoint by restricting attention to possible y values along a ray $R(\widetilde{m},x) = \{y : y = \tilde{\varepsilon}\,\mathrm{y}^F(\widetilde{m},x),\ 0 \leq \tilde{\varepsilon} \leq 1\}$. Note that output-mix vector $\widetilde{m}$ in formulation (3.8) is chosen arbitrarily and bears no link to the output-mix vector m used in DGP (3.1). Recall that y and $\mathrm{y}^F(\cdot)$ are vector valued, whereas $\tilde{\varepsilon}$, a radial efficiency variable, is a scalar. So the latter by construction conforms to the traditional interpretation of a radial efficiency score frequently encountered in DEA or SFA. I am interested in the distribution of such a radial score, when, as in the present case the efficiencies of the data generating process are actually output-specific. The overall probability of observing y from this ray is given as curve integral

$$\int_{R(\widetilde{m},x)} d_Y(y_1,y_2)\,ds \tag{3.6}$$

for some measure s whose variations trace out the whole length of this ray and thus has domain $[0, |\mathrm{y}^F(\widetilde{m})|]$. For convenience I define this measure as

$$s = \alpha\ |\mathrm{y}^F(\widetilde{m})| \quad \text{with } \alpha \in [0,1]. \tag{3.7}$$

This guarantees that s covers the whole range of possible y-values along the ray $R(\widetilde{m}_1)$. Furthermore α could be interpreted as a radial efficiency again just like the $\tilde{\varepsilon}$ used for defining the ray in the first place. Given a specific combination of $(\widetilde{m},x)$-values, the feasible y values under this ray restriction have the following conditional density

$$d_{Y\,|\,\widetilde{M},X}(y) = \begin{cases} \dfrac{d_{Y|X}(y)}{\displaystyle\int_0^1 d_{Y|X}\Big(\alpha \mathrm{y}^F(\widetilde{m},x)\Big)\,\Big|\mathrm{y}^F(\widetilde{m},x)\Big|\,d\alpha} & \text{if } y \in R(\widetilde{m},x) \\ 0 & \text{else} \end{cases} \tag{3.8}$$

Conditioning on output-mix vector $\widetilde{m}$ in (3.8) means geometrically to look at a cross-section of the y-distribution (3.5), where the cross section is defined by a ray (i.e. a line going through the origin) in y-space. Such a ray is exactly the projection path of observed output vectors up to the frontier in radial efficiency measurement. Thus the density of radial efficiency measures for any given $\widetilde{m}$ could theoretically be derived from (3.8), if the functions $\mathrm{y}_s^F(.)$ were given in closed form. Note that this is not the case for DEA type of frontier descriptions. So to investigate the relationship between the distribution of output-specific efficiencies and the distribution of implied radial efficiencies we will rely on a known technology for expositional purposes in the examples to follow. What holds for this case will hold asymptotically for the DEA-estimated frontier case as well, because the latter can be consistently estimated as mentioned above.

From (3.8) the density of implicit radial efficiencies $\tilde{\varepsilon}$ from representation $y = \mathrm{y}^F(\widetilde{m}, x)\,\tilde{\varepsilon}$ can thus be derived principally by substituting $\mathrm{y}^F(\widetilde{m}, x)\,\tilde{\varepsilon}$ for y and normalizing by the overall probability of observing an output vector from this ray as

$$\mathrm{d}_{\tilde{\mathcal{E}}|\widetilde{M},X}(\tilde{\varepsilon}|\widetilde{m}, x) = \frac{d_{Y|X}\left(\tilde{\varepsilon}\,\mathrm{y}^F(\widetilde{m}, x)\right)}{\int_0^1 d_{Y|X}\left(\alpha\,\mathrm{y}^F(\widetilde{m}, x)\right)\,d\alpha} \tag{3.9}$$

$$= \frac{\int\limits_{\Omega(x,y)} d_{Y,M|X}\left(\tilde{\varepsilon}\,\mathrm{y}^F(\widetilde{m}, x), m\right)\,dm}{\int_0^1 \int\limits_{\Omega(x,y)} d_{Y,M|X}\left(\alpha\,\mathrm{y}^F(\widetilde{m}, x), m\right)\,dm\,d\alpha}$$

It is impossible to derive the limit of this distribution as $\widetilde{m}_s \to 1$ for the general case, so I will calculate it for two specific examples. With (3.9) the introductory conjecture to be investigated can now be stated more precisely as:

Conjecture: Under certain conditions $\lim\limits_{\widetilde{m}_s \to 1} \mathrm{d}_{\tilde{\mathcal{E}}|\widetilde{M},X}(\tilde{\varepsilon}|\widetilde{m}, x) \stackrel{?}{=} \mathrm{d}(\varepsilon_s)$

Before continuing it is worth noting an important point about the relationship between output-specific efficiencies and radial efficiencies: The data generating process with output-specific efficiencies and target output-ratios leading to y_i-observations involves $2S-1$ random variables, S output-specific efficiency terms and $S-1$ target output-ratios (one output ratio is always completely predetermined by the remaining $S-1$ output ratios). The density of radial efficiencies conditioned on target output ratios (3.9) on the other hand involves exactly S random quantities, 1 radial efficiency score and $S-1$ target output ratios. So from basic statistical considerations we know that generally it will not be possible to recover the underlying densities of the output-specific efficiencies from the implied radial efficiencies simply because of the reduced dimensionality of the radial perspective and apart from potential dependence amongst output-specific efficiencies.

For the specific example of independent output-specific efficiencies (see below) with $S=2$ it will be shown that the above conjecture nevertheless holds under certain conditions (regarding density values at the border of their respective domains and independence of output-ratios and output-specific efficiencies). But I did not test whether this generalizes to higher dimensional output-spaces, because all of the following developments will be based on the two output-case. Furthermore clearly the DEA case of a common scalar efficiency variable (i.e. the degenerate case of output-specific efficiencies with perfect correlation and equal means) leads immediately to correct estimates of this density (without conditioning upon output-ratios though), if it were just known that indeed a common scalar efficiency variable lies behind the genesis of observed outputs. So the ability of recovering the densities of output-specific efficiencies from radial efficiency scores does not simply amount to the question of whether or not the output-specific efficiencies are independent, as both limiting cases (independence and perfect correlation) in fact can be analyzed in a radial perspective (for the independence case this will be shown below, for the perfect correlation case this is trivial).

2. An example that works

Start with a simple CRS-technology described via input isoquant $\mathrm{y}_1^F(m_1) + \mathrm{y}_2^F(m_1) = 1$ and assume all inputs x to be equal. The latter assumption will help to keep the exposition of this example short. The output-ratios of an individual DMU in this setting are fully determined by a scalar m_1, which will be called output-ratio 1 and which is defined by $m_1 = y_1^F/(y_1^F + y_2^F)$. From this we get $\mathrm{y}_1^F(m_1) = m_1$ and

$\mathrm{y}_2^F(m_1) = 1-m_1$. Define the distributions of the two output-specific multiplicative efficiencies ε_1 and ε_2 as

$$d(\varepsilon_1) = 3\,\varepsilon_1^2 \quad \varepsilon_1 \in [0,1] \tag{3.10}$$

$$d(\varepsilon_2) = 2\,\varepsilon_2 \quad \varepsilon_2 \in [0,1] \tag{3.11}$$

So the joint efficiency density is simply

$$d(\varepsilon_1, \varepsilon_2) = 6\,\varepsilon_1^2\varepsilon_2 \quad \text{for} \quad (\varepsilon_1, \varepsilon_2) \in [0,1]^2 \tag{3.12}$$

The output ratio m_1 shall be treated as random variable with uniform density on $[0,1]$. The complete data generating process is therefore

$$y_1 = \mathrm{y}_1^F(m_1)\,\varepsilon_1 = m_1\varepsilon_1, \quad y_2 = \mathrm{y}_2^F(m_1)\,\varepsilon_2 = (1-m_1)\,\varepsilon_2 \tag{3.13}$$

The joint density of (y_1, y_2) conditional on a given mixture proportion m_1 is derived via transformation technique (based on the Jacobian $|J_{(\varepsilon_1,\varepsilon_2)\to(y_1,y_2)}| = 1/[m_1(1-m_1)])$ as

$$d(y_1, y_2|m_1) = \frac{6\,y_1^2 y_2}{m_1^3(1-m_1)^2} \tag{3.14}$$

Before turning to determination of the distribution of the radial efficiency score ε associated with an observation y I need to get rid of the target output-ratio m_1. This is because the observation y might have been generated from any one of a whole set of possible target output ratios. More precisely y might stem from any m_1 satisfying $y_s \le \mathrm{y}_s^F(m_1)$ for $s = 1, 2$. This unconditional distribution of y, derived from (3.14) and the uniform distribution assumption on m_1 is [1]

$$\begin{aligned} d(y_1, y_2) &= \int_{y_1}^{1-y_2} d(y_1, y_2|m_1)\, d(m_1)\, dm_1 \\ &= \frac{6y_1^2(1-3y_2)}{1-y_2} - \frac{3y_1^2 y_2}{(1-y_2)^2} - \frac{6y_1y_2}{1-y_1} \\ &\quad +18y_1y_2 + 3y_2 + 18y_1^2y_2 \ln\left[\frac{(1-y_1)(1-y_2)}{y_1y_2}\right] \end{aligned} \tag{3.15}$$

Note that the ln-term in density (3.15) has zero-limit for both $y_1 \to 0$ and $y_2 \to 0$ and therefore the $d(y_1, y_2)$ is also defined along the y_1 resp.

[1] using $\int x^{-3}(1-x)^{-2} = -0.5x^{-2} - 2x^{-1} + (1-x)^{-1} + 3\ln|x/(x-1)|$

y_2 axis. Furthermore it is positive along the axis, which is necessary for deriving the limits below. Density (3.15) is graphically represented in Figure 3.1.

Figure 3.1. Joint distribution of outputs, example 1

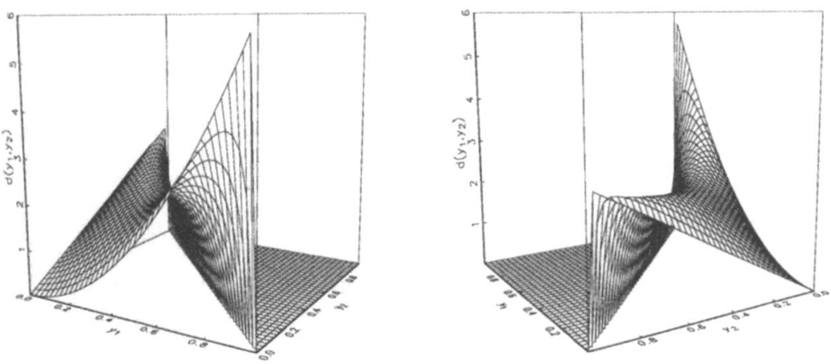

Legend: $d(\varepsilon_1, \varepsilon_2) = 6\varepsilon_1^2\varepsilon_2$, $m_1 \sim \mathcal{U}(0,1)$, $y_1 = m_1\varepsilon_1$ and $y_2 = (1-m_1)\varepsilon_2$.

As explained in section 1 a radial efficiency score ε along a given ray $R(\widetilde{m}_1)$ can now be defined as ratio of the norm of observed output to frontier output for given output-ratio $\widetilde{m}_1$. From equation (3.15) the distribution of this radial efficiency score can be derived analogous to (3.9) as

$$d_{\mathcal{E}|\widetilde{M}}(\varepsilon|\widetilde{m}_1) = \frac{d_Y(\varepsilon \mathrm{y}_1^F(\widetilde{m}_1), \varepsilon \mathrm{y}_2^F(\widetilde{m}_1))}{\int_0^1 d_Y(\alpha \mathrm{y}_1^F(\widetilde{m}_1), \alpha \mathrm{y}_2^F(\widetilde{m}_1))\, d\alpha} \tag{3.16}$$

$$= \frac{d_Y(\varepsilon\widetilde{m}_1, \varepsilon(1-\widetilde{m}_1))}{\int_0^1 d_Y(\alpha\widetilde{m}_1, \alpha(1-\widetilde{m}_1))\, d\alpha}$$

Note that the $|\mathrm{y}^F(\widetilde{m}_1)|$, used in definition (3.7), cancels out from equation (3.16), because it is independent of the integrand α and thus can be factored out from the integral. Using $\lim_{x\to x_0}\int f(x,y)dy = \int[\lim_{x\to x_0} f(x,y)]dy$ we find the two limiting distributions of radial efficiencies to be

$$\lim_{\widetilde{m}_1\to 1} d(\varepsilon|\widetilde{m}_1) = \frac{6\varepsilon^2}{\int_0^1 6\alpha^2 d\alpha} = 3\varepsilon^2 \tag{3.17}$$

$$\lim_{\tilde{m}_1 \to 0} d(\varepsilon|\tilde{m}_1) \quad = \quad \frac{3\varepsilon}{\int_0^1 3\alpha d\alpha} = 2\varepsilon \tag{3.18}$$

So this indeed leads to the marginal densities of output-specific efficiencies (3.10) resp. (3.11) as conjectured above.

3. So why not use simple regression analysis ?

In the light of the above discussion there seems to be a simple strategy to find densities of output-specific efficiencies via estimating the density of an $\tilde{m}$-dependent radial efficiency score and then taking the appropriate limits. The latter could be effected for example by regressing radial DEA efficiency scores on the associated, observed output-ratios m_1, m_2. If we had parameter estimates of this regression we could then take the limits as $m_s \to 1$ and conclude that the expected output-specific efficiencies were equal to the parameters associated with the respective output-ratios.

More specifically assume, that terms w_s, derived from applying a logit transformation to output-specific efficiencies ε_s (i.e. $w_s = \ln[\varepsilon_s/(1-\varepsilon_s)]$) had true means μ_s for $s = 1 \dots S$. But only radial efficiencies $\tilde{\varepsilon}$ were observed with corresponding logits $\tilde{w} = \ln[\varepsilon/(1-\varepsilon)]$. I prefer to work with logit transformed efficiencies because they have domain $(-\infty, +\infty)$ and are thus better suited for standard regression analysis based on normally distributed error terms. Based on a sample of input/output-observations indexed $i = 1 \dots n$ and associated radial (!) efficiency estimates $\tilde{\varepsilon}_i$ (resp. $\tilde{w}_i$) from DEA one might OLS-estimate the following regression equation:

$$\tilde{w}_i = \alpha_1 \tilde{m}_{i,1} + \dots \alpha_S \tilde{m}_{i,S} + \nu_i \quad \text{where } \nu_i \stackrel{iid}{\sim} \mathcal{N}(0, \sigma^2) \tag{3.19}$$

Note that no constant term must be used in this regression, because inclusion of such a term would render the regressor set perfectly collinear $(\sum_{s=1 \dots S} \tilde{m}_{i,s} = 1 \ \forall \ i)$. Denote the resulting parameter estimates as $\hat{\alpha}_1 \dots \hat{\alpha}_S$. The conditional distribution of $\tilde{w}$ given $\tilde{m}$ is therefore defined as

$$[\tilde{w}|\tilde{m}] \sim \mathcal{N}\left(\sum_{s=1}^{S} \hat{\alpha}_s \tilde{m}_s, \sigma^2\right) \tag{3.20}$$

and from this we get

$$\lim_{\widetilde{m}_s \to 1} \mathrm{E}(\widetilde{w}|\widetilde{m}) = \hat{\alpha}_s \tag{3.21}$$

The resulting question with regard to mean output-specific efficiencies thus is whether the expectation of $\hat{\alpha}_s$ under the true distributions of w_s and m_s is indeed μ_s. Or, disregarding the uncertainty with respect to estimation inherent in (3.20): Does the distribution of radial efficiency scores conditional on output-ratios converge to the true distribution of ε_s as $\widetilde{m}_s \to 1$. The next section shall prove by counterexample that (irrespective of the estimation specification!) this is NOT the case in general.

4. A counterexample

Start again with the simple CRS-technology from above described via input isoquant $y_1^F(m)+y_2^F(m) = 1$ and set all inputs equal. This setting shall be investigated along the lines of the previous section but now with two correlated efficiency terms distributed as

$$d(\varepsilon_1, \varepsilon_2) = \varepsilon_1^2\varepsilon_2 + 5\varepsilon_1\varepsilon_2^2, \quad \text{for } 0 \leq \varepsilon_1, \varepsilon_2 \leq 1 \tag{3.22}$$

The two efficiency terms ε_1 and ε_2 are not perfectly correlated, i.e. they are output-specific, with marginal densities being

$$d(\varepsilon_1) = 5\varepsilon_1/3 + \varepsilon_1^2/2 \tag{3.23}$$

$$d(\varepsilon_2) = \varepsilon_2/3 + 5\varepsilon_2^2/2 \tag{3.24}$$

These marginal densities are at the focus of interest here. Stochastic dependence between ε_1 and ε_2 is easy to check by verifying $d(\varepsilon_1, \varepsilon_2) \neq d(\varepsilon_1)d(\varepsilon_2)$. Let m_1 denote the ratio of output 1 to total output, i.e.

$$m_1 = y_1/(y_1 + y_2) \quad \text{with } 0 \leq m_1 \leq 1. \tag{3.25}$$

This mixture proportion is itself treated as random variable with density as defined below. The complete data generating process (a production process subject to inefficiencies) is then defined as

$$y_1 = y_1^F(m_1)\varepsilon_1 = m_1\varepsilon_1, \quad y_2 = y_2^F(m_1)\varepsilon_2 = (1-m_1)\varepsilon_2 \tag{3.26}$$

Only if both efficiencies were equal one an observation (y_1, y_2) would lie on the input isoquant describing best available technology. Now the joint density of (y_1, y_2) conditional on a given mixture proportion m is easily derived via transformation technique, based on the Jacobian $|J_{(\varepsilon_1,\varepsilon_2)\to(y_1,y_2)}| = 1/[m_1(1-m_1)]$, as

$$d(y_1, y_2|m_1) = \frac{y_1^2 y_2}{m_1^3(1-m_1)^2} + \frac{5y_1y_2^2}{m_1^2(1-m_1)^3} \tag{3.27}$$

To determine the distribution of the radial efficiency score ε conditional on ray $\widetilde{m}$ (or output-ratio $\widetilde{m}$) we first need a specification of the distribution of m. For simplicity let this be the uniform distribution, i.e.

$$\mathrm{d}_M(m_1) = \mathcal{U}(0,1) = 1. \tag{3.28}$$

Then the unconditional distribution of y can be derived from (3.27), integrating out the undesired output-ratio variable m_1 to yield: [2]

$$\begin{aligned} d(y_1, y_2) &= \int_{y_1}^{1-y_2} d(y_1, y_2|m_1)\, d(m_1)\, dm_1 \\ &= \frac{y_1^2 - 3y_1^2y_2 - 5y_1y_2}{1-y_2} + \frac{5y_2^2 - 15y_1y_2^2 - y_1y_2}{1-y_1} \\ &\quad + \frac{5y_1 + y_2}{2} + 18y_1y_2 + \frac{y_1^2y_2}{2(1-y_2)^2} - \frac{5y_1y_2^2}{2(1-y_1)^2} \\ &\quad + (3y_1^2y_2 + 15y_1y_2^2)\ln\left[\frac{(1-y_1)(1-y_2)}{y_1y_2}\right] \end{aligned} \tag{3.29}$$

Note that the log-term in density (3.29) has zero-limit for both $y_1 \to 0$ and $y_2 \to 0$ and thus by definition also for $\widetilde{m}_1 \to 1$ and $\widetilde{m}_1 \to 0$. Therefore the unconditional density $d(y_1, y_2)$ is also defined along the y_1 resp. y_2 axis (unlike conditional density (3.27)). Furthermore it is positive along the axis (see Figure 3.2 for a graphical representation), which is necessary for deriving the limits below.

The corresponding density of radial efficiency scores conditional on a fixed output-ratio value $\widetilde{m}$ is hard to calculate in this example. So I will rely on an alternative derivation of the desired density. Note, that the maximum y_s-values are both equal to one under the chosen technology.

[2] using $\int x^{-2}(1-x)^{-3} = 0.5(1-x)^{-2} - x^{-1} + 2(1-x)^{-1} + 3\ln|x/(x-1)|$

Figure 3.2. Joint distribution of outputs, example 2

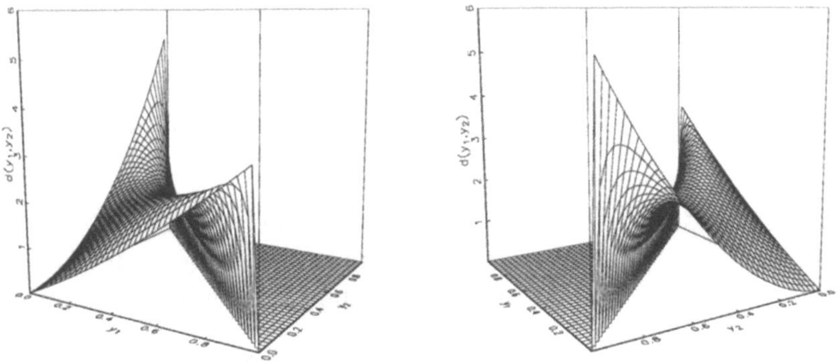

Legend: $d(\varepsilon_1, \varepsilon_2) = \varepsilon_1^2\varepsilon_2 + 5\varepsilon_1\varepsilon_2^2$, $m_1 \sim \mathcal{U}(0,1)$, $y_1 = m_1\varepsilon_1$ and $y_2 = (1 - m_1)\varepsilon_2$.

Therefore the value of y_1, given $y_2 = 0$, is identical to the value of the corresponding radial efficiency measure ε itself. So for this technology we can express the desired limiting distributions of radial efficiencies simply as the limits $\lim_{y_2 \to 0} d(y_1|y_2)$ resp. $\lim_{y_1 \to 0} d(y_2|y_1)$, or more precisely:[3]

$$\lim_{\widetilde{m}_1 \to 1} \mathrm{d}_{\mathcal{E}}(\varepsilon|\widetilde{m}_1) = \lim_{y_2 \to 0} \mathrm{d}_{Y_1|Y_2}(\varepsilon|y_2) \tag{3.30}$$

$$\lim_{\widetilde{m}_1 \to 0} \mathrm{d}_{\mathcal{E}}(\varepsilon|\widetilde{m}_1) = \lim_{y_1 \to 0} \mathrm{d}_{Y_2|Y_1}(\varepsilon|y_1) \tag{3.31}$$

In order to derive the involved conditional distributions I calculated the marginals, which are

$$d_{Y_1}(y_1) = -4y_1^2/4 - 5y_1/3 + 23/12$$

$$d_{Y_2}(y_2) = -5y_2^2/4 - y_2/3 + 19/12$$

With these it is easy to find the desired limits to be

[3] This type of derivation of the desired limits would of course have been possible in the first example as well (for any technology and statistical specification). But one aspect of this chapter is to establish explicitly the link between traditional radial efficiencies and of output specific efficiencies, therefore the first example was solved via limits of the conditional radial efficiency distribution, which is more closely related to what we usually estimate in DEA or SFA (albeit unconditionally).

$$\lim_{\widetilde{m}_1 \to 1} \mathrm{d}_{\mathcal{E}}(\varepsilon|\widetilde{m}_1) = \frac{\lim\limits_{y_2 \to 0} \mathrm{d}_{Y_1,Y_2}(\varepsilon, y_2)}{\lim\limits_{y_2 \to 0} \mathrm{d}_{Y_2}(y_2)} = (5\varepsilon + 2\varepsilon^2)\frac{6}{19} \tag{3.32}$$

$$\lim_{\widetilde{m}_1 \to 0} \mathrm{d}_{\mathcal{E}}(\varepsilon|\widetilde{m}_1) = \frac{\lim\limits_{y_1 \to 0} \mathrm{d}_{Y_1,Y_2}(y_1, \varepsilon)}{\lim\limits_{y_1 \to 0} \mathrm{d}_{Y_1}(y_1)} = (\varepsilon + 10\varepsilon^2)\frac{6}{23} \tag{3.33}$$

So this constitutes a counterexample to the above limit-idea, because the limits (3.32) resp. (3.33) are not even proportional to the marginal densities (3.23) resp. (3.24). Therefore in general it is impossible to derive these marginal output-specific efficiency densities as $m_s \to 1$ limits of an m-dependent radial efficiency distribution. Note that in deriving this result no reference was made to possible strategies for estimating the distribution of radial efficiency scores, because this distribution could be calculated analytically. So this result is not due to possible estimation problems, but arises solely as consequence of the geometry of the problem.

The results from the two examples indicate (although not being proof in a formal sense) that the ability to recover the true underlying output-specific efficiency density from standard estimates of radial efficiency scores (possibly conditioned on observed output ratios) depends in a limited sense on independence between the output specific efficiency terms. But, as the case of perfectly correlated efficiencies proves, such dependence if taken to the extreme itself validates the radial perspective (the DEA case). For the above conjecture to hold in the case of independent output-specific efficiencies furthermore requires density $\mathrm{d}_{Y_1,Y_2}(.)$ to be defined and positive along the axis and, more importantly, that output-specific efficiencies and target output-ratios are independent. The latter will be assumed throughout this book, although the estimation framework to be developed below would basically allow to soften this condition.

But in applied analysis we must not take either of the above favorable scenarios for radial efficiency estimation for granted, in particular because in a statistical sense they should be considered as non-generic cases. This then rules out the seemingly elegant option of regressing radial efficiency scores on observed output-ratios and then taking the limit as described to find the desired output-specific efficiency distributions and thus opens the stage for the subsequently presented approach to output-specific efficiency estimation.

Chapter 4

MARKOV CHAIN MONTE CARLO ANALYSIS

In the following I will give a very brief overview on the background of Markov chain Monte Carlo methodology to the extent, necessary to understand the idea behind the mechanics of the present application. The interested reader will find many textbooks covering the theory in detail, for example Gilks et al., 1996b or Gamerman, 1997. Note also that the present application is formulated in a Bayesian framework, while Markov chain Monte Carlo applications are not restricted at all to Bayesian type of analysis.

The primary target in a Bayesian analysis is the posterior distribution $\pi(b)$ of a vector b of unknowns (parameters, unobserved data) given observed data y. The most interesting components of b in this application are the means and eventually the covariances of the output-specific efficiencies. Furthermore b will also include here the unknown target output-ratios themselves, which are required to define output-specific efficiencies. If we are able to estimate the joint density $\pi(b)$ we can draw inference about the marginal distribution of the means by integrating out the output-ratios (at least numerically). So for expositional purposes I will ignore the composed nature of b for the moment.

In general we are interested in particular features of the posterior distribution like moments, quantiles and so on. All these quantities can be expressed as posterior expectations of functions $g(b)$ of the unknown b. Denoting this expectation by β we thus generally want to find $\beta = \int g(b)d\pi(b)$ as the posterior expectation of $g(b)$ given observed data y.

A Markov chain of realizations of random variates $b^{(t)}$, $t = 1 \dots T$, defined on a state space $\Omega \in \mathbb{R}^S$ is defined via transition kernel $P(\tilde{b}|b^{(t)})$, which determines the probability of observing $\tilde{b} \in \Omega$ at time $t+1$ when $b^{(t)} \in \Omega$ was observed at time t. The very fact, that previous realizations of b (i.e. $b^{(t-1)}, b^{(t-2)}, \dots$) are irrelevant in determining this probability is the Markov property. As a sidenote: If the state space Ω is continuous, the transition kernel $P(\cdot)$ would denote a density.

An irreducible Markov chain is given, whenever the probability to reach any non-empty set from Ω within a finite number of iterations is positive, whatever the start value $b^{(0)}$ of the Markov chain. If we are able to construct such an irreducible Markov chain $b^{(t)}$, $t = 1 \dots T$, with $\pi(\cdot)$ as its stationary distribution, we can then calculate a proxy for β via averaging over the realizations from the Markov chain, i.e. $\hat{\beta}_T = \frac{1}{T}\sum_{t=1\dots T} g(b^{(t)})$.

Furthermore " ... In nice situations $\hat{\beta}_T \to \beta$ almost surely (meaning for almost all sample paths of the Monte Carlo simulation), and the central limit theorem $\sqrt{T}(\hat{\beta}_T - \beta) \xrightarrow{\mathcal{D}} \mathcal{N}(0, \sigma^2)$ gives the size of the Monte Carlo error. The variance σ^2 is difficult to calculate theoretically, but it can be estimated from the Markov chain itself by standard time-series methods ..." (from Geyer, 1992, page 473)

To have convergence in distribution, the chain must also be aperiodic, i.e. the values $b^{(t)}$ must not cycle through a finite number of sets. Under this condition we get $\|P^T(\tilde{b}|b^{(0)}) - \pi(\tilde{b})\| \to 0$ as $T \to \infty$ almost surely (in the same sense as above). See Green, 1999. So (almost) irrespective of the start value $b^{(0)}$, the probability of observing $\tilde{b}$ after T steps is the same as the probability of observing $\tilde{b}$ under the target distribution $\pi(\cdot)$ when T is very large.

Construction of a chain with the above features and with $\pi(\cdot)$ as limiting distribution is simple even for highly complex (and otherwise intractable) target distributions $\pi(\cdot)$ via the Metropolis-Hastings (MH) algorithm (see below). Under mild regularity conditions the chain resulting from application of the MH-algorithm satisfies all of the above conditions necessary to invoke the limit arguments as proven in Tanner and Wong, 1987, Gelfand and Smith, 1990 or Tierney, 1994. Convergence theorems for the resulting sampling distribution are summarized for example in Geyer and Tierney, 1996. Note furthermore that combinations of Markov chains themselves generate a Markov chain, a useful property in combining various methods (the MH-algorithm or a prominent variant thereof: Gibbs sampling) of constructing appropriate chains.

If one wants to get rid of the *almost* (indicating the potential existence of zero-probability sets of problematic start values) in the above theorems, one further has to check for a stronger condition, called Harris recurrence. But this issue will not be pursued here. For a general treatment of limit theorems and convergence rates for Markov chains see Meyn and Tweedie, 1993 and for their particular usage in estimating posterior distributions Tierney, 1994.

1. The Metropolis-Hastings algorithm

To generate the desired Markov chain $\{b^{(t)}\}$ first define a proposal distribution $q(\cdot \mid b^{(t)})$ from which a new *candidate* point $\tilde{b}$ is to be drawn. This proposal distribution might have any form as long as it covers the whole domain of the target distribution. In particular it might depend on some current value $b^{(t)}$ of the vector of unknowns as indicated in the above notation. In general the convergence of $b^{(t)}$ towards the target density $\pi(\cdot)$ will be faster, if proposal $q(\cdot)$ proxies the target $\pi(\cdot)$ well. Then define an acceptance probability $\alpha(b, \tilde{b})$ for this candidate based on the proposal distribution as

$$\alpha(b, \tilde{b}) \equiv \begin{cases} \min \left[\dfrac{\pi(\tilde{b})\, q(b \mid \tilde{b})}{\pi(b)\, q(\tilde{b} \mid b)} \right] & \text{if } \pi(b)\, q(\tilde{b} \mid b) > 0 \\ 1 & \text{otherwise} \end{cases} \tag{4.1}$$

This acceptance probability induces a transition kernel $P(\tilde{b}|b) = q(\tilde{b}|b)\alpha(b, \tilde{b})$ for generating a chain $\{b^{(t)}\}$. The latter will have the above described, desirable characteristics, summarized in the following result due to Mengersen and Tweedie, 1993 and cited after Chib and Greenberg, 1996:

Lemma 1.2 from Mengersen and Tweedie, 1993: If $\pi(b)$ and $q(\tilde{b}|b)$ are positive and continuous for all $(\tilde{b}, b)$ then the resulting transition kernel $P(\tilde{b}|b)$ determining chain $\{b^{(t)}\}$ satisfies all necessary conditions (i.e. has invariant distribution $\pi(\cdot)$, is $\pi(\cdot)$ irreducible and aperiodic) to conclude: $\frac{1}{T}\sum_{t=1\ldots T} g(b^{(t)}) \to \beta$ and $\|P^T(\tilde{b}|b^{(0)}) - \pi(\tilde{b})\| \to 0$ as $T \to \infty$ almost surely.

After specification of a proposal distribution a starting value $b^{(0)}$ needs to be chosen to initiate the iterative sampling process. In general $b^{(0)}$ might be chosen arbitrarily, although in practice the data and the form of $\pi(\cdot)$ often give some useful advice in this regard. Now a chain $\{b^{(t)}\}$ is generated iteratively using the following definition of the $(t+1)$-step value $b^{(t+1)}$ in the following fashion:

1 Draw a candidate $\tilde{b}$ from the proposal distribution $q(\cdot \,|\, b^{(t)})$.
2 Determine the corresponding acceptance probability α. (4.2)
3 Draw a random number u from a uniform distribution on $[0,1]$.
4 Define $b^{(t+1)} = \tilde{b}$ if $u \leq \alpha$ and $b^{(t+1)} = b^{(t)}$ otherwise.

2. Single-component updates

The present problem of estimating output-specific efficiencies is of rather high dimensionality. Suppose we deal with S-dimensional output variables. Then already the DMU-specific unknown target output-ratios will fill $(S-1) \times n$-entries of b. Additionally b will consist of the parameters of the output-specific efficiency distribution and the parameters of the output-ratio distribution. So it might be hard to come up with a satisfactory proposal distribution which enables simultaneous draws of all components of $\tilde{b}$, disregarding other problems which are likely to arise in high-dimensional probability spaces (in particular posterior correlation).

Under such circumstances it is often useful to split up b into several components which can more easily be updated one at a time. Denote these components as $\{b_1 \dots b_C\}$ and a generic component (maybe a vector) as b_c. The corresponding proposal distributions, defined on the domain of component c, shall be labeled $q_c(\cdot)$, $c = 1 \dots C$. Define the vector containing all components but c by $b_{\neg c}$, i.e.

$$b_{\neg c} = \{b_1 \dots b_{c-1}, b_{c+1} \dots b_C\}. \tag{4.3}$$

With this notation I can define an acceptance probability for a single-component MH-algorithm via full conditional distributions $\pi(b_c \,|\, b_{\neg c})$ as follows

$$\alpha(b_{\neg c}, b_c, \tilde{b}_c) \equiv \begin{cases} \min\left[1, \dfrac{\pi(\tilde{b}_c \mid b_{\neg c})\, q(b_c \mid \tilde{b}_c, b_{\neg c})}{\pi(b_c \mid b_{\neg c})\, q(\tilde{b}_c \mid b_c, b_{\neg c})}\right] \\ \qquad \text{if } \pi(b)\, q(\tilde{b}_c \mid b_c, b_{\neg c}) > 0 \\ 1 \text{ otherwise} \end{cases} \tag{4.4}$$

So if conditioning of the proposal is desired (independence proposals would still be allowed), new candidate components must be drawn from the proposal distribution conditional on the most recent values of all components. If updating of the individual components occurs in the order of component subscripts this implies more precisely that

$$b_{\neg c}^{(t)} = \{b_1^{(t+1)} \ldots b_{c-1}^{(t+1)}, b_{c+1}^{(t)} \ldots b_C^{(t)}\}. \tag{4.5}$$

In other words: Sampling candidate $\tilde{b}_c$ from the corresponding proposal at iteration t requires conditioning on the (t+1)-step components $1 \ldots c$–1 and on the t-step components $c \ldots C$. This sequential updating of components $b_c^{(t)}$ will again generate samples $b^{(t)}$ from target distribution $\pi(\cdot)$, see Gilks et al., 1996a.

3. Sampling from conjugate distributions

The acceptance probability (4.4) may appear rather awkward to work with, but under specific conditions, this definition simplifies considerably. One such condition is conjugacy of the distribution of the observed data with respect to the prior distribution of the parameters determining the distribution of the data.

To illustrate the conjugacy condition I will give an example, which will play a prominent role subsequently: Assume that output-specific efficiencies after a logit transformation are normally distributed with mean vector μ and covariance matrix Σ. Denote these logit-transformed output-specific efficiencies of a DMU $w_i \in \mathbb{R}^S$ and assume that all w_i for a sample $i = 1 \ldots n$ are drawn from this S-variate normal Distribution $\mathcal{N}_S(\mu, \Sigma)$. If the prior distribution chosen for the mean vector μ is an S-variate Normal distribution with mean vector μ_0 and covariance matrix Σ (the same as for the data), then, by conjugacy the posterior distribution of μ given the data and Σ is again an S-variate Normal with

$$[\mu \mid w_1 \dots w_n, \Sigma] \sim \mathcal{N}_S\left(\frac{n\,\mathrm{E}_i(w_i) + \mu_0}{n+1}, \frac{\Sigma}{n+1}\right) \tag{4.6}$$

Conjugacy in general means that the posterior density of some unknown variable is of the same parametric family as the prior density of this variable. Furthermore if we use a conjugate prior from which direct sampling is possible this implies that direct sampling is also possible from the posterior. So we might choose this posterior as proposal distribution. Substituting this proposal specification into (4.4) leads to an acceptance probability equal to one, which makes steps 2-4 of the above description of the MH-algorithm superfluous. If this conjugacy argument works for all components of b direct sampling from all full conditional posteriors is possible. This special case of the MH-algorithm is labeled *Gibbs-sampling* after Geman and Geman, 1984.

That conjugacy has wide scope of applicability is rooted in the fact, that conjugate prior distributions are available for the whole family of exponential densities (including the normal used above) according to the following proposition, cited after Robert, 1994:

Proposition Diaconis and Ylvisaker, 1979: If B is an open set in $\mathbb{R}^K$ and b has the prior distribution
$\pi(b|\mu,\tau) = e^{b\mu - \tau\psi(b)}$, then $\mathrm{E}(b) = \mu/\tau$. Therefore, if $w_1, \dots w_n$ are iid $f(w_i|b) = h(w_i)e^{bw_i - \psi(b)}$, then $\mathrm{E}(b|w_1, \dots w_n) = (\mu + \sum_{i=1}^{n} w_i)/(\tau + n)$

For the present application the above proposition implies for example, that if we assume logit efficiencies to be distributed as multivariate normal and the prior distribution of the means also to be of the multivariate normal type, that the posterior distribution of these means of output-specific efficiencies will again be multivariate normal. For the covariance matrix of the multivariate normal the corresponding conjugate prior distribution is the Wishart-distribution. So to work with logit-efficiencies as proposed below, primarily allows an easy handling of output-specific efficiencies within a well analyzed and established statistical framework. But as should have become clear from the MC^2 overview, any other type of efficiency distribution which may seem more appropriate in a specific application could be handled as well with this technique.

Chapter 5

DATA GENERATING PROCESS WITH OUTPUT SPECIFIC EFFICIENCIES

For the statistical foundation of the proposed technique I will use DGP 3 from section 1 of Chapter 2. Furthermore I employ the usual DEA assumption of a convex production technology satisfying strong disposability. This technology will be primarily described by Farrell output-efficient boundaries $\mathrm{Y}^F(x)$ depending on input vector $x \in \mathbb{R}_+^R$. An output-ratio vector $m = \{m_1 \ldots m_S\}$ defined as $m_s = y_s / \sum_{k=1 \ldots S} y_k$ for $s = 1 \ldots S$ together with x then uniquely determines a frontier output vector $\mathrm{y}^F(x,m) = \{\mathrm{y}_1^F(x,m), \ldots ,\mathrm{y}_S^F(x,m)\}$ from $\mathrm{Y}^F(x)$. No closed form functional representation of $\mathrm{y}^F(x,m)$ is required, so in particular a DEA type of frontier description, as derived in the previous section as $\hat{\mathrm{y}}^F(\cdot)$ resp. $\hat{\mathrm{y}}_{BC}^F(\cdot)$ suffices the purpose.

1. Target output ratios

The unobserved target output-ratio vectors m are treated as discrete random variates from a finite grid $\mathbb{M} = \{m_1 \ldots m_G\}$ of possible output-ratios with probability distribution

$$[m|\alpha] \sim \mathrm{d}_M(m;\alpha) \quad m \in \mathbb{M} = \{m_1, \ldots, m_G\} \tag{5.1}$$

where parameterization is via vector α and $\sum_{g=1 \ldots G} \mathrm{d}_M(m_g;\alpha) = 1 \; \forall \; \alpha$. The notation $[m|\alpha] \sim \ldots$ means *the random variable m conditional on variable α is distributed as ...*. The notation $\mathrm{d}(\cdot)$ is used in this paper throughout to denote a generic density function whether discrete or continuous.

This restriction to discrete output-ratios is primarily a convenience feature which enables direct sampling from the posterior conditional density of m_i independent of the specification of $\mathrm{d}_m(\alpha)$. The case of continuous m variates would eventually necessitate a more involved Metropolis-Hastings type of sampling. But this generalization seems not worthwhile given the fact, that the grid $\mathbb{M}$ may be chosen very fine. The discrete version in an ideal setting (based on a true rather than estimated frontier) would also offer the additional advantage of geometric convergence of the sampling distribution to the true joint posterior distribution (see Robert, 1994, p. 346) and I conjecture, that some of this benefit also applies to the case of an estimated frontier.

The set of posterior feasible output-ratios corresponding to an observation (x, y) will be denoted as $\Omega(x, y) \equiv \{m_g : y \leq \mathrm{y}^F(x, m_g)\}$. For fixed grid size G these sets $\Omega(x, y)$ will generally consist of fewer elements for observations closer to the frontier: For highly efficient firms there remains little doubt about the underlying target output-ratios. In the identification discussion to follow in Chapter 6 this issue will play a key role. So it shall be stressed here again as in section 2 of Chapter 2 that an observed output vector y restricts the feasible domain of the associated output-ratio vector m to a subset of $[0, 1]^S$, because the output-specific efficiencies ε_s are restricted to $[0, 1]$. This has been illustrated already in Figure 2.4.

2. Output specific efficiencies

While the random target output ratios combined with frontier information give rise to a distribution of $(y_1 \dots y_S)$-points upon the efficiency frontier, the random efficiencies give rise to a distribution of $(y_1 \dots y_S)$-points in the interior of the technology set. Instead of working with standard multiplicative efficiencies we propose here to work with logit transformed versions thereof.[1] These latter random variates will be denoted as $w \in \mathbb{R}^S$ and will be assumed to follow a multivariate normal

[1] To avoid confusion with a corresponding term often used in the DEA literature it should be noted, that *multiplicative efficiency* here simply means, that multiplication of an (output-specific) efficiency value with the respective frontier output-quantity leads to the observed output quantity.

distribution

$$[w|\mu, \Sigma] \sim \mathcal{N}_S(w; \mu, \Sigma) \tag{5.2}$$

where $\mu = \{\mu_1, \ldots, \mu_S\}$ denotes the mean vector and Σ the $[S \times S]$-dimensional covariance matrix. A w-vector is related to a multiplicative output specific efficiency vector ε through

$$\varepsilon_s = 1/(1 + e^{-w_s}) \text{ for } s = 1...S \text{ with } \varepsilon_s \in [0, 1]. \tag{5.3}$$

The w_s-variates are the logit transformed output-specific efficiencies ε_s. As indicated already these w_s-terms are well suited for a conjugate analysis, which would be impossible for typical distributions on the [0,1]-domain of ε like the Beta-distribution. On the other hand the induced ε-distribution can proxy the typically considered log-Gamma shapes of the latter, so in distributional terms I do not deviate too far from standard SFA.

The covariance matrix Σ is not restricted and supports the full variety of conceivable relationships amongst output-specific efficiencies: Complete output-specificity (no correlation or $\rho_{s,s'} = 0$ for $s \neq s'$), perfect correlation across all outputs ($\rho_{s,s'} = 1$), the implicit assumption (along with equality of output specific mean efficiencies) behind many applied DEA papers. But of course also negative correlation amongst efficiencies is easily accommodated. The latter case might arise if managerial efforts directed towards different outputs are substitutes rather than complements. Whether or not the estimation technique indeed will allow to identify particular types of correlation remains to be analyzed below.

To complete the description of the data generating process I link the involved unobserved random variates w and m to the observed output quantities y_s via frontier mappings as follows:

$$y_s = \mathrm{y}_s^F(x, m) \, \frac{1}{1 + e^{-w_s}} \quad \forall \; s \tag{5.4}$$

Note that once a target output-ratio vector m is given, the output specific efficiencies w_s are defined implicitly by (5.4). In the following the shorthand notation $\mathrm{w}(x, m, y)$ will be used do describe the vector of such logit efficiency terms based on the definition

$$\begin{aligned} \mathrm{w}(x, m, y) \quad &= \quad \{w_1 \ldots w_S\} \\ &\qquad \text{with } w_s = \ln[y_s/(\mathrm{y}_s^F(x, m) - y_s)] \; \forall \; s \end{aligned} \tag{5.5}$$

Definitions (5.1), (5.2) and (5.4) together with mapping $\mathrm{y}^F(x,m)$ now fully describe the DGP with an explicit and general account for output-specific efficiencies.

3. The resulting distribution of output vectors

The posterior analysis will be carried out on the basis of unobserved m and observed y variates which together uniquely determine the w terms. Derivation of the y-distribution requires the Jacobian $|J_{y\to w}|$ of the mapping from Y to W induced by (5.4), which is determined as $\prod_{s=1}^{S} \mathrm{y}_s^F(x,m)/[y_s(\mathrm{y}_s^F(x,m)-y_s)]$. From this we get the desired conditional distribution of y given x, m, μ, Σ

$$\mathrm{d}(y|\, x, m, \mu, \Sigma) = \prod_{s=1}^{S} \frac{\mathrm{y}_s^F(x,m)}{y_s(\mathrm{y}_s^F(x,m)-y_s)}\, \mathcal{N}_S\Big(\mathrm{w}(x,m,y);\, \mu, \Sigma\Big) \qquad (5.6)$$

To describe sample values of x and y I will use generic subscript i. A sample of size n of observations will be denoted $\{x_i, y_i\}$ with corresponding missing variables $\{m_i\}$. I assume that all m_i are identically and independently distributed (iid) according to (5.1) and all y_i conditional on m_i iid according to (5.6). The iid assumption on m_i rules out the possibility of dependency of target output-ratios on inputs. In particular applications this assumption may be considered as too restrictive. But given the already awkward information deficit of the analyst regarding the all important yet unknown target output-ratios this assumption seems a reasonable starting-point for a first attempt to tackle the involved estimation problems. Ultimately of course the justification for this restriction can only be based on context- specific reasoning.

From the iid assumptions invoked it follows that a sample $\{y_1 \dots y_n\}$ of output vectors for given $\{x_1 \dots x_n, m_1 \dots m_n\}$ is thus distributed according to

$$[y_1 \dots y_n|\, x_1, \dots x_n, m_1 \dots m_n, \alpha, \mu, \Sigma] \sim \prod_{i=1}^{n} \{\mathrm{d}(y_i|\, x_i, m_i, \mu, \Sigma)\} \qquad (5.7)$$

which corresponds to the likelihood of the observed data in Non-Bayesian terms if target output-ratios m_i were known. Table 5.1 summarizes the above described structure.

Table 5.1. Statistical structure for MC^2 estimation of output-specific efficiencies with logit-normal efficiencies

observed variables	**latent variables**
$\begin{bmatrix} y_1 \\ \vdots \\ y_i \\ \vdots \\ y_n \end{bmatrix} = \begin{bmatrix} y_{11} & y_{12} & & y_{1S} \\ & \vdots & & \\ y_{i1} & y_{i2} & \dots & y_{iS} \\ & \vdots & & \\ y_{n1} & y_{n2} & & y_{nS} \end{bmatrix}$	$\begin{bmatrix} m_1 \\ \vdots \\ m_i \\ \vdots \\ m_n \end{bmatrix} = \begin{bmatrix} m_{11} & m_{12} & & m_{1S} \\ & \vdots & & \\ m_{i1} & m_{i2} & \dots & m_{iS} \\ & \vdots & & \\ m_{n1} & m_{n2} & & m_{nS} \end{bmatrix}$
$[y_i \vert x_i, m_i] \sim$ $\prod_{s=1}^{S} \frac{y_s^F(x_i, m_i)}{y_{is}[y_s^F(x_i, m_i) - y_{is}]}$ $\times \mathcal{N}_S\Big(\mathrm{w}(x_i, m_i, y_i);\ \mu, \Sigma\Big)$	$m_i \overset{iid}{\sim} \mathrm{d}_M(m_i;\ \alpha)$
parameters: $\mu \in \mathbb{R}^S$, $\Sigma \in \mathbb{R}^{S \times S}$, α	

Chapter 6

IDENTIFICATION

To discuss the issue of identifiability we need the marginal likelihood of observing the sample outputs $\boldsymbol{y}=\{y_1 \dots y_n\}$ for given sample inputs $\boldsymbol{x}=\{x_1 \dots x_n\}$ and given parameters of the involved density functions. This likelihood is derived by integrating out the latent (unobserved) variables m_i from density $d(\boldsymbol{y}, \boldsymbol{m}|\boldsymbol{x}, \mu, \Sigma, \alpha)$ (i.e. density (5.7) multiplied by the joint density of the m_i-terms) leading to

$$
\begin{aligned}
\mathrm{d}(\boldsymbol{y}|\boldsymbol{x}, \mu, \Sigma, \alpha) &= \qquad\qquad (6.1)\\
&= \int\limits_{\Omega_1} \cdots \int\limits_{\Omega_n} \prod_{i=1}^{n} \{\mathrm{d}(y_i|\, x_i, m_i, \mu, \Sigma)\, \mathrm{d}(m_i \,|\, \alpha)\}\, dm_1 \cdots dm_n \\
&= \prod_{i=1}^{n} \int\limits_{\Omega_i} \mathrm{d}(y_i|\, x_i, m_i, \mu, \Sigma)\, \mathrm{d}(m_i|\alpha)\, dm_i
\end{aligned}
$$

The vector of unknown parameters of this distribution consists of all terms from μ, Σ and α, for which we shall use the shorthand notation $\theta = \{\mu, \Sigma, \alpha\}$. As usual let $\mathcal{L}(\theta|\boldsymbol{x}, \boldsymbol{y})$ denote the likelihood function which is actually nothing but (6.1) in different notation. From the maximum likelihood perspective identification of parameter $\theta \in \Theta$ would require verification of the following:

If $\mathcal{L}(\theta'|\boldsymbol{x}, \boldsymbol{y}) \geq \mathcal{L}(\theta|\boldsymbol{x}, \boldsymbol{y})$ and $\mathcal{L}(\theta''|\boldsymbol{x}, \boldsymbol{y}) \geq \mathcal{L}(\theta|\boldsymbol{x}, \boldsymbol{y})$
for all $\theta \in \Theta$ then $\theta' = \theta''$.

So all we ask is whether a unique vector θ^* exists which maximizes this likelihood. For the particular likelihood function (6.1) this condition can not be verified analytically because this density is not available in closed form (remember the $y_s^F(.)$-terms). Nevertheless I will try to shed some light on the specific identification problems involved in the present context by investigating the major conceptual issues in this regard. The following section will deal with the basic tradeoff between distributional parameters with regard to sample likelihood, section 2 analyzes the role of domain information in identification and section 3 provides complementary insights based on graphical analysis of likelihood surfaces.

1. The basic tradeoff in an expectational perspective

To discuss the basic potential obstacle to identifiability in the context of estimating output-specific efficiencies I focus on the simple two-output case for expositional purposes. To start the discussion lets look at the prior expectations of the two outputs y_1, y_2 conditional on some input vector x. Based on the assumed independence of target-output ratios and output-specific efficiencies (which themselves may still be correlated) and definition $y_s = \mathrm{y}_s^F(x, m_1)\, \varepsilon_s$ (the analogue to definition 5.4, but with standard multiplicative efficiencies replacing the logit versions and a scalar m_1 output-ratio replacing the possibly vector valued m therein) these prior expectations are simply derived as

$$\begin{aligned} \mathrm{E}(y_1) &= \mathrm{E}[\mathrm{y}_1^F(x, m_1)]\, \mathrm{E}(\varepsilon_1) \\ \mathrm{E}(y_2) &= \mathrm{E}[\mathrm{y}_2^F(x, m_1)]\, \mathrm{E}(\varepsilon_2) \end{aligned} \tag{6.2}$$

All we know a priori about the mapping $\mathrm{y}_s^F(x, m_1)$ from the convexity assumption is that $m_1 < \widetilde{m}_1$ implies $\mathrm{y}_1^F(x, m_1) \leq \mathrm{y}_1^F(x, \widetilde{m}_1)$ and $\mathrm{y}_2^F(x, m_1) \geq \mathrm{y}_2^F(x, \widetilde{m}_1)$ and that this mapping is continuous in the sense $\lim_{\alpha \to 0} \mathrm{y}_s^F(x, m_1 + \alpha) = \mathrm{y}_s^F(m_1)\ \forall\ m_1 \in [0, 1]$. So for example increasing the mean of random variable m_1 would increase the expectation $\mathrm{E}[\mathrm{y}_1^F(x, m_1)]$ and lower the expectation $\mathrm{E}[\mathrm{y}_2^F(x, m_1)]$. Furthermore changes in frontier points due to changes in target-output ratio m_1 occur smoothly and with known direction.

Assume that the density for output specific efficiencies is parametrized as $\mathrm{d}_{\mathcal{E}}(\varepsilon_1, \varepsilon_2 \,|\, \mu_1, \mu_2, \Sigma)$ with $\mu_1 = \mathrm{E}(\varepsilon_1)$ and $\mu_2 = \mathrm{E}(\varepsilon_2)$ being the respective means and Σ any additional parameters. Further let $\mathrm{d}_M(m_1 | \alpha_1, \alpha_2)$

be the density of target output ratio 1 with $\alpha_1 = \mathrm{E}(m_1)$ being the mean thereof and α_2 (possibly a vector) any additional parameters of the target output-ratio distribution.

Start from some given values of parameters μ_1, μ_2, α_1 with associated expectations for the two outputs and imagine then a decrease in μ_1, i.e. a lower expected efficiency in producing output 1. If this decrease is accompanied by an appropriately chosen increase in α_1, i.e. an increased expectation of target output-ratio 1, the decrease in $\mathrm{E}(\varepsilon_1)$ will be exactly offset by the increase in $\mathrm{E}[\mathrm{y}_1^F(x, m_1)]$ and the resulting expectation $\mathrm{E}(y_1)$ will be left unchanged compared to the one associated with the start values. The increase in α_1 at the same time implies a decreased expectation $\mathrm{E}[\mathrm{y}_2^F(x, m_1)]$, but by appropriately choosing a higher μ_2 the increase in expected efficiency $\mathrm{E}(\varepsilon_2)$ of producing output 2 will offset this decrease in $\mathrm{E}[\mathrm{y}_2^F(x, m_1)]$ again exactly, leaving also the expectation $\mathrm{E}(y_2)$ unchanged.

If we reinterpret the y_1, y_2 values in the above argument as sample means, i.e. $y_s = \frac{1}{n}\sum_{i=1}^{n} y_{is}$, the logic unfolded would get more of an empirical flavor. It would then tell, that in an average sense a sample of output observations might be the result of quite distinct underlying populations of target output-ratios and output-specific efficiencies with the same tradeoff at work as for a single y_1, y_2-pair. Thus it becomes obvious, that additional aspects of the involved distributions must also be considered to eventually identify the unknown population parameters including the means. Consequently the distributional forms assumed a priori for these distributions play an important role in identification.

The above argument highlights the dominating problem underlying identification of output-specific efficiencies based on unknown target output-ratios: There is always a possible tradeoff between mean efficiencies and mean target output-ratios such that two distinct sets of the corresponding mean parameters command similar (if not equal) plausibility for any given sample of input/output observations. And this problem will be reflected also in the discussion below formulated in terms of the likelihood function proper.

2. The role of domain observations in identification

Now I want to approach the identification issue from the angle of observed domains of the key variables. The competing influence of the means for ε_i and m_i on the likelihood is exercised indirectly through the overall probability of the prespecified ranges of feasible m_i and ε_{is} values for given y_i's. So these domains play a crucial role in the posterior (likelihood) perspective.

Recall the definition of the feasible range for m_{i1} as defined for the two output case in (2.10) of Chapter 2. Note also that fixing a target output-ratio m_{i1} for given observation y_i also determines ε_{i1} and ε_{i2} for this observation through $\varepsilon_{i1} = y_{i1}/\mathrm{y}_1^F(m_{i1})$ resp. $\varepsilon_{i2} = y_{i2}/\mathrm{y}_2^F(m_{i1})$. So the range $[m_{i1}^{\min}, m_{i1}^{\max}]$ of feasible m_{i1} implies a posteriori feasible ranges for output-specific efficiencies

$$\varepsilon_{i1} \in \left[\frac{y_{i1}}{\mathrm{y}_1^F(x_i, m_{i1}^{\max})}, 1\right] \tag{6.3}$$

$$\varepsilon_{i2} \in \left[\frac{y_{i2}}{\mathrm{y}_2^F(x_i, m_{i1}^{\min})}, 1\right] \tag{6.4}$$

where $m_{i1}^{\min}$ resp. $m_{i1}^{\max}$ are defined analogous to (2.8) resp. (2.9) of Chapter 2. Clearly full efficiency $\varepsilon_{is} = 1$ in producing output s always marks the upper boundary reachable by choosing the corresponding minimum target output ratio m_{is} compatible with observation y_i. And furthermore the variation of m_{i1} to effect integration in 6.1 goes along with unique variation in $\varepsilon_{i1}, \varepsilon_{i2}$.

If the underlying densities of output-specific efficiencies and target output-ratios were multimodal and thus potentially also the (multidimensional) likelihood surface, the effect of changing parameter values upon the likelihood (6.1) in general were unclear. Under such circumstances quite disparate sets of parameter values might be associated with modes of possibly similar value of the likelihood function making identification almost impossible, or to say the least: extremely demanding from an estimation viewpoint.

So I will assume unimodality of all involved densities instead. Then the problem becomes tractable at least conceptually (technical tractability in the sense of estimator performance has yet to be investigated). The basic tradeoff, analyzed in the previous section via the impact of different parameter-combinations of general efficiency and target output-ratio distributions upon expected output observations y_i (an ex ante perspective), shall now be discussed for unimodal distributions via the impact of y_i and the implied domains of the individual target output-ratios m_i (or equivalently: the implied domains of efficiencies ε_i) upon the resulting likelihood (the ex post perspective). It is clear, that the identifying role of y_i observations must be exercised exactly through these implied domains, because the y_i observations themselves are merely the handle to determine the integration ranges of the feasible target output-ratios for calculating the likelihood values via 6.1. And only owing to the restriction to unimodal densities will the tradeoff between mean parameters μ_1, μ_2, α_1 in this likelihood perspective still have determinate signs for each of these variables. With regard to variance parameters matters are less clear.

For illustrative purposes I will resort to a numerical example with 5 observations based on a technology described via input-isoquant $y_{i1}^3 + y_{i2}^3 = 1$ and equal inputs for all DMU's. The underlying distributional specifications with regard to the means of m_1, ε_1 resp. ε_2 are $\alpha_1 = 0.33$, $\mu_1 = 0.73$ resp. $\mu_2 = 0.95$. The sample data are given in Table 6.1 and contain the unobserved target output-ratios (with associated frontier points) and output specific efficiencies as well as the observed output quantities. A graphical representation of this example, particularly of the implied domains is given in Figure 6.1.

Table 6.1. A numerical example

DMU	m_1	$y_1^F(m_1)$	$y_2^F(m_1)$	ε_{i1}	ε_{i2}	y_{i1}	y_{i2}
A	0.22	0.28	0.99	0.54	0.75	0.15	0.74
B	0.29	0.40	0.98	0.50	0.92	0.20	0.90
C	0.57	0.89	0.67	0.40	0.85	0.36	0.57
D	0.60	0.92	0.61	0.68	0.95	0.63	0.58
E	0.72	0.98	0.38	0.38	0.95	0.37	0.36

The implied domain restrictions per DMU with regard to m_1 are displayed in the top right graph of Figure 6.1. The bottom horizontal line within this graph shows the domain $\Omega(y_A)$ of feasible output ratios m_{i1}

Figure 6.1. Posterior domains of variables

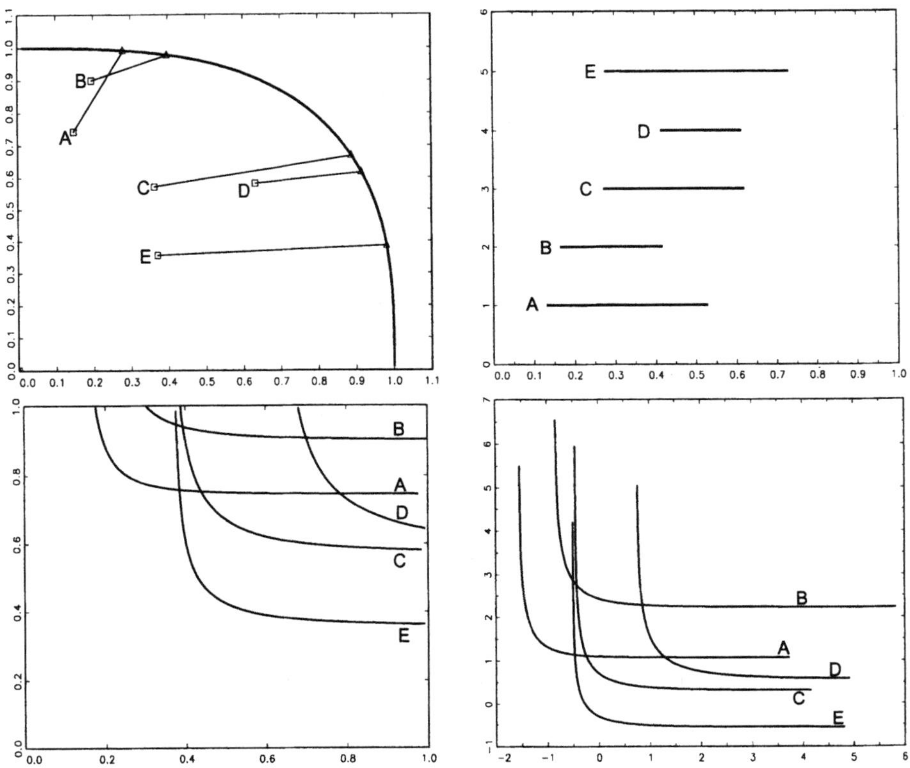

for DMU A, stretching from 0.13 to 0.54. The next line above that gives the domain for DMU B and so on. Visual inspection thus tells for example that the output-ratio domain $\Omega(y_A)$ has roughly twice length of $\Omega(y_D)$, while any sort of average efficiency (over the two outputs) of DMU A is considerably lower than a corresponding efficiency measure for DMU D. Analogous observations hold for pairwise comparisons between the other DMU's. So there is clear negative correlation between an efficiency of a DMU (measured as some directional distance from the frontier) and the length (the area in higher dimensional spaces) of the implied domain of feasible target output-ratios.

Consider for a moment the possibility of estimating the distribution $\mathrm{d}_M(\alpha)$ of target output-ratios separately, based solely on such domain information, derived from observation y_i and knowledge of the efficiency frontier. This will yield general insights about the impact of the degree of inefficiency upon identifiability. It should be kept in mind though, that such an estimation strategy which ignores the associated inefficiencies strictly speaking is inconsistent, because in the presence of output specific efficiencies we will not even asymptotically be able to recover true mean target output-ratios from such domain information alone.

To make the point assume now that each observed domain is equally informative. In a Bayesian perspective, as employed throughout this work, and lacking additional information this would be a reasonable prior assumption for estimating the distribution of target output ratios. So the domain information $\Omega(y_i)$ could be translated into standard sample point information by constructing an equal-sized and equal-spaced grids of output ratios for each of the DMU specific domains $\Omega(y_i)$ and then one could estimate $\mathrm{d}_M(\alpha)$ based on all these grid points (parametrically or non-parametrically does not matter here). Equal sized grids of course would typically lead to higher concentration of output-ratios for DMU's closer to the frontier, i.e. DMU's with higher efficiency. So clearly the more efficient DMU's would be more influential in determining the estimate of $\mathrm{d}_M(\alpha)$.

This observation carries over to the setting where $\mathrm{d}_M(\alpha)$ and the distribution of output-specific efficiencies are estimated jointly. So I conclude that identification of the parameters of both involved distributions will be owed particularly to more efficient observations. Thus for a sample from a population with very low average efficiency it will be rather easy to combine changing parameters of the target output-ratio distribution with changing parameters of the output-specific efficiency distribution to yield similar likelihood values, such that these different sets of parameter values will be hard to distinguish based on the likelihood function. This argument should be kept in mind when interpreting the performance results in Chapter 8, which are based on mean efficiencies of 0.7 for output 1 resp. 0.93 for output 2. From the above we thus may expect that estimator performance particularly in terms of variance would be worse (better) for lower (higher) mean efficiencies.

The posterior domains of $(\varepsilon_{i1}, \varepsilon_{i2})$-pairs associated with the observations listed in Table 6.1 are displayed in the bottom left graph of Figure 6.1. Again we observe that the length of these domain lines is inversely related to the underlying efficiencies, just like for the m_i-domains. But instead of discussing the issue at stake within the realm of the domains of efficiencies proper I want to switch perspective and look at the implied domains in logit space $w_{is} = \ln(\varepsilon_{is}/(1-\varepsilon_{is}))$ as displayed in the bottom right graph of Figure 6.1. The domains in this perspective can not be drawn at full length as all of the associated lines would stretch further into infinity whenever one of the involved output-specific efficiencies approaches 1. But the picture is complete enough for our discussion here, because the missing portions of the picture would contain almost linear vertical resp. horizontal extensions of the visible lines and thus would not provide much additional information.

Assume next we were given an estimate $\hat{\alpha}_1$ of mean output ratio 1 higher than any feasible m_i, i.e. $\hat{\alpha}_1 > \max\{m_1 : m_1 \in \cup_{i=1}^{5}\Omega(y_i)\}$. Given unimodality of the involved distribution such an α_1-estimate of course is very unlikely given the fixed domains $\Omega(y_i)$, as all latent target output-ratios would then necessarily lie to the left of the mean. But we could nevertheless try to lend as much plausibility as possible to this scenario by appropriately choosing a low $\hat{\mu}_1$ estimate and a high $\hat{\mu}_2$ estimate. This would imply DMU-specific posterior expected output-ratios at the far right end of the respective domains drawn in the top right graph and the expected logit output-specific efficiencies would be concentrated somewhere far in the vertical portions of the respective domains in the bottom right graph. By the invoked maximum likelihood principle the mean logit efficiency estimators will be located in the center of this scatter of resulting (w_{i1}, w_{i2})-points.

If we then were to lower $\hat{\alpha}_1$ somewhat and find again the most likely accompanying $\hat{\mu}_1$, $\hat{\mu}_2$ values we would get a new scatter of expected (w_{i1}, w_{i2})-points, which follows this movement in $\hat{\mu}_1$, $\hat{\mu}_2$ downward along the vertical portions of the respective domains. The target output-ratio mean estimator $\hat{\alpha}_1$ on the other hand would clearly come closer to the mean of posterior expected m_i-values, because the latter will remain rather stuck close to their respective upper domain boundaries for small changes in $\hat{\alpha}_1$. So the net effect of this simultaneous change in parameter values will be an increase in likelihood owed to increased plausibility of observing these posterior m_i-values, because only negligible effect upon the likelihood is to be expected from changing the efficiency distribution parameters. Analogous reasoning of course is possible for the opposite scenario with a very low $\hat{\alpha}_1$ start value. Approaching the identification problem from extreme values of $\hat{\alpha}_1$ thus highlights the role of the m_i-domains in this regard. In distinguishing between $\hat{\alpha}_1$-values within $\{\cup_{i=1}^{5}\Omega(y_i)\}$ on the other hand the assumed shape of the involved distributions will become the primary identifying force.

With regard to the potential for identifying the variance parameters of output specific efficiencies the above argument based on the domain graphs gives rise to concern. The particular L-shape of the $(\varepsilon_{i1}, \varepsilon_{i2})$-domains, owed to the convexity of the underlying technology and displayed in the bottom right graph for logit-efficiencies, is a feature likely to dominate useful distributional information contained in the dispersion of these domains. In an attempt to best describe the dispersion of the $(\varepsilon_{i1}, \varepsilon_{i2})$-points with a normal distribution these equally L-shaped domains constitute the only available hard information about the form of this normal distribution from (x_i, y_i) observations. Given this limited type of information let's again look at the likelihood impact of changing $\hat{\alpha}_1$ values, which an MC^2 estimation technique generates while scanning the parameter space.

We realize that accommodating (likelihood maximizing) support of these changes in $(\varepsilon_{i1}, \varepsilon_{i2})$-space from a normal distribution might require drastic changes in the variance components when the bulk of posterior expected $(\varepsilon_{i1}, \varepsilon_{i2})$ points switches between the vertical and the horizontal portions of the domains: In a region of almost vertical domains the variance of output-1 efficiencies is almost fixed, while the variance of output-2 efficiency may be varied to achieve higher likelihood and vice versa in the region of almost horizontal domains. The covariance component on the other hand will remain almost constant for movements along the vertical resp. horizontal portion of the efficiency domains. But when switching between them the sign of the covariance term is likely to fluctuate strongly. In any case these accommodating changes in variance components will be primarily induced by the L-shape and will have little to do with the underlying true variance components of output-specific efficiencies.

Summarizing I conjecture that identification of the variance components of output specific efficiencies may be extremely difficult. A fortiori this conjecture also holds for correlation coefficients, which summarize variance information from two components: If each of the latter is hard to identify individually, a compound correlation measure will be even harder to identify. Consequently I suspect the distribution of a correlation estimator for output-specific efficiencies in any given distributional setting to be rather flat over the [-1,1]-range of possible values, no matter what the true correlation coefficient is. This is discouraging inasmuch, as the question of positively or negatively correlated efficiencies across outputs might be of considerable practical interest.

3. Studying the likelihood surface

Now we shall graphically investigate the likelihood surfaces of a specific sample $\{x_i, y_i\}_{i=1}^n$ of observations (different from the one used in the previous section) under the maintained assumptions about the data generating process described in Chapter 5. This will help to identify potential problems caused for example by multi-modality, by high posterior correlation of parameters or very flat likelihoods over large ranges of parameter values and complements the analytical analysis in the previous section.

The ideal situation (in a two parameter setting) would be nicely bump-shaped surfaces like the one for a bivariate zero correlation Normal distribution with circular contour lines. Finding likelihood surfaces of this type (which I henceforth will simply call *regular*) would in general promise that MC^2 scans of the parameter space will return frequently to the modal (from the likelihood perspective) values, no matter where the scan starts and what remote places it occasionally may visit. Unfortunately we will not find this regular type of surface for the present problem of estimating output-specific efficiencies under the standard parameterization. This indicates potential difficulties with convergence and motivates the search for better parameterizations. The subsequent analysis will again be based on the likelihood function defined in (6.1).

In the following a random sample of size $n = 30$ based on a two-output technology $y_1^3 + y_2^3 = 1$ will be studied, where inputs are assumed equal for all DMU's (or equivalently where a constant returns to scale technology is assumed based on a single input). Output-specific random efficiency vectors $\varepsilon_i = \{\varepsilon_{i1}, \varepsilon_{i2}\}$ for each DMU are constructed by independent sampling of vectors $w_i = \{w_{i1}, w_{i2}\}$ (the now familiar logit-efficiencies) from a bivariate Normal with mean vector $(\mu_1, \mu_2) = (1, 4)$ and covariance matrix Σ (where $\sigma_1^2, \sigma_2^2 = 0.8$ and $\sigma_{12} = 0.3$) and then setting $\varepsilon_{is} = 1/(1 + e^{-w_{is}})$. This specification implies a mean efficiency in producing output 1 of roughly 0.73 and of 0.99 of producing output 2. If these were the characteristics of a real-world example it seems worthwhile devoting some effort to the estimation of this highly product specific distribution of managerial abilities.

Output-ratios are independently drawn from a Dirichlet distribution with parameter vector $(\alpha_1, \alpha_2) = (2, 4)$. This specification of the Dirichlet distribution implies an expected target ratio of output 1 to total output of 0.33 with standard deviation of 0.18. Thus the maintained assumption is that the management of a typical DMU from this population would want to produce 2 times as much of output 2 than of output 1.

3.1 The case of (μ_1, μ_2) and (α_1, α_2)

Based on these parameters the likelihood (6.1) will be evaluated in this section. Each of the following graphs depicts the likelihood surface resulting from varying two parameters at a time while all remaining parameters are set to their true values. While we are necessarily confined to look at the likelihood surface in $\mathbb{R}^3$-space the full likelihood surface in the present example stretches out in $\mathbb{R}^8$-space and covers variation in 2 mean terms, 3 distinct covariance terms for the efficiency distribution, 2 terms describing the output-ratio distribution and the likelihood variation itself.

In the following four-part figures the two top row graphs show the likelihood surface from the perspective of the two varying parameters involved respectively. The bottom row graphs show the same likelihood surface from two additional perspectives for further curvature information. The vertical axis in each case depicts the corresponding mean log-likelihood values. The maximum mean log-likelihood values in each graph are the same because that the maximum occurs within the displayed range of parameter values. On the other hand the vertical axis covers different ranges of possible likelihood-values and so it is not meaningful to compare the degree of curvature of the surface between the graphs.

Figure 6.2 displays variations in the likelihood due to variations in the means (μ_1, μ_2). The top left graph of this figure shows the μ_1 values along the horizontal axis and peaks at around 1.2, not too far from the target value of 1. The top right graph instead, displaying the same information but with μ_2 represented on the horizontal axis, peaks at around 3.8, pretty close to the target value of 4. Peaking in both cases is not very pronounced but in the ballpark range. So even for the small sample chosen for illustration there is reason to hope that the corresponding estimator should be able to identify the underlying difference in the means of output-specific efficiencies.

The likelihood surface with regard to the shape parameters (α_1, α_2) of the output-ratio distribution on the other hand appears rather flat over a large range of plausible values as can be seen from Figure 6.3. In

Figure 6.2. Mean log-likelihood for different (μ_1, μ_2) combinations.

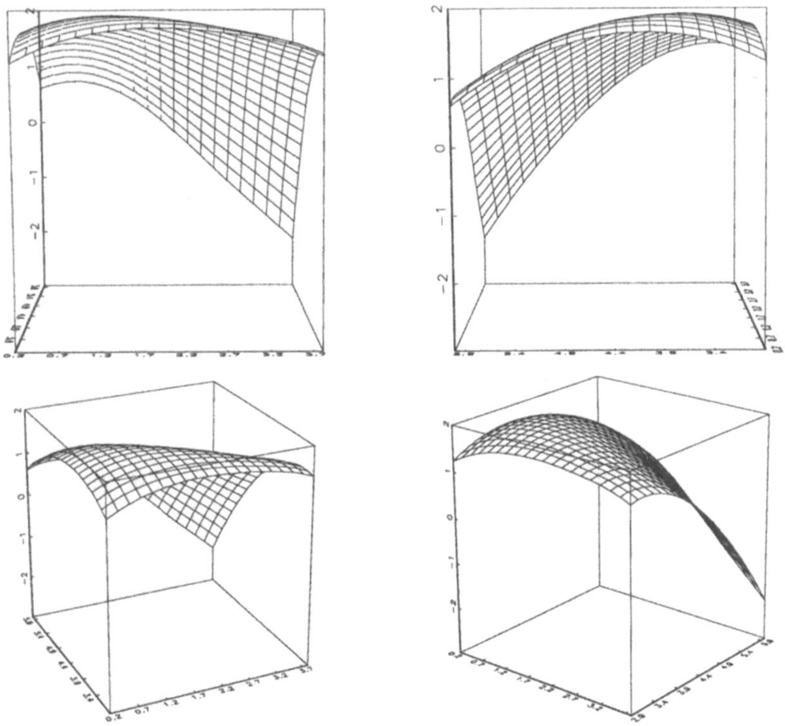

particular it can be seen from the bottom left graph in this figure that for a certain ratio α_1/α_2 of roughly 4/9 (compared to the true ratio of 2/4) of these parameter values reaches the highest likelihood values. So at least with respect to the expected target output-ratio, which depends solely upon this α_1/α_2-ratio the likelihood surface has a useful curvature for estimation purposes. But at the same time the likelihood values along this line of α_1, α_2 values with constant ratio does not change very much. So it is not obvious whether curvature is sufficient to identify the two parameters separately and whether it truly peaks close to the target values of $(\alpha_1, \alpha_2) = (2, 4)$.

Figure 6.3. Mean log-likelihood for different (α_1, α_2) combinations.

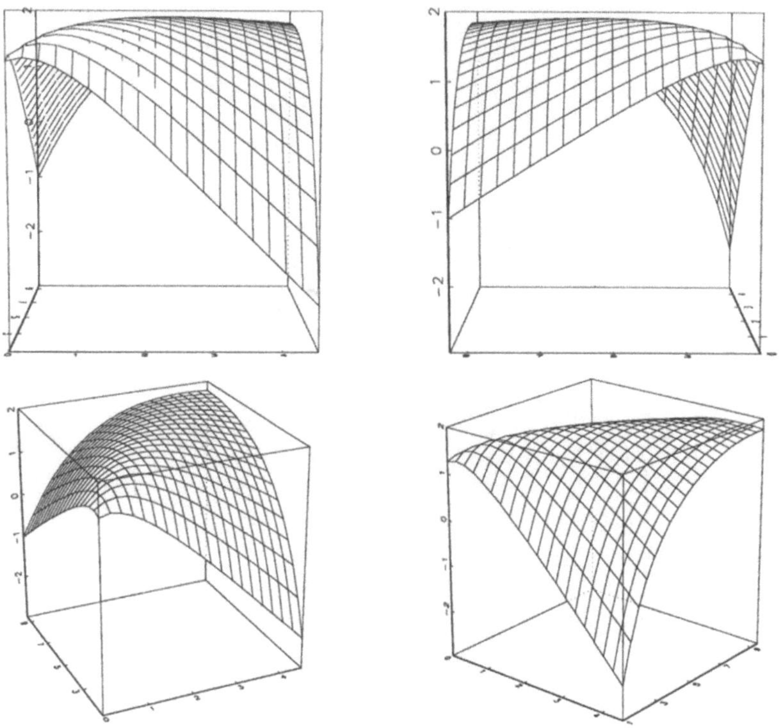

3.2 An example of a reparameterization

The above analysis provides some confidence that at least the expectation of target output-ratios seems to be identified. So I want to approach the problem again based on a parameterization in terms of the expectation $\alpha_1/(\alpha_1 + \alpha_2)$ and the sum $\alpha_1 + \alpha_2$. The likelihood-surface for this parameterization is depicted in Figure 6.4 and it is immediately visible that the likelihood now peaks more clearly. In particular as can be seen in the top left graph depicting $\alpha_1/(\alpha_1 + \alpha_2)$-values along the horizontal axis the mode of the likelihood is at roughly 0.32 while the true value of $\alpha_1/(\alpha_1 + \alpha_2)$ is $2/6 \sim 0.33$. Thus this ratio, which defines the expectation of the ratio of output 1 to total output under the chosen Dirichlet distribution, is very close to target. The mode of the

Figure 6.4. Mean log-likelihood of $(\mathrm{E}(m_1), \alpha_1+\alpha_2)$ combinations.

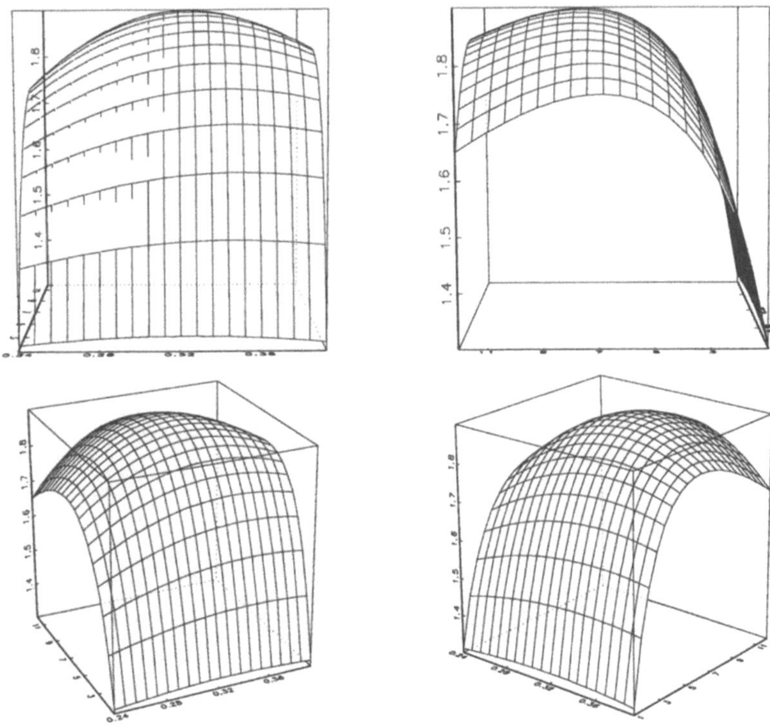

likelihood seen from the $\alpha_1 + \alpha_2$ perspective (the top right graph) on the other hand is even more pronounced. But the corresponding $\alpha_1 + \alpha_2$ value of roughly 7 is relatively further away from the target 6 compared to $\alpha_1/(\alpha_1 + \alpha_2)$. As $\alpha_1 + \alpha_2$ plays a prominent role in determining the variance of output-ratios I therefore expect that the latter can be less reliably estimated.

It must be emphasized here that in both figures, 6.3 and 6.4, the range of α_1 resp. α_2 values covered is identical. But as can be verified by comparing the values of the vertical axis in both figures the corresponding ranges of likelihood-values differ significantly: [-3,2] in 6.3 and [1.3,1.9] in 6.4. Obviously the parameterization in terms of $\alpha_1/(\alpha_1+\alpha_2)$ and $\alpha_1+\alpha_2$ leads to generally higher likelihood-values, while the α_1, α_2 parameterization seems to cover also some rather unlikely parameter-combinations.

The reason for this difference of course is, that the combinations of two parameters matter, rather than there individual values. I want to illustrate the difference between the two parameterizations with an example. This will also help to clarify the link between a certain parameterization and the potential use of prior information from the data in the context of output-specific efficiency estimation. It will become clear how prior information in this context can be obtained and why it may apply to one parameterization but not to the other.

Assume the observed outputs indicate an expectation $\mathrm{E}(m_1) = \alpha_1/(\alpha_1 + \alpha_2)$ which should be at least 0.3 and at most 0.5. The rationale for such a minimum value could be derived in an applied context from the data and the estimated efficiency frontier via implied m_i domains: Project the output of a DMU upon the efficiency frontier so as to maximize its output 1 efficiency and then take the m_1-value associated with this projection point, i.e. the lower boundary of the m_i-domain. Repeat this for all DMU's and then calculate the corresponding mean of the m_1-values. This leads to a plausible minimum $\mathrm{E}(m_1)$ value supported by the data. Projection so as to maximize output 2 efficiency leads to the corresponding maximum $\mathrm{E}(m_1)$ value.

So it is the data underlying the efficiency analysis which gives this type of prior information with regard to a plausible range for the means of target output-ratios. The distributional assumptions have nothing to do with this prior information. We can thus apply this prior information to restrict the range of $\alpha_1/(\alpha_1+\alpha_2)$ values, which define the relevant expectation under the Dirichlet distribution. In a parameterization including this term such prior information will be of obvious help, while it would be useless for example in the α_1, α_2 parameterization used before. For the sake of exposition I will furthermore restrict the $\alpha_1+\alpha_2$ values to lie in the [1,12]-range. This range is not data driven, but it is associated with a huge range of implied standard deviations around the true value of 0.18.

To compare the usefulness of prior information for both parametrizations I construct first a rough grid for the parameterization in terms of $(\alpha_1/(\alpha_1+\alpha_2), \alpha_1+\alpha_2)$, which will be labeled parametrization 2. This leads to the parameter combinations given in columns 1 and 2 of Table (6.2):

These parameter combinations then induce corresponding pairs of (α_1, α_2) values which are given in columns 3 and 4 of Table (6.2). Now take

Table 6.2. Prior information for parametrization 2

$\left(\frac{\alpha_1}{\alpha_1+\alpha_2},\right.$	$\left.\alpha_1+\alpha_2\right)$	$\Rightarrow$	$(\alpha_1,$	$\alpha_2)$
0.3	1		0.3	0.7
0.3	6		1.8	4.2
0.3	12		3.6	8.4
0.4	1		0.4	0.6
0.4	6		2.4	3.6
0.4	12		4.8	7.2
0.5	1		0.5	0.5
0.5	6		3.0	3.0
0.5	12		6.0	6.0

the induced minimum and maximum values for α_1 (0.3 resp. 6.0) and α_2 (0.5 resp. 8.4) and construct an evenly spaced grid of (α_1, α_2) values based on these limits. This leads to α_1, α_2 values as given in columns 1 and 2 of Table (6.3) and in turn induce pairs of $(\alpha_1/(\alpha_1+\alpha_2),\ \alpha_1+\alpha_2)$ values, which are reported in columns 3 and 4 of Table (6.3). As can be seen, these induced values are outside the above defined range for both variables in several instances (the grey-shaded figures in the table). Clearly the above argument also applies to continuous parameter-spaces.

So using prior information for parameterization 1 might force the estimator to search in highly implausible regions of the parameter-space despite the fact, that individually the α_1 and α_2 values are restricted to the same range as is induced by prior information for parameterization 2. In particular this use of prior information for parameterization 1 may lead to severe estimation problems if the likelihood profile has multiple modes and some of these are in the implausible regions of (α_1, α_2)-space. In such cases the MC^2 iterations might get stuck in such regions leading to slow convergence or no convergence at all. The unimodal shapes of the likelihood depicted above (based on the true values for all non-graphed parameters!) should not deceive the reader in this respect, as they are no guarantee for unimodal and nicely peaking likelihood surfaces when some of the non-graphed parameters are off there target values.

3.3 Variance components of the efficiency distribution

In Figure 6.5 the likelihood surface is drawn for various $(\ln(\sigma_1^2), \ln(\sigma_1^2)$-combinations. The modes are roughly at 0.4 resp. -0.5 for $\ln(\sigma_1^2)$ resp. $\ln(\sigma_2^2)$. This implies likelihood maximizing values for σ_1^2 of approximately 1.5 and of 0.6 for σ_2^2. Particularly the $\sigma_1^2 = 1.5$ is significantly off the target value 0.8 indicating hard times for an estimator in the attempt to find the corresponding underlying population parameters for samples as small as $n = 30$. Note furthermore that it leads to only small losses of likelihood if both variances are increased beyond the two observed modes, while decreases lead to comparatively large losses, which indicates the potential problem of overestimation the variance components of the output-specific efficiencies.

Note that in deriving figure 6.5 the underlying correlation amongst the two efficiencies was kept constant at the true value of $0.3/0.8 = 0.375$. Keeping the covariance term σ_{12} constant at the true value of 0.3 instead would lead to eventual violation of the definition of a covariance matrix (being positive definite) for some of the σ_1^2, σ_2^2 combinations considered.

An interesting variable for practical purposes is the correlation $\rho = \sigma_{12}/(\sigma_1\sigma_2)$ amongst output-specific efficiencies. In Figure 6.6 the like-

Table 6.3. Prior information for parametrization 1

$(\alpha_1,$	$\alpha_2)$	$\Rightarrow$	$\left(\frac{\alpha_1}{\alpha_1+\alpha_2},\right.$	$\left.\alpha_1+\alpha_2\right)$
0.3	0.5		.375	0.8
0.3	4.0		.070	4.3
0.3	8.4		.034	8.7
3.0	0.5		.857	3.5
3.0	4.0		.429	7.0
3.0	8.4		.263	11.4
6.0	0.5		.923	6.5
6.0	4.0		.600	10.0
6.0	8.4		.417	14.4

Figure 6.5. Mean log-likelihood for different $(\ln(\sigma_1^2), \ln(\sigma_1^2))$ combinations.

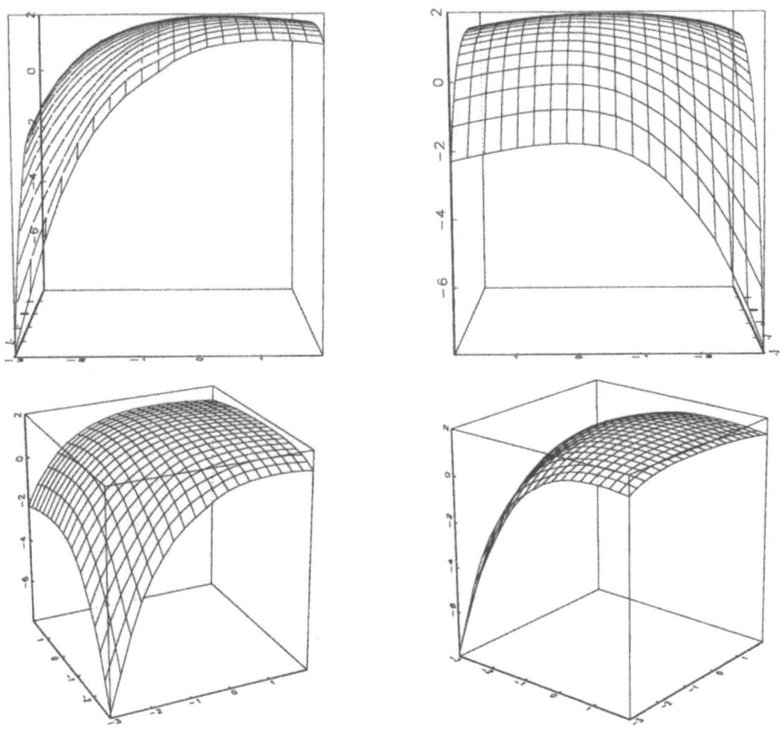

lihood profile for different combinations of $\ln(\sigma_1^2)$ and this correlation coefficient $\rho \in [-0.9, +0.9]$ are shown for given true values for σ_2^2 and all other parameters. While from the σ_1^2-perspective (the top left graph) the maximum of the likelihood exhibits some variation with a marginal peak at around 0.4 again, the ρ-perspective (the top right graph) is purely frustrating: Over most of the range of possible ρ values the likelihood appears completely flat for the approximate modal $\ln(\sigma_1^2)$-value of 0.4.

In fact I found similar problems when considering combinations of ρ along with any other parameter. Therefore changes in the likelihood due to variation of any other parameter are likely to dominate changes in the likelihood due to variation of ρ. So if a random sampling mechanism scans the domain of ρ (as will be explained below) along with that

Figure 6.6. Mean log-likelihood for different ($\ln(\sigma_1^2)$, ρ) combinations.

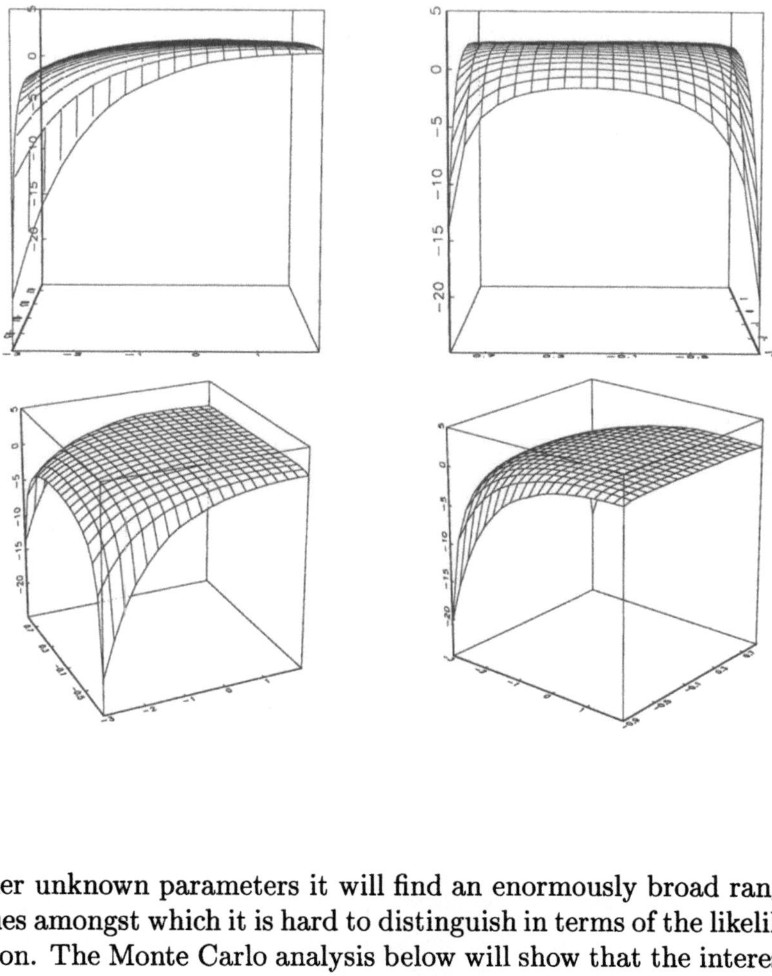

of other unknown parameters it will find an enormously broad range of ρ-values amongst which it is hard to distinguish in terms of the likelihood function. The Monte Carlo analysis below will show that the interesting question about the type of correlation between output-specific efficiencies underlying a sample thus can not be answered reliably with this sort of parametrization and motivates the future search for better ones.

Chapter 7

DERIVING POSTERIOR DISTRIBUTIONS

Density (5.7) can not be expressed in closed form or at least approximated for the general case (for example by linearization), when a closed form representation of $\mathrm{y}_s^F(x_i, m_i)$ is missing. This is exactly the case with a DEA estimated frontier. So parameter estimation based on analytical evaluation of this likelihood in applied work (with unknown frontier) is impossible. On the other hand the quantities $\mathrm{y}_s^F(x_i, m_i)$ can be consistently estimated for every x_i, m_i via DEA applied to $\{x_i, y_i\}$, as has been mentioned above.

1. The prior assumptions

So to use (5.7) for parameter estimation I will instead resort to MC^2 methodology (as described generally in Chapter 5) in a Bayesian setup treating the unknown parameters μ, Σ, α as random variates following certain prior distributions and the latent m_i-terms as variables to be estimated along the way. With respect to the functional form of these prior distributions I rely on conjugacy as much as possible for easily tractable posterior distributions. So I assume that parameter vector μ is multivariate normally distributed and the inverse covariance matrix Σ^{-1} as Wishart distributed. The Wishart distribution, defined on the space of symmetric positive semi-definite matrices, is defined as

$$\mathcal{W}_S(\Sigma^{-1}; r, W) \equiv \frac{|W|^r}{\pi^{S(S-1)/4} \prod_{s=1}^{S} \Gamma(\frac{2r+1-s}{2})} \times |\Sigma^{-1}|^{r-(S+1)/2} \exp\{-\mathrm{tr}(W\Sigma^{-1})\} \quad (7.1)$$

Apart from conjugacy considerations a general guideline for choosing prior distributions is to make them as little informative as possible to get data driven rather than assumption driven results. As long as we don't need the prior distributions themselves we can afford to leave the hyperparameters of these prior distributions unspecified. This is the case here for μ and Σ, whose posterior distributions are from known parametric families owing to conjugacy. Thus I simply assume μ to follow a multivariate Normal distribution $\mathcal{N}_S(\cdot,\cdot)$ and Σ to follow the Wishart distribution $\mathcal{W}_S(.,.)$. These prior distributions are called improper and can only be evaluated a posteriori based on (y_i, m_i) data.

The least informative prior distribution possible for α depends on the specification of $\mathrm{d}_M(m_i;\alpha)$. To accommodate eventually non conjugate specifications of the target output ratio distributions as well, I assume for the moment that the parameter vector α follows a distribution from a parametric family $\mathrm{d}_\alpha(\gamma_0)$ with prespecified vector γ_0 of hyperparameters. In many cases a mildly informative uniform on α will suffice, which would only require domain determination.

Summarizing the above assumptions we get the following prior structure:

$$\mu \sim \mathcal{N}_S(\cdot,\cdot), \quad \Sigma^{-1} \sim \mathcal{W}_S(\cdot,\cdot), \quad \alpha \sim \mathrm{d}_\alpha(\gamma_0) \quad (7.2)$$

2. Sampling from the full conditional posterior distributions

From (5.1), (5.2), (5.7), the iid assumptions and the priors (7.2) the conditional posterior distributions, the key elements of MC^2 analysis, can now be derived. The unobserved target output ratios, confined to a finite grid of possible values (see section 1 of Chapter 5), are independent also in the posterior perspective with probabilities of the feasible values defined by

$$d(m_i|x_i, y_i, \alpha, \mu, \Sigma) = \frac{d(y_i|\, x_i, m_i, \mu, \Sigma)\; d_M(m_i;\, \alpha)}{\sum_{m_g \in M(x_i, y_i)} d(y_i|\, x_i, m_g, \mu, \Sigma)\; d_M(m_g;\, \alpha)} \tag{7.3}$$

Sampling from (7.3) is straightforward via the cumulative distribution technique, because the posterior cumulative distribution of m_i given values for parameters μ, Σ and α can be calculated exactly. For a given sample $\{m_i\}$ of output-ratio vectors generated from (7.3), given Σ and α values, the conditional posterior distribution of μ is found to be the following multivariate Normal:[1]

$$\begin{aligned}[\mu|x_1 \ldots x_n, y_1 \ldots y_n, m_1 \ldots m_n, \Sigma] \; &\sim \\ \mathcal{N}_S\left(\frac{1}{n}\sum_{i=1}^{n} \mathrm{w}(x_i, y_i, m_i),\; \frac{\Sigma}{n}\right)\end{aligned} \tag{7.4}$$

So this conditional distribution is exactly known and sampling a new value therefrom is a routine job for statistical or mathematical software.[2] The covariance matrix Σ also has an exactly known conditional posterior distribution which by conjugacy is

$$\begin{aligned}[\Sigma^{-1}|\, x_1 \ldots x_n, m_1 \ldots m_n, y_1 \ldots y_n, \mu] \; &\sim \\ \mathcal{W}_S\Big(0.5n, 0.5\, \mathrm{M}_C[\mathrm{w}(x_i, y_i, m_i), \mu]\Big)\end{aligned} \tag{7.5}$$

where $\mathrm{M}_C[\cdot]$ indicates the second central moment operator

$$\begin{aligned}\mathrm{M}_C[\mathrm{w}(x, y, m), \mu] \; &= \; \sum_{i=1}^{n_2} [w_{i1} - \mu_1, \ldots, w_{iS} - \mu_S,] \\ &\quad \times \; [w_{i1} - \mu_1, \ldots, w_{iS} - \mu_S,]' .\end{aligned}$$

Note that occasionally a different parameterization for the Wishart is chosen, as for example in Gilks et al., 1996b, which would accordingly

---

[1] If we had chosen an informative Normal prior for μ instead, i.e. $\mu \sim \mathcal{N}(\mu_0, \Sigma_0)$, the conditional posterior would be $[\mu|w_1 \ldots w_n, \Sigma] \sim \mathcal{N}(\mu^*, \Sigma^*)$ with $\Sigma^* = (\Sigma_0^{-1} + n\Sigma^{-1})^{-1}$ and $\mu^* = \Sigma^*[\Sigma_0^{-1}\mu_0 + n\Sigma^{-1}\mathrm{E}(w_i)]$.

[2] I used the normal random number generator implemented in the GAUSS programming package, used for all calculations in this book.

lead to a different specification of the posterior. The presented specification is due to Bernardo and Smith, 1994. A Wishart-random generator is not implemented in GAUSS, the software used for calculations for the present study. So I followed the proposal for programming such a generator given in Johnson, 1987. Finally the conditional posterior distribution for the parameter vector α of target output-ratios is found to be proportional ($\propto$) to

$$[\alpha|m_1 \dots m_n] \;\propto\; \mathrm{d}_\alpha(\alpha; \gamma_0) \prod_{i=1}^{n} \mathrm{d}_M(m_i;\, \alpha). \tag{7.6}$$

Knowing this distribution only up to a factor of proportionality suffices for sampling a new value from this distribution by the Metropolis-Hastings updating mechanism (4.2). For specific distributions of output-ratios m_i the above posterior might be amenable to conjugate analysis as well, but I still do not want be as specific about this distribution at the moment.

After fixing the hyperparameters γ_0 and defining arbitrary start values $\mu^{(0)}$, $\Sigma^{(0)}$ and $\alpha^{(0)}$ iterative sampling from (7.3)-(7.6) can start. First a sample of output-ratios is drawn from (7.3) conditional on the values $\mu^{(0)}$, $\Sigma^{(0)}$ and $\alpha^{(0)}$. This sample shall be denoted $\{m_i^{(1)}\}_{i=1}^n$. Conditional on this sample and covariance matrix $\Sigma^{(0)}$ a new mean vector $\mu^{(1)}$ is drawn from posterior distribution (7.4). Next a new covariance matrix $\Sigma^{(1)}$ is generated from distribution (7.5) conditional on sample $\{m_i^{(1)}\}_{i=1}^n$ and mean vector $\mu^{(1)}$.

Finally the parameter vector α is updated based on the sample $\{m_i^{(1)}\}_{i=1}^n$. If $\mathrm{d}_M(m_i;\alpha)$ is not from the conjugate family and the posterior distribution not from a known parametric family this last step will require prior specification of a proposal distribution $q(\cdot)$ to apply updating rule (4.2). A widely used proposal distribution leading to geometric convergence under fairly mild regularity conditions (see Roberts and Tweedie, 1994) is a Normal centered at the old values of the corresponding parameters, i.e.

$$q(\tilde{\alpha}|\alpha^{(0)}) \equiv \mathcal{N}(\tilde{\alpha};\, \alpha^{(0)}, \sigma_\alpha^2). \tag{7.7}$$

Updating based on proposals of type (7.7) is labeled random walk Metropolis and leads to $q(\tilde{\alpha}|\alpha^{(0)}) = q(\alpha^{(0)}|\tilde{\alpha})$. So the acceptance rate (4.1) for this candidate value is determined solely by the posterior odds of new vs. old α values and the new value $\alpha^{(1)}$ will be set to the candidate value $\tilde{\alpha}$ if accepted and otherwise set equal to $\alpha^{(0)}$. Choosing the variance parameter σ_{α}^2 will require some tuning to achieve a desired average acceptance probability for proper mixing. Roberts et al., 1994 and Gelman et al., 1995 have come up with an approximate range [0.15,0.5] for optimal acceptance rates in the general case.

Sequentially updating all unknown quantities T times in the iterative manner just described will generate a sequence $\{m_1^{(t)} \dots m_n^{(t)}, \mu^{(t)}, \Sigma^{(t)}, \alpha^{(t)}\}_{t=1}^T$ whose limiting distribution ($T \to \infty$) is the joint distribution of the parameters and the missing data conditional on observations $\{x_i, y_i\}$. The expectation of any posterior quantities of interest (including functions of the estimated quantities) can then be calculated from these sampled parameters and missing data, relying on the ergodicity feature of the constructed chains as detailed in the Lemma of Mengersen and Tweedie, 1993 cited in section 1 of Chapter 4. As an example consider the sample means $\bar{\varepsilon}_s^{(t)} = \frac{1}{n} \sum_{i=1 \dots n} 1/[1+\exp(-w_{is}^{(t)})]$ of output-specific efficiencies, which are functions of the estimated target output ratios $m_i^{(t)}$ by definition (5.5). Ergodicity of the DMU-specific $\{m_i^{(t)}\}$ chains then implies

$$\text{Prob}\left[\frac{1}{T}\sum_{t=1}^{T} \bar{\varepsilon}_s^{(t)} \;\to\; \text{E}(\bar{\varepsilon}_s | \, x, y)\right] = 1. \tag{7.8}$$

The present proposal for output-specific efficiency estimation thus may be summarized as the following sequence of steps:

- Estimate $\mathrm{y}^F(x_i, m_g)$ via DEA for all x_i and all $m_g \in \mathbb{M}$ based on sample $\{x_i, y_i\}$ and use these estimates $\hat{\mathrm{y}}^F(x_i, m_g)$ to proxy the unknown frontier points in the following steps where required
- Treat the m_i-terms as missing observations, identically and independently distributed according to (5.1) and treat the parameters μ, Σ and α as random variates from prior distributions (7.2)
- Choose hyperparameters for the prior distributions and proposal distributions as necessary
- Sample iteratively from the conditional posterior distributions (7.3) - (7.6) of $m_1 \dots m_n, \mu, \Sigma, \alpha$ to generate Markov chains of these variables
- Conduct inference about the unknown quantities (means, quantiles, functions of...) based on these Markov chains considering them as approximate samples from the true posterior distributions

The key element of this data-augmentation approach applied to output specific efficiency estimation consists of repeated sampling of target output-ratios from their posterior distribution (7.3), because all other posterior distributions are conditioned on such a sample of these values. As shown such sampling within the described stochastic setting based on a finite grid of a priori feasible target output-ratios is particularly straightforward. If one instead prefers to work with continuous target output ratios it would in general no longer be possible to sample directly from the conditional posterior distribution of m_i . But in this case one could rely again on mechanism (4.2) just like I did above for updating of α.

A computational problem with continuous types of output-ratios is the fact, that the m_i variates enter the stochastic model primarily via mappings $\mathrm{y}_s^F(x_i, m_i)$, for which no closed form representations are available when the frontier estimate is based on DEA. For continuous m_i's this mapping thus will have to be reevaluated in each iteration step, which can be extremely time consuming for large data sets or higher dimensional settings. By restricting the analysis as proposed to a finite grid of m_i values instead the estimates $\hat{\mathrm{y}}_s^F(x_i, m_g)$ have to be calculated only once for all $i = 1 \dots n$ and all $g = 1 \dots G$ before the iterations actually start. Because I will perform large scale Monte Carlo simulations (each based on thousands of iteration loops) for an assessment of small sample performance of the proposed approach, I did not consider the case of continuous output ratios.

In any particular MC^2 application questions about the necessary number of replications, optimal burn-in time, removal of serial correlation and convergence checking will have to be dealt with in detail. But rather than performing according diagnostics on a sample by sample basis in the Monte Carlo analysis itself I relied on extensive preliminary testing of a few typical samples to come up with a general rule. For general discussions of the involved issues the reader is referred to Raftery and Lewis, 1996, Gilks et al., 1996b or Cowles and Carlin, 1996. The two most widely followed recommendations with regard to convergence diagnosis are to be found in Gelman and Rubin, 1992 and Geweke, 1992. In the application to follow, I will follow the relevant approach of Geweke, 1992 and explain it's use in more detail.

3. Scale Invariance

An important question in efficiency estimation is whether or not the results depend on two specific types of data manipulations: Rescaling one or more of the input/output variables and adding constants to these variables. The first type of manipulation most naturally occurs when changing the units of measurement of the data. If this does not affect the results, the estimator would be called unit invariant or, synonymously, scale invariant. It seems like a modest criteria for the usefulness of an efficiency estimator to be scale invariant, because clearly the relative performance of a DMU vs. its competitors should not be affected by measuring a quantity output in tons or kilograms resp. a value output in dollars or thousands of dollars. Yet for example the traditional additive DEA model does not have this property. The second type of manipulation may be necessary in applications, where certain data of specific DMU's are originally negative (think of negative profits as output variable), in which case the standard LP optimization routines required for efficiency estimation could not be applied. An efficiency estimator which is not affected by adding constants to the variables is labeled translation invariant. In the following the scale invariance property of the proposed estimator shall be established, while translation invariance clearly must be rejected as the underlying frontier estimation technique does not have this property either. An overview about scale invariance and translation invariance features of various types of DEA models is given for example in Cooper et al., 2000, p. 102.

The question of scale invariance in the present context arises at two distinct levels. At the basic level one may ask, whether introducing the concept of non observed random target-output ratios for determining the proper reference points (as such being random variables themselves!) preserves the scale invariance property available for the underlying frontier estimation technique BCC-DEA. Answering this question involves the calculation of expected output-specific efficiencies based on known distributions in order to get rid of the unobserved target output ratios. There is no analogue to the calculation of such expectations in standard DEA, because there the unique reference points (for each DMU) are singled out from all those available by prior choice of a projection technique, which lacks any statistical rationale.

At the estimation level instead one would ask, whether the estimated distribution of output-specific efficiencies (i.e. the parameters like the μ

and Σ from (5.2 determining this distribution) is the same when based on some original data set resp. a rescaled version thereof. To answer this question one would need a closed form solution for parameter estimates (like it is available in the classical regression context) for explicit comparison. Here we have no such closed form solutions to offer due to the DEA step involved in describing the efficiency frontier in random piecewise linear fashion (recall that the frontier description itself is based on random observations!). So this question must remain unanswered.

Before proceeding it must be noted, that scale invariance does indeed hold for the radial efficiency scores derived from BCC-DEA, the frontier estimation technique underlying the present approach. This is easy to verify from analyzing the maximization problem (2.1): Multiplying any input or output (of each DMU!) with a positive, input/output-specific constant does not alter any of the optimization conditions. These constants can be factored out from the respective left hand and right hand side of each inequality constraint and therefore be cancelled. Furthermore these constants do not appear in the objective function, so it is trivial to conclude, that the efficiency scores from a rescaled data set are exactly equal to the efficiency scores from the original data set.

A trivial corollary associated with this scale invariance property of efficiency scores will be important in proving scale invariance of the present estimator as well. To establish this corollary define a transformed or rescaled data set (indicated via tilde$^{\sim}$) without loss of generality by rescaling just the first variable via some positive constant β as follows:

$$\tilde{y}_{i1} = \beta y_{i1} \quad \text{and } \tilde{y}_{is} = y_{is} \; \forall s \neq 1 \quad \text{with } \beta > 0 \qquad (7.9)$$

Then denote the BCC-DEA estimated radial efficiency scores of DMU i in the original scaling of the variables as ε_i and the corresponding estimate from the rescaled data set as $\tilde{\varepsilon}_i$. Likewise denote a target output ratio applying to DMU i in this newly defined output space as $\widetilde{m}_i$. For the moment it shall be left unspecified how $\widetilde{m}_i$ relates to m_i, as the corollary should hold for arbitrary output ratio definitions. Now the scale invariance of radial efficiency scores, i.e. $\varepsilon_i = \tilde{\varepsilon}$, by definition of such scores also implies $y_{i1}/\mathrm{y}_1^F(x_i, m_i) = \tilde{y}_{i1}/\tilde{\mathrm{y}}_1^F(x_i, \widetilde{m}_i)$, where the output ratios corresponding to observations are denoted as m_i resp. $\widetilde{m}_i$. Using (7.9) we may substitute βy_{i1} for $\tilde{y}_{i1}$ resp. y_{is} for $\tilde{y}_{is}$ (for $s = 2 \ldots S$) and then get immediately

$$\tilde{\mathrm{y}}_1^F(x_i, \widetilde{m}_i) = \beta \mathrm{y}_1^F(x_i, m_i), \quad \mathrm{y}_s^F(x_i, m_i) = \tilde{\mathrm{y}}_s^F(x_i, \widetilde{m}_i) \; \forall \; s \neq 1, \quad (7.10)$$

whatever definition of output ratios we may use. But note, that the relationships (7.10) do not just hold for the output-ratios corresponding to the respective observations, but for any arbitrary output-ratios, as long as they are defined in the same manner for the original output variables and the rescaled ones. This general relationship between any points on the efficiency frontiers associated with the respective data sets shall be illustrated geometrically with Figures 7.1 and 7.2 for a two-output case with $\beta = 2$ which extends easily to models of arbitrary dimensionality.

Figure 7.1. Original output space

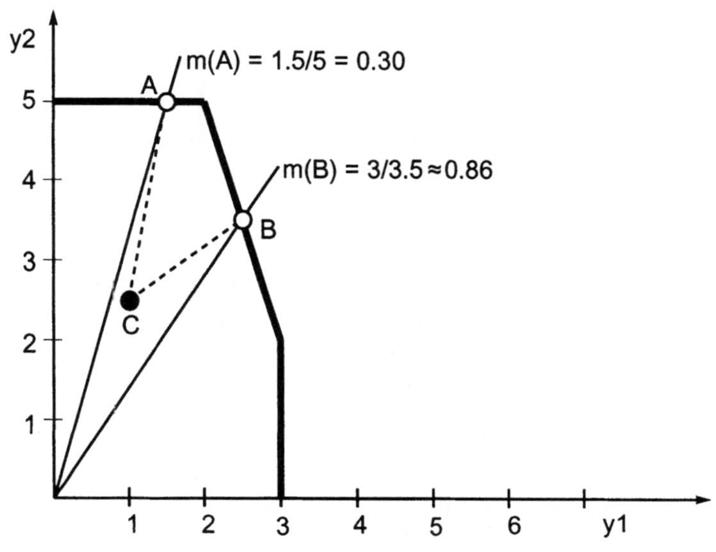

DEA estimated frontiers (not only of the BCC types) by construction are closest convex hulls around the data points.[3] So if some output vector (y_1, y_2) was on the (Farrell) efficiency frontier calculated from the original data and these data were rescaled according to (7.9) with $\beta = 2$, then $(2y_1, y_2)$ must be an output vector on the efficiency frontier calculated from this rescaled data set (like points A and A' resp. B and B' in the graphs). Furthermore if the target output-ratio of DMU 1 in the graph actually determined point A as reference point for efficiency com-

[3] An exception to this are so called *free disposal hulls* as proposed in Meeusen and van den Broeck, 1977, which are not considered here.

Figure 7.2. Transformed output space ($\tilde{y}_1 = 2y_1$)

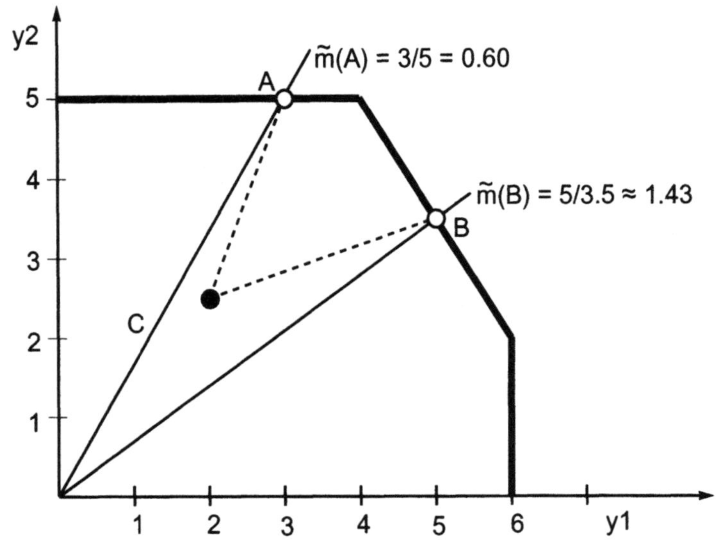

parisons in the original output space, then the uniquely corresponding target output-ratio of DMU 1 in the transformed space must be the one associated with point A' and analogously for any other target output ratio (for example the one leading to B resp. B').

While the above is an argument for scale invariance for given target output-ratios, we actually need a result proving this for unknown target output-ratios. So the only remaining step to establish scale invariance for the present approach is to construct expected output-specific efficiencies by integrating (averaging, if you prefer) over the density of the unobserved target output-ratios, because the latter ultimately determine the output-specific efficiencies via the $\mathrm{y}_s^F(x_i, m_i)$ terms. But since output-ratios indeed are affected by rescaling of outputs (a fact reflected in 7.10), so will be their distributions. Thus one might suspect, that the scale dependence of output-ratios and the implied change in m-distributions between original and rescaled output space leads to scale dependence of output-specific efficiency scores. It will be shown, that this suspicion is wrong.

At the basic level, for which we want to prove scale invariance, we deal with known distributions of target output-ratios and output specific efficiencies and known frontier. From this information we shall derive the conditional posterior distribution of target output-ratios for given observations on inputs and outputs of a specific DMU in original and rescaled output space respectively and then compare the conditionally expected output specific efficiencies for both output spaces. For a particular type of efficiency distribution (to be used in Chapter 8) the corresponding posterior distribution has been derived in (7.3). For the present argument we want a more general description of this conditional posterior density, so we reformulate the data generating process as

$$\begin{aligned} y_{is} &= \mathrm{y}_s^F(x_i, m_i)\, \varepsilon_s \quad \forall\; s = 1, \dots S \\ \text{with} \quad & m_i \overset{iid}{\sim} \mathrm{d}_M(m_i), \quad m_i = (m_{i1}, \dots, m_{i(S-1)}) \\ \text{and} \quad & \varepsilon_i \overset{iid}{\sim} \mathrm{d}_\mathcal{E}(\varepsilon_i), \quad \varepsilon_i = (\varepsilon_{i1}, \dots, \varepsilon_{iS}) \end{aligned} \tag{7.11}$$

From this we find the joint density of $y_i = (y_{i1}, \dots, y_{iS})$ and m_i to be

$$\begin{aligned} &\mathrm{d}_{Y,M|X}(y_i, m_i | x_i) = \\ &\prod_{s=1}^{S} \frac{1}{\mathrm{y}_s^F(x_i, m_i)} \; \mathrm{d}_\mathcal{E}\left(\frac{y_{i1}}{\mathrm{y}_1^F(x_i, m_i)}, \dots, \frac{y_{iS}}{\mathrm{y}_S^F(x_i, m_i)}\right) \mathrm{d}_M(m_i) \\ &\text{if } y_{is} \leq \mathrm{y}_s^F(x_i, m_i)\; \forall\; s, \text{otherwise } 0 \end{aligned} \tag{7.12}$$

and finally the posterior distribution of m_i given x_i, y_i as

$$\mathrm{d}(m_i | x_i, y_i) = \mathrm{d}_{Y,M|X}(y_i, m_i | x_i) \Bigg/ \int_{\substack{m\, \in \\ \Omega(x_i, y_i)}} \mathrm{d}_{Y,M|X}(y_i, m | x_i)\, dm \tag{7.13}$$

Via frontier description $\mathrm{y}_s^F(x_i, m_i)$ the output specific efficiencies are tied to target output ratios m_i through

$$\varepsilon_{is} = y_{is} / \mathrm{y}_s^F(x_i, m_i), \tag{7.14}$$

i.e. they are functions of the unobserved target output ratios. The expectation of output specific efficiencies of DMU i conditional on observed input and output vectors (x_i, y_i) must therefore be defined as

$$\mathrm{E}_{M|X_i,Y_i}\left[\frac{y_{is}}{\mathrm{y}_s^F(x_i,m)}\right] = \frac{\int\limits_{\Omega_i} \frac{y_{is}}{\mathrm{y}_s^F(x_i,m)}\ \mathrm{d}_{Y,M|X_i}(y_i,m|x_i)\ dm}{\int\limits_{\Omega_i} \mathrm{d}_{Y,M|X_i}(y_i,m|x_i)\ dm} \tag{7.15}$$

where the indicated integration is actually a sequence of integration steps of the form

$$\int\limits_{\Omega_i}(\cdots)\ dm = \int\limits_{\Omega_{i(S-1)}} \cdots \int\limits_{\Omega_{i1}} (\cdots)\ dm_1 \ldots dm_{S-1} \tag{7.16}$$

with integration ranges Ω_{is} defined as intervals

$$\begin{aligned} \Omega_{is} = \Big[&\min_{m_1 \ldots m_s} \{m_s : y_{ik} \leq \mathrm{y}_k^F(x_i,m)\ \forall\ k\}, \\ &\max_{m_1 \ldots m_s} \{m_s : y_{ik} \leq \mathrm{y}_k^F(x_i,m)\ \forall\ k\}\Big] \\ \forall\ s = 1 \ldots (S-1)& \end{aligned} \tag{7.17}$$

So to determine the integration range Ω_{i1} we minimize resp. maximize over m_1 for given values $m_2 \ldots m_{(S-1)}$, to determine the integration range Ω_{i2} we minimize resp. maximize over (m_1, m_2) for given values $m_3 \ldots m_{(S-1)}$ and so on. Now let's describe the relationship between m and $\widetilde{m}$ with general functions as follows

$$\begin{aligned} m_s &= f_s(\widetilde{m}) \quad \forall\ s = 1 \ldots (S-1) \\ \text{and } m &= f(\widetilde{m}) = \{f_1(\widetilde{m}), \ldots f_{S-1}(\widetilde{m})\}, \end{aligned} \tag{7.18}$$

respectively

$$\begin{aligned} \widetilde{m}_s &= g_s(m) \quad \forall\ s = 1 \ldots (S-1) \\ \text{and } \widetilde{m} &= g(m) = \{g_1(m), \ldots g_{S-1}(m)\} \end{aligned} \tag{7.19}$$

For example we may once again define a generic output ratio (applying to target output ratios as well as to output ratios of observed points) in the two-output case as $m_1 = y_1/(y_1 + y_2)$ resp. $\widetilde{m}_1 = \tilde{y}_1/(\tilde{y}_1 + \tilde{y}_2)$. By (7.9) this leads to $\widetilde{m}_1 = \beta y_1/(\beta y_1 + y_2)$ and therefore

$$m_1 = \frac{\widetilde{m}_1}{\beta + (1-\beta)\widetilde{m}_1} \quad \text{and } \widetilde{m}_1 = \frac{\beta m_1}{1 + (\beta - 1) m_1}. \tag{7.20}$$

To each of the equation systems (7.18) and (7.19) corresponds a Jacobian matrix of first partial derivatives which will be denoted $\mathrm{J}_{\widetilde{m}\to m}$ for (7.18) resp. $\mathrm{J}_{m\to\widetilde{m}}$ for (7.19). It is easy to check that equation system (7.18) and the associated Jacobian $\mathrm{J}_{\widetilde{m}\to m}$ satisfy the basic regularity conditions required by transformation Theorem on page 65. So we can express the distribution of $\widetilde{m}$ via the distribution of m as

$$\mathrm{d}_{\widetilde{M}}(\widetilde{m}) = |\det(\mathrm{J}_{\widetilde{m}\to m})|\ \mathrm{d}_M(f(\widetilde{m})) \tag{7.21}$$

and furthermore the joint distribution of output observations and target output-ratios in the transformed output space as

$$\begin{aligned} &\mathrm{d}_{\tilde{Y},\widetilde{M}|X}(\tilde{y}_i, \widetilde{m}_i|x_i) = \\ &\quad \prod_{s=1}^{S} \frac{1}{\tilde{\mathrm{y}}_s^F(x_i,\widetilde{m}_i)}\ \mathrm{d}_{\mathcal{E}}\left(\frac{\tilde{y}_{i1}}{\tilde{\mathrm{y}}_1^F(x_i,\widetilde{m}_i)}, \ldots, \frac{\tilde{y}_{iS}}{\tilde{\mathrm{y}}_S^F(x_i,\widetilde{m}_i)}\right) \\ &\quad \times |\det(\mathrm{J}_{\widetilde{m}\to m})|\ \mathrm{d}_M(f(\widetilde{m})) \\ &\quad \text{if } \tilde{y}_{is} \le \tilde{\mathrm{y}}_s^F(x_i,\widetilde{m}_i)\ \forall\ s, \text{otherwise } 0 \end{aligned} \tag{7.22}$$

Using (7.9) and (7.10) this can be expressed as

$$\begin{aligned} \mathrm{d}_{\tilde{Y},\widetilde{M}|X}(\tilde{y}_i, \widetilde{m}_i|x_i) &= \beta^{-1}\ |\det(\mathrm{J}_{\widetilde{m}\to m})| \\ &\times \mathrm{d}_{Y,M|X}(\tilde{y}_{i1}/\beta, \tilde{y}_{i2}, \ldots\tilde{y}_{iS}, f(\widetilde{m}_i)|x_i). \end{aligned} \tag{7.23}$$

Now substitute y_i for $\tilde{y}_i$ based on definition (7.9), which leads to the following conditional expectation of output s-specific efficiency of DMU i in the transformed space:

$$\mathrm{E}_{\widetilde{M}|X_i,\tilde{Y}_i}\left[\frac{\tilde{y}_{is}}{\tilde{\mathrm{y}}_s^F(x_i,\widetilde{m})}\right] = \mathrm{E}_{\widetilde{M}|X_i,\tilde{Y}_i}\left[\frac{y_{is}}{\mathrm{y}_s^F(x_i,f(\widetilde{m}))}\right] =$$

$$\frac{\displaystyle\int_{\widetilde{\Omega}_i} \frac{y_{is}}{\mathrm{y}_s^F(x_i,f(\widetilde{m}_i))}\ |\det(\mathrm{J}_{\widetilde{m}\to m})|\ \mathrm{d}_{Y,M|X}\Big[y_i, f(\widetilde{m}_i)\Big|x_i\Big]\ d\widetilde{m}_i}{\displaystyle\int_{\widetilde{\Omega}_i} |\det(\mathrm{J}_{\widetilde{m}\to m})|\ \mathrm{d}_{Y,M|X}\Big[y_i, f(\widetilde{m})\Big|x_i\Big]\ d\widetilde{m}} \tag{7.24}$$

where the sequence of integrations to be performed and the corresponding integration limits are analogous to those defined in (7.16) and (7.17), but with $\widetilde{m}$ resp. $\tilde{y}_i$ replacing m resp. y_i. So in order to prove that this expectation over $\widetilde{m}$ is indeed the same as the one over m we only need to show that the integration over the components of $\widetilde{m}$ can be replaced by an integration over components of m, such that the involved Jacobian cancels and the implied change in integration limits leads to the integration limits in original space.

Let's show this first for the two output case (for which output-ratios are scalars) with output-ratios for which a reversible mapping exists, such that we may write $m = f(\widetilde{m})$, $\widetilde{m} = f^{-1}(m)$ and $\det(\mathrm{J}_{\widetilde{m}\to m}) = f'(\widetilde{m})$. For this case we find the two involved integrals of (7.24) via substituting the integrand m for $f(\widetilde{m})$ to be

$$\int\limits_{\widetilde{m}\,\in\,\widetilde{\Omega}(x_i,\tilde{y}(y_i))} \ldots |f'(f^{-1}(m))|\ \mathrm{d}_{Y,M|X}(y_i, m|x_i)\ (f^{-1})'(m)\, dm \qquad (7.25)$$

But $(f^{-1})'(m) = 1/f'(\widetilde{m}) = 1/f'(f^{-1}(m))$ and from the relationship between original and transformed space we know that $f'(.) > 0$, i.e. the relationship between $\widetilde{m}$ and m is monotone and increasing. So $|f'(.)| = f'(.)$ and we may continue to argue as follows: If the minimum of feasible $\widetilde{m}$ for given $x_i, \tilde{y}_i$ is defined as $\underline{\widetilde{m}} = \min_{\widetilde{m}}\{\widetilde{m} : \tilde{y}_{is} \leq \tilde{\mathrm{y}}_s^F(x_i, \widetilde{m})\}$ then also $\underline{\widetilde{m}} = \arg\min_{\widetilde{m}}\{f_1(\widetilde{m}) : \tilde{y}_{is} \leq \tilde{\mathrm{y}}_s^F(x_i, \widetilde{m})\} = \arg\min_{\widetilde{m}}\{f_1(\widetilde{m}) : y_{is} \leq \mathrm{y}_s^F(x_i, f_1(\widetilde{m})\}$ holds and therefore $f_1(\underline{\widetilde{m}}) = \arg\min_m\{m : y_{is} \leq \mathrm{y}_s^F(x_i, m)\}$. Denoting the minimum feasible m for given x_i, y_i as $\underline{m}$ we thus have $\underline{m} = f_1(\underline{\widetilde{m}})$. Analogous reasoning establishes $\overline{m} = f_1(\overline{\widetilde{m}})$ so that after substituting the integrand m for $\widetilde{m}$ we get exactly the integral (7.15) which defines the expectation of output specific efficiencies in the original output space, which concludes the proof of scale invariance at the basic level for the two-output case and general definitions of output-ratios.

For ease of exposition in the multiple output case we restrict attention to generic output ratio definitions as follows:

$$m_s = y_s/y_S \quad \forall\ s = 1\ldots(S-1) \qquad (7.26)$$

From this and the definition of rescaled outputs (7.9) we immediately get the relationships

$$m_1 = f_1(\widetilde{m}) = \widetilde{m}_1/\beta, \quad m_s = f_s(\widetilde{m}) = \widetilde{m}_s \text{ for } s = 2\ldots(S-1) \qquad (7.27)$$
$$\widetilde{m}_1 = g_1(m) = \beta m_1, \quad \widetilde{m}_s = g_s(m) = m_s \text{ for } s = 2\ldots(S-1) \qquad (7.28)$$

with associated Jacobian $\det(\mathrm{J}_{\widetilde{m}\to m}) = 1/\beta$. So the Jacobian is independent of $\widetilde{m}$ and can be factored out from both integrals (appearing in nominator and denominator) in 7.24 and thus cancelled. Furthermore the integration variables $\widetilde{m}_2 \ldots \widetilde{m}_{S-1}$ can simply be replaced by $m_2 \ldots m_{S-1}$. So 7.24 in this particular case reads

$$\mathrm{E}_{\widetilde{M}|X_i,\tilde{Y}_i}\left[\frac{\tilde{y}_{is}}{\tilde{\mathrm{y}}_s^F(x_i,\widetilde{m})}\right] = \frac{\displaystyle\int\limits_{\widetilde{\Omega}_i} \frac{y_{is}}{\mathrm{y}_s^F(x_i,m')}\, \mathrm{d}_{Y,M|X}\Big[y_i, m'\Big|x_i\Big]\, d\widetilde{m}}{\displaystyle\int\limits_{\widetilde{\Omega}_i} \mathrm{d}_{Y,M|X}\Big[y_i, m'\Big|x_i\Big]\, d\widetilde{m}} \tag{7.29}$$

where $m' = \{f_1(\widetilde{m}_1), m_2, \ldots, m_{S-1}\}$, $d\widetilde{m} = d\widetilde{m}_1\ dm_2 \ldots dm_{S-1}$ and the integration sequence and the integration intervals are again defined analogous to (7.16) and (7.17). Finally substitute m_1 for $f_1(\widetilde{m}_1)$ and $d\widetilde{m}_1 = \beta dm_1$ to get the desired result of scale invariance at the basic level for the multi-output case as well. It has to be noted, that the present restriction to a particular type of output-ratio underlying this proof is only required to keep the proof short for general dimensions of output-vectors. The proof is possible for other types of output-ratio definitions as well but then becomes increasingly laborious for higher dimensional output-spaces.

III

EVALUATING THE CONCEPT

Chapter 8

MONTE CARLO ANALYSIS OF ESTIMATOR PERFORMANCE

For applied efficiency analysis the main intended benefit from the proposed approach is the ability to identify differences in the means of output-specific efficiencies. So the primary questions of the following Monte Carlo analysis will be whether this ability is merely a theoretical one having only asymptotic appeal or whether it is also practically useful for typical sample sizes encountered in applied efficiency analysis. This ability is ultimately owed to the joint estimation of most likely DMU-specific target output-ratios from the large set of theoretically feasible target output-ratios. For determining the latter the bias corrected version of DEA as described in section 3 of Chapter 2 will be used, while output-specific efficiency estimation proper will be affected via MC^2 based on the posterior distributions derived in section 2 of Chapter 7, with some missing specifications yet to be added.

1. Sample generation

The following Monte Carlo simulations will be based on a two output-technology, the smallest possible dimension to study the problem at hand. As will be seen, the proposed technique performs moderately well in this two-output case but as first experience with higher dimensional models indicates, performance deteriorates rapidly with the dimensionality of the problem. This of course may have to do more with the known poor convergence of DEA rather than with particular MC^2 features. Whatever the reason the extremely time consuming nature of the involved simulations ruled out large scale experiments to get more conclusive evidence for higher dimensional models, so I will not enter into speculations about the likely performance of the proposed approach for such settings.

The technology used for the present Monte Carlo simulation is a constant returns to scale technology with a single input and two outputs related via transformation function

$$y_{i1}^{\gamma} + y_{i2}^{\gamma} = 1, \quad \text{where } \gamma \geq 1. \tag{8.1}$$

This formulation describes a constant elasticity of transformation (CET) input-isoquant and because no input levels are involved the specification (8.1) essentially applies only to a constant returns to scale technology. A CET input-isoquant may be part of a more general input/output separable formulation of a production function as is often used in multi-output analysis as for example in Kumbhakar, 1996 or Fernández et al., 2000.[1]

The elasticity of transformation ϱ corresponding to (8.1) is $1/(\gamma - 1)$. I will consider models with three different values for γ: A full substitutability model with $\gamma = 1$ ($\varrho = \infty$), a medium substitutability model with $\gamma = 3$ ($\varrho = 0.5$) and a Leontief-like model with $\gamma = 10$ ($\varrho \simeq 0.11$). These different values are supposed to cover the most likely range of transformation elasticities encountered in real world applications of frontier and efficiency estimation techniques and will allow to assess the influence of production function curvature on the quality of the estimators.

To get an idea of sample size impact on the performance of the proposed approach and a idea about the speed of convergence I considered sample sizes $n = 30$, $n = 100$ and $n = 300$. These may appear as rather small, but the proper meaning of sample size particularly in a DEA context

[1] An input-output separable form of a production relationship with input vector x and output vector y is most generally defined as $g(y) = f(x)$. For a CET function $g(y)$ with two outputs the corresponding specification would be $A[by_1^{\gamma} + (1-b)y_2^{\gamma}]^{\nu/\gamma} = f(x)$, where $\nu > 0$ is the degree of homogeneity of function $g(y)$. So the implicit assumption of specification (8.1) is $b = 0.5$, while ν is essentially left unspecified. Note that ν by itself does not tell anything about the nature of returns to scale of such a production relationship. This would instead require a comparison of ν with the degree of homogeneity of $f(x)$. So the constant returns to scale assumption implicit in formulation (8.1) might result from any ν, as long as the degree of homogeneity of $f(x)$ is also ν. For a general discussion of the properties of such functional forms, although in input space, see Beattie and Taylor, 1985.

is revealed only when related to the dimensionality of the problem. As has been noted for example in Simar, 1996, the *curse of dimensionality* is much more of a problem in DEA than in parametric frontier estimation approaches. Given the assumption of constant returns to scale the technology chosen here has actually a dimension of only two: One input-isoquant in $\mathbb{R}^2$ suffices to describe this technology. Therefore in my opinion a range of 30 to 300 observations implies amounts of curvature information which covers also many applied settings with much more observations, but typically also with much higher dimensionality.

For describing the output-ratio distribution I use a discrete variant of the standard Dirichlet density

$$\mathcal{D}(m|\alpha) = \frac{\Gamma(\sum_{s=1..S}\alpha_s)}{\prod_{s=1..S}\Gamma(\alpha_s)} \prod_{s=1..S} m_s^{(\alpha_s-1)}.$$

With only two outputs as in the present case the output ratio vectors may be represented as two-dimensional vectors $m_i = (m_{i1}, m_{i2})$ from the unit simplex, i.e. $m_{i1} + m_{i2} = 1$ and $m_{is} \geq 0 \ \forall \ s, i$. For the simulations the corresponding two-dimensional parameter vector of the Dirichlet density is chosen as $\alpha = \{2, 4\}$. The a priori feasible output ratios m_i are confined to an equispaced grid $\mathbb{M} = \{m_1 ... m_G\}$ of points with $G = 100$. So the specification of (5.1) for the present purpose with discrete output-ratios is

$$\text{Prob}(m_i|\alpha) = \frac{\prod_{s=1}^{2} m_{is}^{\alpha_s-1}}{\sum_{g=1}^{G}\prod_{s=1}^{2} m_{gs}^{\alpha_s-1}}, \quad m_i \in \mathbb{M}, \quad \forall\, i = 1 \ldots n \qquad (8.2)$$

Clearly the proportionality factor (involving the Gamma-function applied to the parameters only) appearing in the standard Dirichlet specification given above can be factored out from nominator and denominator and thus cancelled in this discrete version of a Dirichlet density.

As m_{i2} is fully determined via $1 - m_{i1}$ this specification is equivalent to a Beta distribution of m_{i1} alone with parameters α_1, α_2. I will stick to the Dirichlet representation because it easily generalizes for descriptions of output-ratio distributions in higher dimensional problems. So the prior expectation of target output ratios is $\text{E}(m_{is}) = \alpha_s/(\alpha_1+\alpha_2)$ for $s = 1, 2$ with variances $\text{V}(m_{is}) = \text{E}(m_{is})[1 - \text{E}(m_{is})]/(1+\alpha_1+\alpha_2)$. For the chosen coefficients of α this leads to expectations $\text{E}(m_{i1}) \simeq 0.33$, $\text{E}(m_{i2}) \simeq 0.67$ and variances $\text{V}(m_{i1}) = \text{V}(m_{i2}) \simeq 0.0316$.

The assumed distribution of target output-ratios thus is unimodal with a standard deviation of roughly 0.18. For a ratio restricted to the [0,1]-interval the latter value appears as compromise between a completely flat (uniform) distribution and a very peaked one. It must be recalled, that target output-ratios in practice will reflect perceived price ratios of outputs under the profit maximization hypothesis. So assuming unimodality on the part of target output-ratios amounts to the assumption of an unimodal price-ratio distribution for the maintained assumption of a homothetic technology defined in 8.1. If the latter instead were multimodal serious doubts would have to be raised about the implicit assumption of sufficient product homogeneity underlying comparative efficiency studies. In this sense I consider the unimodality assumption as a mere reflection of basic conditions that should be satisfied in efficiency analysis anyway, whether or not being output-specific.

The prior distribution of the parameters α_1, α_2 of the Dirichlet distribution is chosen as uniform over a grid of points from $[1, 2, \ldots 10] \times [1, 2, \ldots 10]$. These parameter values cover a wide range of forms of the target output-ratio distribution from uniform to highly concentrated. The restriction to a grid of feasible α-values allows to sample these values from the posterior distribution (7.6) directly, which speeds up the simulations. Experiments with continuous α and a Metropolis Hastings update step replacing direct sampling from the posterior indicate almost no change in performance of the estimators but a non-negligible loss of time compared to the discrete case. This loss of time is prohibitive when thousands of samples have to be evaluated so I confined simulations to the discrete α case.

The distribution of logit efficiencies w_i is specified as multivariate Normal with mean vector μ and covariance matrix Σ. The motivation for the above choice was given in section 2 of Chapter 5. The prior distribution of μ is chosen as multivariate Normal, while the prior distribution of the inverse covariance matrix is assumed to be of the Wishart type (see section 1 of Chapter 7). The latter two distributions were left improper, i.e. without specifying the eventually associated hyperparameters, and are thus as uninformative as possible. The means of logit-efficiencies were chosen as $\mu = (1, 3)$ with variance components $\sigma_1^2 = \sigma_2^2 = 0.8$ and $\sigma_{12} = 0.3$.

The implied means $\bar{\varepsilon}_1$ resp. $\bar{\varepsilon}_2$ of the corresponding proper multiplicative efficiencies $\varepsilon_{i1}, \varepsilon_{i2}$, are approximately 70% for producing output 1 and 93% for producing output 2 with standard deviations of 0.17 and 0.06 respectively and a correlation of 0.33. The systematic difference between the two output-specific efficiencies as expressed by their means is thus 23 percentage points. This difference on one hand is large enough to raise doubts about the usefulness of radial efficiency estimates and thus constitutes a serious case for output-specific efficiency estimation instead. On the other hand this difference in the light of the chosen standard deviations is small enough for a meaningful analysis, i.e. the two efficiency distributions exhibit enough overlap of probability mass to make the problem non trivial. The choice of a correlation factor of 0.33 is considered as an intermediate case between the standard assumption of perfect correlation and the idea of two production divisions working fully independent in managerial terms.

Based on convergence checking along the lines of Geweke, 1992 of some prototype samples I have chosen the numbers of MC^2 replications just high enough for the iteration means to stabilize sufficiently. This led to 3000, 2000 and 1000 replications for sample sizes 30, 100 and 300 respectively. In an applied context these numbers would be chosen much higher (50.000 in the application to follow) for more reliability of the results and of course convergence checking would be done on a sample by sample basis. This option was ruled out for the simulations here due to time constraints. The numbers of burn-in iterations discarded from each run were chosen as 500, 200 and 100 for sample sizes 30,100 and 300 respectively, again determined in advance based on several runs for the prototype samples.

Computational aspects

All calculations are executed via GAUSS, a high level mathematical programming language, for which I wrote all the routines (particularly the data generator, the bootstrapped DEA and MC^2 step) repeatedly needed in the course of the simulations. For each sample data set these calculations roughly took on average 6 minutes on an old PII-333MHz computer. Between 500 and 1000 (depending on sample size) Monte Carlo samples were created and then analyzed for each of the nine settings leading to a final pure processing time of roughly 20 days. Clearly 6 minutes for an individual sample is almost nothing from an applied point of view and leaves plenty of time for improvements on a sample by sample basis. Particularly the number of loops in bootstrapping the

DEA frontier estimator and the number of loops for constructing Markov chains could be increased easily in applied work by a factor of 10 or even 100, leading to more reliable results.

On the other hand 6 minutes per sample may turn out to be a very long time when it comes to large scale simulations for a variety of settings. It is clear that Monte Carlo evidence from the particular settings chosen can not be conclusive for the general case. Maybe different prior assumptions about the underlying distributions would lead to completely different results. Based on small scale experience with quite diverse settings I doubt this to be the case, but the primary reason for not covering additional settings is exactly the 6 minutes per sample it takes to come up with moderately reliable estimators.

2. Results based on a DEA-estimated frontier

All of the presented results are based on prior DEA of the data to generate frontier point estimates as described in detail in section 3 of Chapter 2. These estimates are then used in the MC^2 estimation as described instead of the unknown true frontier points. But for comparison purposes I will also report results for the case of a known frontier in a subsequent section. This will help to clarify the individual contributions of DEA resp. MC^2 to overall estimator performance in terms of bias and variance.

For presentation of the results I will mainly rely on boxplots of the Monte Carlo Distribution of the various estimators. The main performance features will be easy to spot by visual inspection of these boxplots, which include minimum, median and maximum as well as the 90% interpercentile range and 50% interpercentile range of estimators. For completeness the results are given numerically as well in the Appendix.

The Monte Carlo distributions of an estimator for different sample sizes and technologies will be depicted as boxplots on top of each other with a common scale within a single frame. The three boxplots at the bottom of each frame describe results for the Leontief-like technology with $\rho \simeq 0.11$, the next three for the intermediate elasticity of transformation case $\rho = 0.5$ and the three topmost for the case $\rho = \infty$. Within each of these triple-blocks of boxplots the one at the bottom depicts the $n = 300$ case, the one in the middle the $n = 100$ case and the topmost the $n = 30$ case. This arrangement should make for easy comparison amongst models with different elasticities of transformation and for getting a rough idea of convergence as sample size increases from 30 to 300. In each graph a vertical line through the whole frame will indicate the true value of the underlying parameter to assess bias.

In addition to parameter estimates I will also present results for the difference between the sample means of output-specific efficiencies and for the sample correlation amongst the two output-specific efficiencies. The former quantity is of most practical interest amongst the quantities estimated. It has to be noted, that these latter two quantities are not parameters of the stochastic specifications but functions of the estimated DMU-specific efficiencies, i.e. functions of the latent variables.

Figure 8.1. MC-distribution of $\mathrm{E}(w_{i1})$ estimator

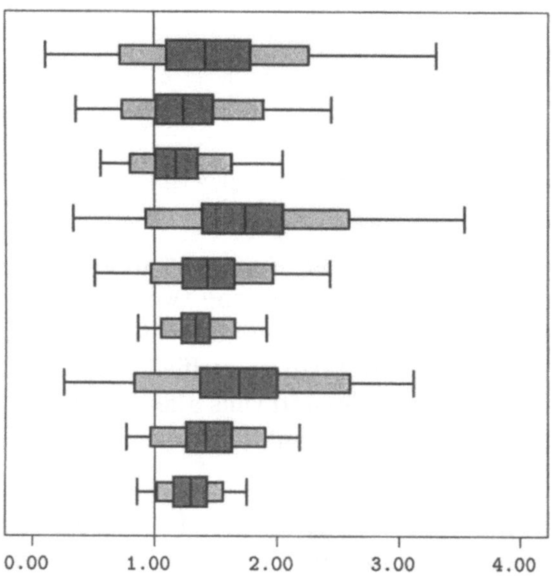

Vertical line: true parameter value; Leftmost and rightmost line of bars: minimum resp. maximum; Light shaded bars: 90% interpercentile range; Dark shaded bars: 50% interpercentile range. The individual boxplots, from top to bottom, refer to the following scenarios: 1: ($n=30$, $\rho=\infty$), 2: ($n=100$, $\rho=\infty$), 3: ($n=300$, $\rho=\infty$), 4: ($n=30$, $\rho=0.5$), 5: ($n=100$, $\rho=0.5$), 6: ($n=300$, $\rho=0.5$), 7: ($n=30$, $\rho \simeq 0.11$), 8: ($n=100$, $\rho \simeq 0.11$), 9: ($n=300$, $\rho \simeq 0.11$).

Figures 8.1 and 8.2 display the distributions for the estimators of mean logit-efficiencies μ_1 and μ_2 whose true values were 1 resp. 3. The first observation emerging from Figure 8.1 is that μ_1 is generally overestimated

Figure 8.2. MC-distribution of $\mathrm{E}(w_{i2})$ estimator

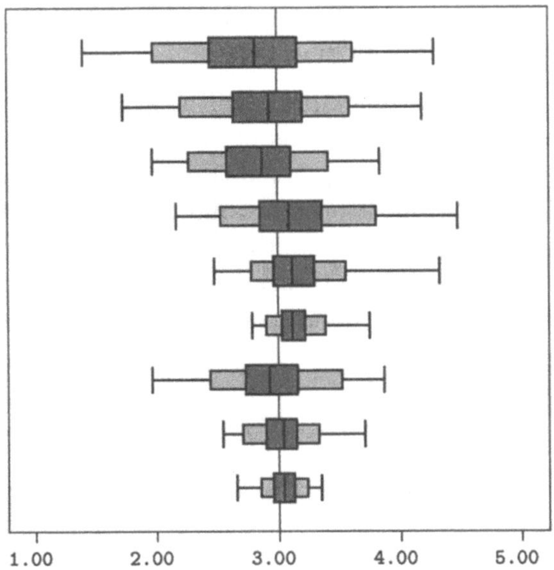

Legend: See Figure 8.1

while the μ_2-estimator is more on target as can be seen from Figure 8.2. I thus expect the difference between the two means of output-specific efficiencies to be underestimated generally, with the extent yet to be determined. On the other hand it can be verified that the 90% range of the two estimators does not overlap and thus allows to reject the hypothesis of equal means with reasonable confidence even for the smallest sample sizes across all models.

The evidence with regard to the influence of curvature of the isoquant on estimation performance is mixed. The-μ_2 estimator does comparatively well in terms of median bias in case of a Leontief-like technology (the bottom three bars), while the μ_1 estimator does so for a technology with infinite elasticity of transformation.

On the other hand the range between minimum and maximum of the two estimators is invariably smallest for a Leontief-like technology for all sample sizes. The latter finding indicates that such a low elasticity of transformation technique gives better advice with regard to parameter bounds for the MC^2 random scans than a high elasticity of transformation technique. Similar observations will also be made for the other estimators and constitutes a general finding worth some more explanation.

With infinite elasticity of transformation an input isoquant for a two-output technology is a straight line. Thus identification of parameters may be hard, as a small increase in expected target output 1 ratio (i.e. $\alpha_1/(\alpha_1+\alpha_2)$ in the present parameterization) for example accompanied by a small decrease in mean output 1 efficiency μ_1 and a small increase in mean output 2 efficiency will lead only to a small change of the overall likelihood. For a Leontief-isoquant on the other hand the same increase of expected target output 1 ratio needs a much larger accompanying change in one of the efficiency means (depending on whether the frontier points are concentrated on the horizontal or the vertical portion of the isoquant) to achieve a similar likelihood. So I conjecture that for more curved isoquants an MC^2 estimator in general will return sooner from parameter combinations in the tails of the posterior distribution than for less curved isoquants, thus lowering the expected maximum deviations from the modal values during the course of the simulation.

Figure 8.3. MC-distribution of VAR(w_{i1}) estimator

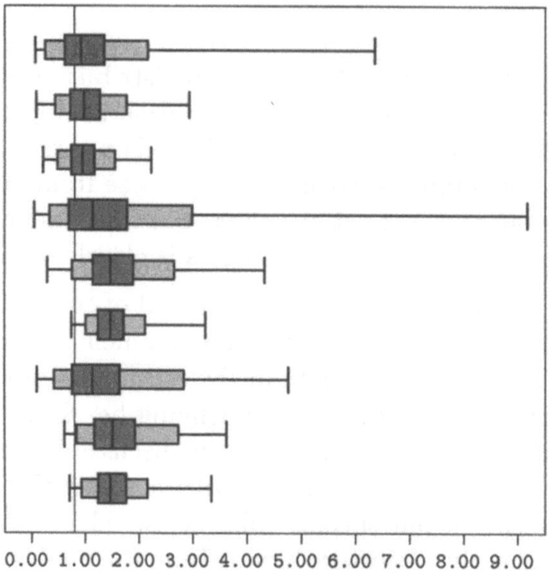

Legend: See Figure 8.1

Figure 8.4. MC-distribution of VAR(w_{i2}) estimator

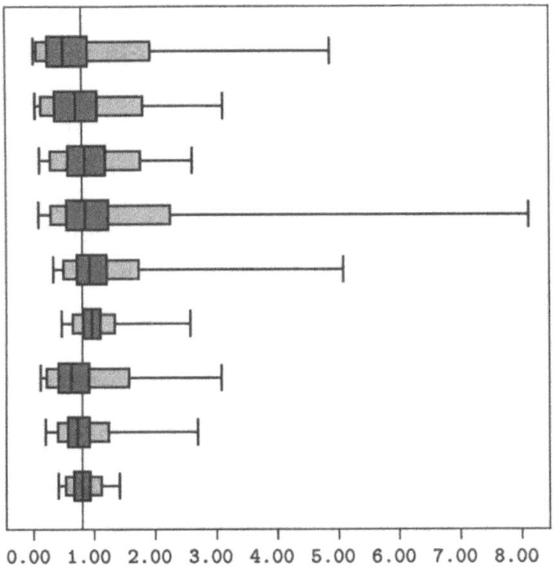

Legend: See Figure 8.1

Figures 8.3 and 8.4 display the Monte Carlo distributions of the estimators for the two variances σ_1^2 resp. σ_2^2. Positive bias for σ_1^2 is evident from the boxplots, while the σ_2^2-estimator is well on target. Convergence is obviously not monotone. Increasing sample size from 30 to 100 leads to increased median bias in 4 out of 6 cases, but this tendency is reversed as sample size is further increased to 300 as is clearly visible.

The results for estimators of covariance σ_{12} and of correlation ρ are displayed in Figures 8.5 and 8.6. I will only comment on the correlation factor which summarizes features from the estimators of the covariance matrix entries and has a natural accompanying benchmark for hypothesis testing. As was already indicated in discussing identification in Chapter 6, it seems hard to come up with a reasonable estimator of correlation amongst output-specific efficiencies. The Monte Carlo analysis confirms this early conjecture arising from the analysis of likelihood profiles. The results indicate that a one-sided test to identify at least the correct sign of the correlation estimator would not allow to reject the Null hypothesis $\mathcal{H}_0 : \rho \leq 0$ versus the alternative $\mathcal{H}_0 : \rho > 0$ in

Figure 8.5. MC-distribution of COV(w_{i1},w_{i2}) estimator

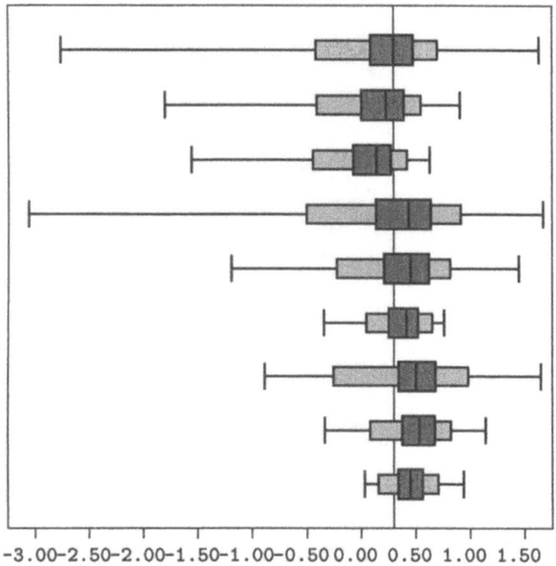

Legend: See Figure 8.1

an uncomfortably high proportion of cases. And this although the true correlation was as high as 0.375.

Particularly from observations based on an infinite elasticity of transformation model it seems impossible to recover the correlation factor: Not only do the estimators exhibit significant bias and large variance, but also convergence seems flawed. Matters improve for lower transformation elasticities, but still remain unsatisfactory. Only for a sample size of 300 and a Leontief-like technology does the correlation estimator display positive correlation consistently and has bias and variance small enough to be of practical use. Note also that for sample size 30 the estimator has consistently positive bias pointing erroneously towards perfect correlation no matter which model I consider. And this systematic failure comes along with systematic overestimation of output 1 efficiency, as results displayed in Figure 8.1 confirm. So a generally useful estimation strategy with regard to the correlation amongst output-specific efficiencies under the maintained assumptions has yet to be developed and clearly requires a better designed model parametrization than the one employed here.

Figure 8.6. MC-distribution of CORR(w_{i1},w_{i2}) estimator

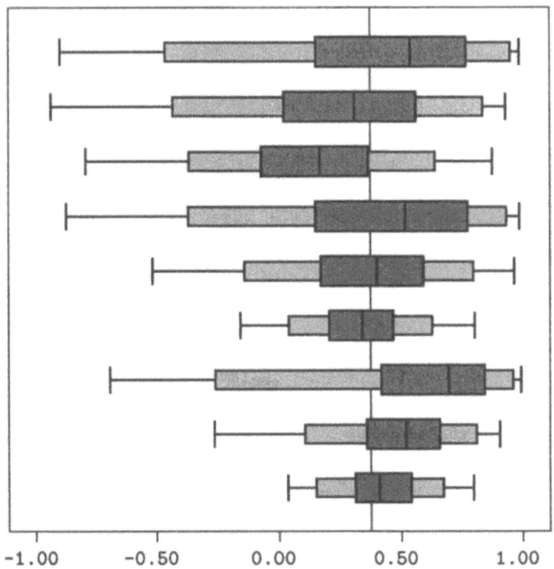

Legend: See Figure 8.1

Results for the estimators of the Dirichlet parameters α_1 and α_2 are displayed in Figures 8.7 resp. 8.8 (rather than for the actual underlying parameterization in terms of $\alpha_1/(\alpha_1+\alpha_2)$ and $\alpha_1+\alpha_2$). They will be of interest to analysts who are interested in the underlying distribution of target output-ratios themselves, rather than just the implied efficiency measures. Bias for the smallest sample size is regularly positive at roughly 20% of respective target value and decreases to roughly 5% for the largest samples considered. Convergence is monotone at a satisfying rate, regardless of the underlying model. Recall that for estimation I relied on parameterization $\alpha_1/(\alpha_1+\alpha_2)$, $\alpha_1+\alpha_2$ and used prior information on $\alpha_1/(\alpha_1+\alpha_2)$ from the data and the DEA estimated frontier for specifying the prior distribution (see the details given in section2 of Chapter 6). This additional information might have contributed to the comparatively consistent results with regard to bias and convergence across models.

Of most practical interest will be the results displayed in Figures 8.9 and 8.10 for the estimated sample means $\mathrm{E}_i(\varepsilon_{i1})$ resp. $\mathrm{E}_i(\varepsilon_{i2})$ of output specific efficiencies. These results are easier to interpret than the cor-

Figure 8.7. MC-distribution of α_1 estimator

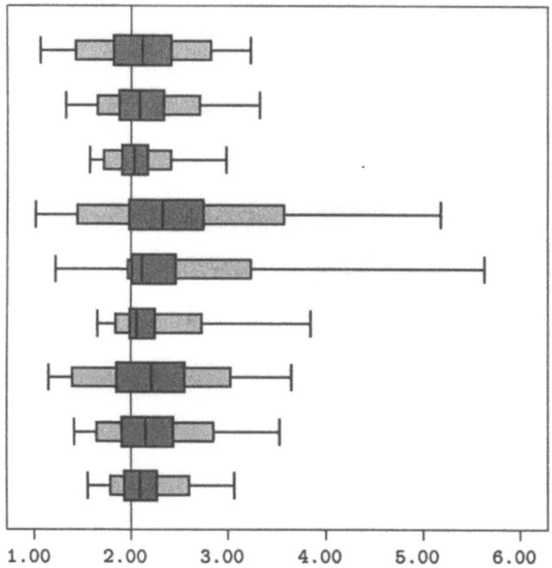

Legend: See Figure 8.1

responding and qualitatively similar results for the estimated means of logit-efficiency terms μ_1, μ_2, because they are normalized to the familiar scale of multiplicative efficiency scores. Thus it will be possible to assess the performance of the approach based on accuracy requirements in applied work.

Again we observe consistent positive median bias in estimating mean output 1 efficiency of roughly 12% in terms of target value for the smallest sample size 30. This bias reduces to roughly 4% when sample sized is increased to 300. Bias for the estimator of mean output 2 efficiency on the other hand is, if at all, an issue only under the infinite elasticity of transformation model (an unlikely case to occur in practice anyway) where it is below 3% for all sample sizes. Bias for the other models considered is consistently below 1% in terms of target value and should thus be of no practical concern. Convergence is monotone and pronounced for the estimator of mean output 1 efficiency but non monotone for the estimator of mean output 2 efficiency. In the light of the low bias of the latter estimator this again seems to be of no practical concern.

Figure 8.8. MC-distribution of α_2 estimator

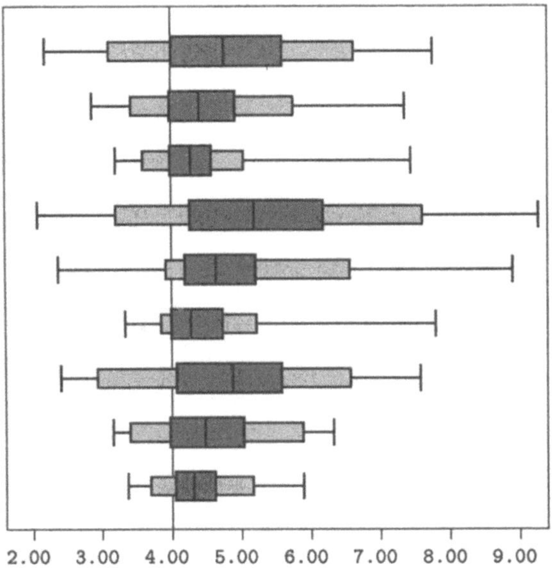

Legend: See Figure 8.1

Reliable claims about systematic efficiency differences across outputs requires sufficiently little overlap of the distributions of these two output-specific efficiency means. It can verified from the figures, that this requirement is met for sample sizes of at least $n = 100$ for all elasticity of transformation scenarios. In particular the upper 95% quantile of the mean output 1 efficiency is consistently lower than the lower 95% quantile of the mean output 2 efficiency. So in less than 5% of all cases (the overlap not necessarily applies to single runs!) would the analyst get the wrong advice regarding the output of primary concern in a performance perspective. For sample size $n = 300$, the overlap is zero for all but the infinite elasticity of transformation case (the zero is just a proxy for the true, most likely small positive figure which would result from comparing the distributions based on infinitely many Monte Carlo samples). Based on these findings I conclude that a difference-between-efficiency-means estimator based on the proposed approach and at least 100 observations will reliably reveal eventual systematic efficiency differences across outputs in a single-input, two-output scenario.

Figure 8.9. MC-distribution of $E(\varepsilon_{i1})$ estimator

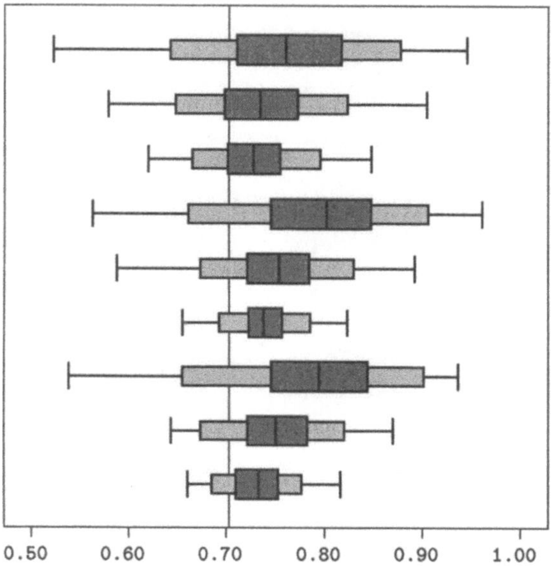

Legend: See Figure 8.1

3. Comparison with estimators based on a known frontier

A natural question arising from the above discussion of results concerns the potential bias introduced into MC^2 estimation of output-specific efficiencies by estimating the required frontier points via DEA rather than using the true (but usually unknown) frontier points. After all, DEA (whether or not bias corrected) yields consistent frontier point estimates, but this gives little guidance with regard to expectable results from small samples as the ones investigated in the present simulations. To answer the above question I will present results for estimators based on a known frontier and compare them to the results derived via DEA-estimated frontier as above. I will only consider the model with medium elasticity of transformation ($\rho = 0.5$) for this comparison as the qualitative conclusions drawn are the same for the other models, which are based on different transformation elasticities.

Figures 8.11 and 8.12 display results for the means μ_1 resp. μ_2 of the logit-efficiency terms. Comparing the upper three boxplots (for the esti-

Figure 8.10. MC-distribution of $E(\varepsilon_{i2})$ estimator

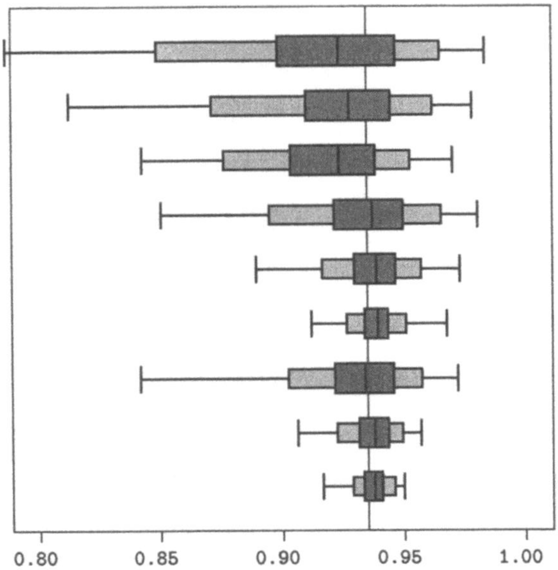

Legend: See Figure 8.1

mator based on a known frontier) and the lower three boxplots (for the same estimator based on a DEA estimated frontier) it is obvious that running the MC^2 estimator on a DEA estimated frontier rather than a known frontier introduces considerable additional error. This holds particularly for parameter μ_1 whose target value is 1. But as can be seen, the introduced error comes primarily in the form of bias rather than additional variance. Note also, that convergence is painfully slow for the DEA-based estimators, a non-surprising result given the findings for DEA frontier point estimators of Kneip et al., 1998.

We expect this type of result to carry over to all other DEA-based MC^2-estimators, like the one for the correlation coefficient ρ. Results for the latter are graphically summarized in Figure 8.13. Apparently they seem to escape this conjecture, as they are less biased than the corresponding estimators based on the true frontier and at the same time have comparable variability. Unfortunately the bias for the DEA-based estimator reverses sign and thus it is unclear from the limited sample sizes considered, how convergence would proceed for increasingly larger samples.

Figure 8.11. MC-distribution of $E(w_{i1})$ estimators

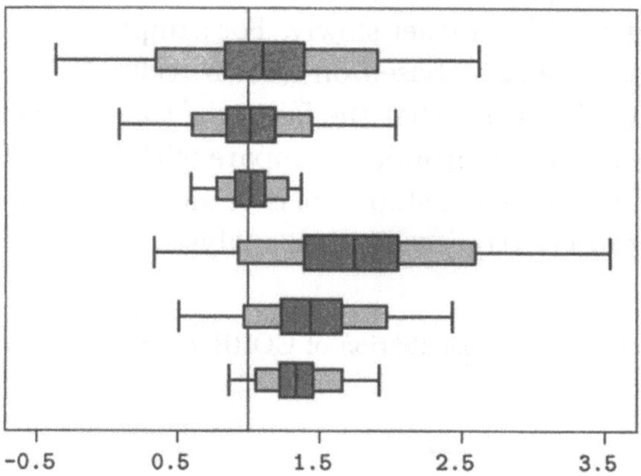

Vertical line: true parameter value. Leftmost and rightmost line of bars: minimum resp. maximum. Light shaded bars: 90% interpercentile range. Dark shaded bars: 50% interpercentile range. The upper three boxplots give results for the estimator based on true frontier, the lower three boxplots the corresponding results for the estimator based on a DEA estimated frontier. The ordering within each boxplot-triple from top down is $n = 30$, $n = 100$, $n = 300$. The elasticity of transformation of the underlying model is $\rho = 0.5$.

Figure 8.12. MC-distribution of $E(w_{i2})$ estimators

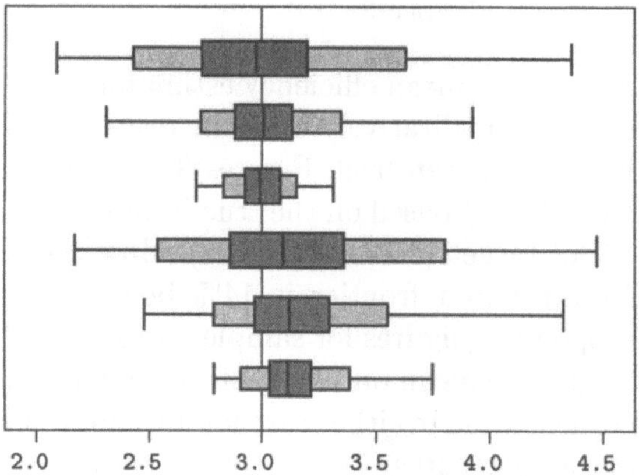

Legend: See 8.11.

The MC^2 correlation estimator based on the true frontier does not seem to exhibit that sort of behavior.

Apart from these differences there is one thing the estimators have in common: A strong upward bias (towards perfect correlation) for small sample sizes that vanishes rather slowly. For sample size 100 the median of the correlation estimator based on known technology is still as high as 0.59. I conclude from this that the failure of the correlation estimator based on a DEA-estimated frontier (compare with Figure 8.6) is not due to this prior DEA estimation step, but is of more intrinsic nature to the problem and definitely requires further analysis.

Figure 8.13. MC-distribution of CORR(w_{i1},w_{i2}) estimators

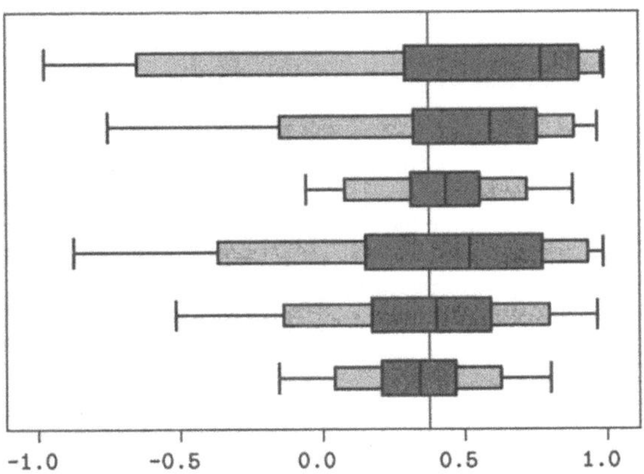

Legend: See 8.11.

With regard to the sample mean efficiency estimators E(ε_{i1}) resp. E(ε_{i2}) results should not differ qualitatively from the results for the logit means μ_1 resp. μ_2. This can be seen from Figures 8.14 and 8.15. For sample size 30 the estimator E(ε_{i1}) based on the true frontier has positive bias of approximately 3% of target (0.725 vs. 0.703) while the same estimator based on a DEA estimated frontier is 14% beyond target (0.802 vs. 0.703). The corresponding figures for sample size 300 are 1.2% vs. 4.9%. The estimator for sample mean output 2 efficiency has bias smaller than 0.5% relative to target value in either case for all sample sizes considered. This 4-times as large percentage bias for mean output 1 efficiency thus is about the price to be payed in applied efficiency analysis for lacking knowledge of both the frontier and the output-specific efficiencies, rather than the output-specific efficiencies alone.

Figure 8.14. MC-distribution of $E(\varepsilon_{i1})$ estimators

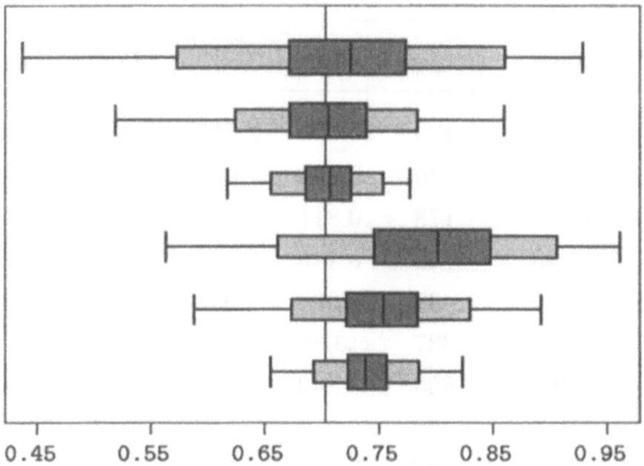

Legend: See 8.11.

Figure 8.15. MC-distribution of $E(\varepsilon_{i2})$ estimators

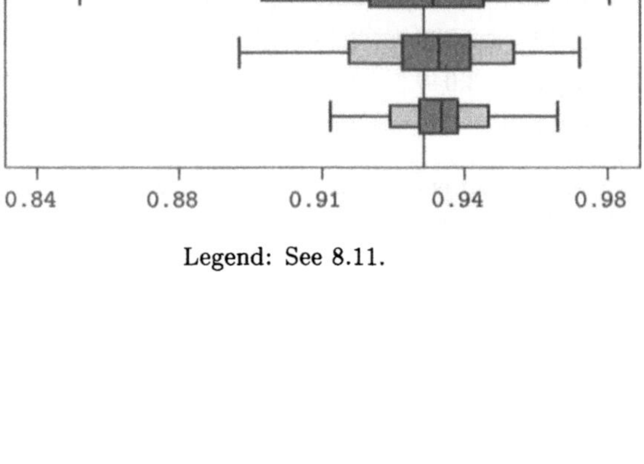

Legend: See 8.11.

APPENDIX 8.A: Numerical results

Table 8.A.1. MC-Distribution of μ_1 estimates

ϱ	n	Mean	Median	5%	95%	Bias	STD	MSE
∞	30	1.456	1.423	0.730	2.251	0.456	0.481	0.439
	100	1.266	1.240	0.744	1.887	0.266	0.345	0.190
	300	1.197	1.178	0.811	1.626	0.197	0.248	0.100
0.5	30	1.740	1.745	0.940	2.583	0.740	0.499	0.797
	100	1.450	1.437	0.981	1.962	0.450	0.298	0.291
	300	1.345	1.337	1.065	1.650	0.345	0.179	0.151
0.11	30	1.700	1.693	0.842	2.590	0.700	0.498	0.738
	100	1.442	1.420	0.975	1.897	0.442	0.269	0.268
	300	1.296	1.297	1.028	1.552	0.296	0.168	0.116

Legend: μ_1 mean of logit efficiencies in producing output 1, true value: 1, ϱ = elasticity of transformation, n = sample size.

Table 8.A.2. MC-Distribution of μ_2 estimates

ϱ	n	Mean	Median	5%	95%	Bias	STD	MSE
∞	30	2.821	2.819	1.993	3.608	-0.179	0.509	0.291
	100	2.916	2.935	2.217	3.578	-0.084	0.410	0.175
	300	2.855	2.873	2.281	3.404	-0.145	0.340	0.137
0.5	30	3.118	3.092	2.541	3.797	0.118	0.374	0.154
	100	3.144	3.119	2.791	3.546	0.144	0.240	0.078
	300	3.132	3.114	2.913	3.379	0.132	0.142	0.038
0.11	30	2.949	2.930	2.450	3.512	-0.051	0.316	0.102
	100	3.027	3.040	2.715	3.321	0.027	0.180	0.033
	300	3.041	3.040	2.863	3.226	0.041	0.109	0.014

Legend: μ_2 mean of logit efficiencies in producing output 2, true value: 3, ϱ = elasticity of transformation, n = sample size.

Table 8.A.3. MC-Distribution of σ_1^2 estimates

ϱ	n	Mean	Median	5%	95%	Bias	STD	MSE
∞	30	1.046	0.924	0.275	2.147	0.046	0.634	0.404
	100	1.028	0.982	0.456	1.749	0.028	0.410	0.169
	300	0.973	0.954	0.497	1.533	-0.027	0.315	0.100
0.5	30	1.342	1.139	0.353	2.970	0.342	0.899	0.926
	100	1.546	1.464	0.769	2.632	0.546	0.566	0.619
	300	1.507	1.467	1.028	2.091	0.507	0.353	0.382
0.1	30	1.317	1.135	0.441	2.813	0.317	0.777	0.704
	100	1.606	1.506	0.863	2.713	0.606	0.556	0.676
	300	1.505	1.467	0.956	2.141	0.505	0.362	0.386

Legend: σ_1^2 variance of logit efficiencies in producing output 1, true value: 0.8, ϱ = elasticity of transformation, n = sample size.

Table 8.A.4. MC-Distribution of σ_2^2 estimates

ϱ	n	Mean	Median	5%	95%	Bias	STD	MSE
∞	30	0.683	0.500	0.080	1.909	-0.317	0.638	0.507
	100	0.788	0.701	0.150	1.787	-0.212	0.525	0.320
	300	0.909	0.847	0.301	1.744	-0.091	0.444	0.206
0.5	30	0.997	0.849	0.306	2.231	-0.003	0.656	0.430
	100	1.006	0.932	0.515	1.714	0.006	0.412	0.169
	300	0.978	0.963	0.665	1.320	-0.022	0.234	0.055
0.1	30	0.715	0.622	0.230	1.555	-0.285	0.399	0.240
	100	0.775	0.723	0.419	1.223	-0.225	0.287	0.133
	300	0.811	0.798	0.550	1.100	-0.189	0.171	0.065

Legend: σ_2^2 variance of logit efficiencies in producing output 2, true value: 0.8, ϱ = elasticity of transformation, n = sample size.

Table 8.A.5. MC-Distribution of ρ_{12} estimates

ϱ	n	Mean	Median	5%	95%	Bias	STD	MSE
∞	30	0.427	0.538	-0.457	0.945	0.127	0.440	0.210
	100	0.278	0.309	-0.425	0.831	-0.022	0.370	0.138
	300	0.154	0.168	-0.360	0.635	-0.146	0.296	0.109
0.5	30	0.426	0.517	-0.362	0.928	0.126	0.408	0.182
	100	0.376	0.402	-0.132	0.792	0.076	0.284	0.086
	300	0.338	0.343	0.047	0.623	0.038	0.177	0.033
0.1	30	0.579	0.694	-0.253	0.956	0.279	0.362	0.209
	100	0.494	0.520	0.112	0.804	0.194	0.221	0.086
	300	0.421	0.410	0.156	0.667	0.121	0.150	0.037

Legend: ρ_{12} correlation between logit-efficiencies in producing output 1 resp. output 2, true value: 0.375, ϱ = elasticity of transformation, n = sample size.

Table 8.A.6. MC-Distribution of α_1 estimates

ϱ	n	Mean	Median	5%	95%	Bias	STD	MSE
∞	30	2.123	2.116	1.440	2.812	0.123	0.411	0.184
	100	2.123	2.089	1.666	2.699	0.123	0.321	0.118
	300	2.046	2.033	1.731	2.404	0.046	0.196	0.040
0.5	30	2.407	2.329	1.459	3.561	0.407	0.641	0.576
	100	2.309	2.113	1.983	3.224	0.309	0.465	0.311
	300	2.152	2.059	1.856	2.719	0.152	0.276	0.099
0.1	30	2.218	2.212	1.406	3.014	0.218	0.486	0.284
	100	2.200	2.151	1.660	2.842	0.200	0.378	0.183
	300	2.123	2.095	1.800	2.591	0.123	0.247	0.076

Legend: α_1 first parameter of Dirichlet distribution of output-ratios, true value: 2, ϱ = elasticity of transformation, n = sample size.

Table 8.A.7. MC-Distribution of α_2 estimates

ϱ	n	Mean	Median	5%	95%	Bias	STD	MSE
∞	30	4.808	4.765	3.131	6.608	0.808	1.057	1.770
	100	4.494	4.405	3.448	5.739	0.494	0.718	0.759
	300	4.305	4.282	3.612	5.025	0.305	0.457	0.302
0.5	30	5.249	5.190	3.226	7.592	1.249	1.320	3.302
	100	4.827	4.633	3.936	6.548	0.827	0.867	1.435
	300	4.414	4.272	3.864	5.203	0.414	0.520	0.441
0.1	30	4.819	4.870	2.956	6.555	0.819	1.064	1.803
	100	4.536	4.469	3.416	5.871	0.536	0.719	0.803
	300	4.352	4.304	3.709	5.152	0.352	0.446	0.323

Legend: α_2 second parameter of Dirichlet distribution of output-ratios, true value: 4, ϱ = elasticity of transformation, n = sample size.

Table 8.A.8. MC-Distribution of $E(\varepsilon_1)$ estimates

ϱ	n	Mean	Median	5%	95%	Bias	STD	MSE
∞	30	0.762	0.760	0.644	0.877	-3.238	0.071	10.489
	100	0.736	0.735	0.649	0.823	-3.264	0.053	10.655
	300	0.729	0.728	0.667	0.795	-3.271	0.038	10.702
0.5	30	0.795	0.802	0.663	0.905	-3.205	0.072	10.279
	100	0.753	0.754	0.675	0.829	-3.247	0.047	10.546
	300	0.740	0.738	0.694	0.784	-3.260	0.028	10.632
0.1	30	0.791	0.794	0.656	0.900	-3.209	0.072	10.306
	100	0.751	0.750	0.675	0.819	-3.249	0.042	10.558
	300	0.732	0.733	0.687	0.775	-3.268	0.028	10.679

Legend: Sample $E(\varepsilon_1)$ mean of efficiencies in producing output 1, true value: 0.703, ϱ = elasticity of transformation, n = sample size.

Table 8.A.9. MC-Distribution of $E(\varepsilon_2)$ estimates

ϱ	n	Mean	Median	5%	95%	Bias	STD	MSE
∞	30	0.919	0.924	0.850	0.965	-3.081	0.036	9.494
	100	0.925	0.928	0.872	0.962	-3.075	0.027	9.457
	300	0.920	0.923	0.877	0.952	-3.080	0.023	9.486
0.5	30	0.935	0.937	0.896	0.965	-3.065	0.021	9.397
	100	0.938	0.939	0.917	0.957	-3.062	0.012	9.377
	300	0.939	0.939	0.927	0.950	-3.061	0.007	9.371
0.1	30	0.932	0.934	0.903	0.957	-3.068	0.017	9.410
	100	0.937	0.938	0.923	0.949	-3.063	0.008	9.382
	300	0.937	0.938	0.929	0.946	-3.063	0.005	9.380

Legend: Sample $E(\varepsilon_2)$ mean of efficiencies in producing output 2, true value: 0.935, ϱ = elasticity of transformation, n = sample size.

IV

PUTTING THE CONCEPT TO WORK

Chapter 9

AN APPLICATION: QUALITY VS. QUANTITY IN UK PRIVATE SECONDARY EDUCATION

The data to be analyzed in this first application of the methodology outlined and investigated in the previous chapters concern graduation from secondary schools in the UK. The two outputs to be considered here are the quality and the quantity of sixth-form grading (the corresponding exams are called A-level exams in the UK). There is an ongoing debate in the UK about education policy and in particular about whether or not it is desirable that secondary schools focus on grading quality and neglect grading quantity to a large extent. It has been argued, that it instead would be in societies interest to have a greater quantity of graduates per year, but that schools instead would tend to drive many average talented pupils from school before they reach the sixth form, where they would become candidates to take the A-level exams. A good and regularly updated account of this debate can be found on the webpage of the Department for Education `www.dfee.gov.uk` and the webpage of The Times Educational Supplement `www.tes.co.uk`.

One element of this UK schooling debate is the ranking of 1000 secondary schools published regularly in the Financial Times (FT), which is also the data source for the present application. The FT-ranking, known as the FT-1000 league tables, is solely based on quality criteria and ignores quantity considerations completely. One quantity aspect of education is for example the probability of an average entrant into some school of ever reaching the final exams of this school. From a parental perspective this is likely to be an influential piece of information with regard to the schooling decision to be made, but of course this information will be considered jointly with information about schooling quality. For a detailed account of the parental schooling decision see Collins and Snell, 2000.

A repeated claim in schooling debates, not just in the UK, regarding quantity vs. quality is that there exists an inevitable tradeoff between these two aspects. So one question to be asked here is, whether this tradeoff is indeed a relevant issue for UK private secondary schools. If it were found for example, that it is possible to increase quantity without sacrificing quality because of large efficiency improvement potentials, this tradeoff may turn out to be of merely theoretical concern. Another, related question to be asked is, whether any systematic differences can be found between the efficiency in providing grading quality and the efficiency in providing grading quantity. If so, we should be able to tell whether the dominating performance problems of schools concern quality or quantity provision. But it will also be interesting to see, how the ranking based on output specific efficiencies relates to the FT-ranking and how the output specific efficiency scores relate to certain school characteristics like size, proportion of boys and girls or religious orientation of the school. I will analyze these questions by estimating output-specific efficiencies in the manner described above, but with a slightly different statistical structure and a few new elements regarding the update mechanism.

1. A brief review of related literature

[1]

Hanushek, 1986 surveys 147 studies of educational production functions, all aiming at comparative measurement of school performance. He characterizes the "achievements of individual students" as the output of the educational process resulting from consuming inputs related to school characteristics, teachers qualifications and curricula. For state schools he proposes to use expenditures to proxy these inputs. Analogously I proxy them by the parents' willingness to pay for tuition in the present case of private schools. With regard to proper output measures Hanushek dis-

[1] This survey draws heavily upon research of Susanne Warning, who screened the relevant literature.

tinguishes between two general groups of educational output: qualitative output (presented mostly by test scores) and quantitative output (like school continuation rates or attendance rates). Wenger, 2000, making the same point about the two basic education outputs, adds school completion to the list of potential quantity output measures. He shows that test scores and school completion are indeed substitutes in a production theoretic perspective.

The only comparative study of school performance explicitly using quantitative and qualitative output and using an analytical framework similar to mine is Ray and Mukherjee, 1998. They use the percentage of graduating students continuing further education as quantitative output. This measure, like earnings proposed early on in Mincer, 1974 and used in applied analysis for example in Behrman and Birdsall, 1983, refers to post schooling experiences of former pupils. I lack such type of data and therefore my quantity output measure refers solely to experiences during schooling time.

So schooling output can be conceived as at least a two-dimensional matter, involving quality and quantity aspects. The following survey of other relevant studies is therefore divided into three groups: The first one only considering quality outputs, the second one focusing on quantity aspects and the third one including both types of characteristics, although often not under the labels of quantity and quality outputs.

The first group only considers qualitative output measures. [2] Amongst these studies are Bessent and Bessent, 1980, Authella M. Bessent and Reagan, 1982, Authella M. Bessent and Long, 1984, Chalos, 1997, Ray and Mukherjee, 1998 and Ruggiero, 1999, which all treat school performance in a production theoretic fashion. While they all use different output measures, their common input variable is expenditures per pupil, in line with the present approach. Some authors additionally use the ratio of administrative to instructional expenditures as input variable like Bessent and Bessent, 1980, Mayston and Jesson, 1988 or Chalos, 1997. I do not have this type of data and therefore could not follow this approach.

[2] Note that for internal evaluations of schools performed by the UK Department of Education so called valued-added models are being used, where quality aspects of pupils on entry are compared to quality aspects of the same cohort at later stages of schooling. In such models quality variables thus enter as inputs as well as outputs.

The studies within the second group refer explicitly to quantity output measures and use DEA for efficiency evaluation, so they are closely related in a basic methodological aspect to the present study. These studies include Mancebon and Moliero, 2000 (for primary schools in Hampshire), who found neither significant influence of the proportion of girls in the class nor the size of school, while religious orientation (Church of England) is found to have significant positive influence on efficiency. The findings presented below by and large stand opposite to these findings. Like Mancebon and Moliero, 2000 also Noulas and Ketkar, 1998, McCarthy and Yaisawarng, 1993, Engert, 1996 and (Färe et al., 1989) interpret pass-levels at different exams as quantity outputs.

The third group of studies includes qualitative as well as quantitative outputs and therefore is closest in spirit to the present work. Thanassoulis, 1996b, Thanassoulis, 1996a and Thanassoulis and Dunstan, 1994 are particularly relevant here, as they also deal with secondary schools in the UK (although looking at state schools rather than private schools). They consider placement ratios to jobs after graduation as quantity output and test scores as quality output. Behrman and Birdsall, 1983 also incorporate quality and quantity aspects of schooling into their analysis (regression of earning functions), but their target is not efficiency evaluation but rather a comparison of social rates of return for these two basic types of outputs.

In terms of variable specification the study most similar to the present one, are Ray and Mukherjee, 1998, mentioned above, and Ruggiero and Vitalino, 1999. The latter analyzes cost efficiency of New York State schools with a variable returns-to-scale DEA model and use expenditures per pupil as single input, quantity output variables based on dropout and graduation rates and qualitative output variables based on test scores. One result from their study and contrasting mine, is that school size (measured as total pupils) does not significantly influences efficiency.
Lovell et al., 1994 examine secondary schools with regression analysis and find a positive influence of school size and elite schools on efficiency. They also find that the religious orientation (catholic vs. non-catholic in their paper) has a negative impact on efficiency in the long term, in basic accordance with my findings.

2. Estimating technology

The following description of the frontier estimation step deviates in minor respects from the description given in Section 2. In particular I will not apply bias correction to the original frontier point estimates, which inevitably means that some observations will appear as fully efficient under a radial perspective.[3] For the later output-specific efficiency estimation step this will necessitate a clear distinction between the inefficient and the efficient subsample of DMU's, because the statistical model will not be defined for radially efficient DMU's. Furthermore I will work with logit output-ratios, so the mapping (2.6) will require a corresponding adaptation.

As common start off point with the discussion so far I use the radial distance measures θ_j^* for all $j = 1 \dots n$ from program (2.1).[4] These imply radial output-efficiency scores $\varepsilon_j^* = 1/\theta_j^*$ for all DMU's. Some of these scores will be one giving rise to the definition of a set of size $n_1 \leq n$ of DMU's with $\varepsilon_j^* = 1$ (the efficient DMU's) and another one of size $n_2 < n$ with $\varepsilon_j^* < 1$ (the inefficient DMU's), where $n_1 + n_2 = n$. I will refer to a DMU from the efficient set as $(x_j^\bullet, y_j^\bullet)$ for $j = 1...n_1$ and to a DMU from the inefficient set as (x_i°, y_i°) for $i = 1...n_2$. Only the efficient DMU's determine the shape of the frontier.

Now denote output-ratio vectors as $\widetilde{m}$ (rather than m as in Section 2) and define them as:

$$\widetilde{m} = \{\widetilde{m}_1 \dots \widetilde{m}_S\} \quad \text{with } \widetilde{m}_k = \frac{y_k}{\sum_{s=1}^S y_s} \quad \text{and} \sum_{s=1\dots S} \widetilde{m}_s = 1 \tag{9.1}$$

and real numbers $\kappa_i \in \mathbb{R}_+$ as

$$\kappa_i = \min_s \{y_{is}^\circ : y_{is}^\circ > 0\} \quad i = 1 \dots n_2. \tag{9.2}$$

Using these definitions I construct fictitious observations $(x_i^\circ, \widetilde{m}\kappa_i)$ which are unambiguously inefficient under the frontier defined via observations

---

[3] No bias correction will be employed here, because the sample size (237) of the present application relative to the dimensionality of the problem (2 outputs, 1 input) is rather large and therefore the potential gains from bias correction are rather small.

[4] As in program (2.1) I will rely here on a variable returns to scale (VRS) model. But while this choice was arbitrary in Section 2 (all subsequent derivations would have been unchanged for a constant returns to scale mode), this choice is necessary for the present application due to output-specifications involving an output given as percentage. The option of using a CRS model is ruled out, because it would eventually lead to frontier points with percentages beyond 100.

$\{x_j^\bullet, y_j^\bullet\}_{j=1}^{n_1}$. So with respect to the pooled sample $(x_i^\circ, \widetilde{m}\kappa_i) \cup \{x_j^\bullet, y_j^\bullet\}_{j=1}^{n_1}$ the radial, output oriented efficiency of fictitious DMU $(x_i^\circ, \widetilde{m}\kappa_i)$ can be calculated via program

$$\max_{\gamma_1 \dots \gamma_{n_1}, \zeta_i} \zeta_i \quad \text{s.t.:} \quad \zeta_i \widetilde{m}_s \kappa_i \leq \sum_{i=1}^{n_1} \gamma_j \, y_{js}^\bullet \quad \forall \, s \tag{9.3}$$

$$x_{ir}^\circ \leq \sum_{i=1}^{n_1} \gamma_j \, x_{jr}^\bullet \quad \forall \, r, \quad \sum_{i=1}^{n_1} \gamma_j = 1$$

Denoting the $\widetilde{m}$ and x_i°-dependent maximum value of the objection function of (9.3) as $\zeta_i^*(x_i^\circ, \widetilde{m})$ a technology representation for an output-ratio vector $\widetilde{m}$ and an observed input vector x_i° is defined as in Section 2 but with $\widetilde{m}$ replacing the former m and the input arguments restricted to input vectors from inefficient DMU's:

$$\tilde{\mathrm{y}}^F(x_i^\circ, \widetilde{m}) = \begin{bmatrix} \tilde{\mathrm{y}}_1^F(x_i^\circ, \widetilde{m}) \\ \vdots \\ \tilde{\mathrm{y}}_S^F(x_i^\circ, \widetilde{m}) \end{bmatrix} = \begin{bmatrix} \zeta^*(x_i^\circ, \widetilde{m}) \, \widetilde{m}_1 \kappa_i \\ \vdots \\ \zeta^*(x_i^\circ, \widetilde{m}) \, \widetilde{m}_S \kappa_i \end{bmatrix}. \tag{9.4}$$

Deviating from the developments in earlier sections I will now switch to a logit representation m_i of the original output ratios $\widetilde{m}_i$, defined as $m_i = \ln(\widetilde{m}_i/(1-\widetilde{m}_i))$ with $m_i \in (-\infty, +\infty)$. The advantage of working on the logit scale is that this enables the use of the Normal distribution to statistically characterize the target output-ratios. It should be kept in mind though, that the implied distribution of the original output-ratios under a logit-Normal specification is necessarily unimodal (unlike the Dirichlet distribution used so far), which in certain applied contexts may be regarded as overly restrictive. In any case the technology representation in this logit perspective will be

$$\mathrm{y}^F(x_i^\circ, m_i) = \tilde{\mathrm{y}}^F(x_i^\circ, 1/(1 + e^{-m_i})). \tag{9.5}$$

3. The statistical model

As throughout this book the emergence of output observations under a given technology, represented now via (9.5), is modelled as the result of the combined influence of the chosen target output-ratios and realized output-specific efficiencies. While the following statistical model deviates in some details from the one used above for the simulations, the core element thereof, the treatment of target output-ratios as unobserved (latent) random quantities, will remain the same.

3.1 The data generating process

Denoting the involved efficiency variables as $\varepsilon_{is} \in (0,1)$, the relationship between logit target output-ratios, inputs, output observations and output-specific efficiencies is then defined as

$$\varepsilon_{is} = y^{\circ}_{is} \,/\, \mathrm{y}^{F}_{s}(x^{\circ}_{i}, m_i) \;\forall\; i, s. \tag{9.6}$$

The logit target output-ratios are considered as random variates from some parametric distribution. The present application has only two outputs and consequently only one independent output-ratio, so m_i may be modeled as scalar. I define it as the logit ratio between output 1 and the sum of both outputs, i.e.,

$$m_i = \ln\left(\frac{y_{i1}/(y_{i1}+y_{i2})}{1-y_{i1}/(y_{i1}+y_{i2})}\right) = \ln\left(\frac{y_{i1}}{y_{i2}}\right) \tag{9.7}$$

with $m_i \in (-\infty, +\infty)$. Analogous to the preceding sections I will work with a discrete version of m_i, restricting feasible values to a finite grid of points represented as set $\mathbb{M} = \{m_1 \dots m_G\}$, where indices reflect an ordering such that $m_g < m_{g+1}$ for $g = 1 \dots G-1$. As indicated, this will allow direct sampling from the posterior distributions of the individual m_i's when it comes to construct Markov Chains (see below). Using parameter vector $\alpha = \{\alpha_1, \alpha_2\}$ the probabilities of these logit output ratios m_i shall be defined as discrete version of the univariate Normal:

$$\begin{aligned} \mathrm{p}(m_g \,|\, \alpha) \stackrel{iid}{=} \;& \Phi(0.5(m_g + m_{g+1});\, \alpha_1, \alpha_2) \\ & -\Phi(0.5(m_{g-1} + m_g);\, \alpha_1, \alpha_2) \quad \forall\; i. \end{aligned} \tag{9.8}$$

where $\Phi(\cdot; \alpha_1, \alpha_2)$ denotes the Normal cumulative density function with mean α_1 and precision α_2 (the inverse of the usual variance parameter) and where the notational convention $m_0 = -\infty$ and $m_{G+1} = +\infty$ is used. Definition (9.8) of a discretized Normal density (rather than more familiar $\mathrm{p}(m_g|\alpha) = \phi(m_g|\alpha)/\sum_{g\in\mathbb{M}} \phi(m_g|\alpha)$ for a uniformly distributed set of m_g values) is necessary, because I will not rely on a uniform grid of

m_g points. It is easy to verify, that an equally spaced grid of m_g points on the logit scale leads to high concentrations of $\widetilde{m}_g$ values at the upper and lower end of the original [0,1] domain of $\widetilde{m}_g$. This is undesirable, as the feasible output-ratios are typically (as in the present application) concentrated somewhere in the middle of this original domain. So I will instead work with a uniform grid of $\widetilde{m}_g$ points (additionally restricted to the range of feasible points associated with observed y_i's) and then will transform them into corresponding m_g values on the logit scale. This will ensure, that for any given size of set $\mathbb{M}$ we achieve a much larger set of options for possible target output-ratios for each individual DMU than by using a uniform grid of m_g points.

The implied distribution on $\widetilde{m}_i$ arising from specification (9.8) is supposed as proxy for other conceivable unimodal distributions on the $[0,1]$-interval, although it is not defined at the borders 0 resp. 1. So definition (9.8) restricts applicability of the model to cases with output-ratios from $(0,1)$, in other words: strictly positive outputs. The data set of the present application satisfies this condition.

The two involved efficiency variables are also considered as random variates and it will be assumed that the logits

$$w_{is} = \ln(\varepsilon_{is}/(1-\varepsilon_{is})) \tag{9.9}$$

of these variables follow a bivariate Normal distribution. For estimation purposes I will parameterize this density different than usual and different than in the previous sections: If the standard mean parameters of a bivariate Normal distribution are denoted as μ_1, μ_2, I will parameterize instead via $\beta = \{\beta_1, \beta_2\}$ where $\beta_1 = \mu_1 - \mu_2$ and $\beta_2 = 0.5(\beta_1 + \beta_2)$. From preliminary testing I found this parameterization to work better than the standard one. So it will be assumed, that the logit efficiencies are distributed as follows:

$$\mathrm{d}_W(w_{i1}, w_{i2} \,|\, \beta, \Sigma) \stackrel{iid}{=} \mathcal{N}_2\left(\begin{bmatrix} w_{i1} \\ w_{i2} \end{bmatrix}; \begin{bmatrix} \beta_2 + 0.5\beta_1 \\ \beta_2 - 0.5\beta_1 \end{bmatrix}, \Sigma \right) \quad \forall\, i. \tag{9.10}$$

Note also that specification (9.10) given (9.9) is not defined for $\varepsilon_s = 1$. So in the process of estimating output-specific efficiencies only the inefficient observations will be used. This may appear as nothing but a practical necessity but it can be justified statistically noting that the likelihood of full efficiency and thus of an observation not deviating from the frontier is zero for logit efficiencies as defined in (9.10). Consequently observations which constitute this frontier and thus appear efficient (whether they are indeed or not) can never be part of a sample used for output-specific efficiency estimation.[5]

Using definition (9.9) the data generating process can now be specified as relationship between logit target output-ratios m_i, output-specific efficiency terms w_i and observed output vectors as y_i:

$$y_{is}^{\circ} = \mathrm{y}_s^F(x_i^{\circ}, m_i)\,\frac{1}{1+e^{-w_{is}}} \qquad s = 1,2. \tag{9.11}$$

Given m_i and x_i° thus the output specific efficiency terms w_{is} are implicitly defined by (9.11). For better readability and to emphasize dependency of w_i-terms on m_i-terms I will often use functional notation $\mathrm{w}(x_i^{\circ}, m_i, y_i^{\circ})$ to describe the vector $w_i = \{w_{i1}, w_{i2}\}$ of the corresponding logit efficiencies, i.e.

$$\mathrm{w}(x_i^{\circ}, y_i^{\circ}, m_i) = \{w_{i1}, w_{i2}\} \tag{9.12}$$

$$\text{with} \quad w_{is} = \ln[\,y_{is}^{\circ}\,/(\mathrm{y}_s^F(x_i^{\circ}, m_i) - y_{is}^{\circ})] \tag{9.13}$$

although this definition includes the mapping $\mathrm{y}^F(x_i^{\circ}, m_i)$, which is not given in closed form. The DGP process involving output-specific efficiencies is now fully described via definitions (9.5), (9.8), (9.10) and (9.11).

From definition (9.11) the posterior feasible domain of the logit target output-ratio can be derived for each individual DMU. To determine this feasible range note that a frontier point $(\mathrm{y}_1^F(x_i^{\circ}, m_i), \mathrm{y}_2^F(x_i^{\circ}, m_i))$ possibly associated with observation $(x_i^{\circ}, y_i^{\circ})$ must satisfy

$$y_s^{\circ} \leq \mathrm{y}_s^F(x_i^{\circ}, m_i) \quad s = 1,2. \tag{9.14}$$

So the corresponding minimum and maximum m_i-values can be derived as

$$m_i^{\min} = \min\{m_i : \mathrm{y}_1^F(x_i^{\circ}, m_i) \geq y_{i1}^{\circ}\} \tag{9.15}$$

$$m_i^{\max} = \max\{m_i : \mathrm{y}_2^F(x_i^{\circ}, m_i) \geq y_{i2}^{\circ}\} \tag{9.16}$$

[5] For the chosen distributional specifications the observations appearing efficient in a DEA perspective are known to be inefficient indeed, a reflection of the general upward bias of DEA efficiency estimates for deterministic frontiers. An alternative procedure would be to bias correct the frontier estimate first as described in Section 3 of Chapter 2.

This gives rise to the definition of the feasible set $\Omega(x_i^\circ, y_i^\circ)$ of logit output-mix vectors m_i corresponding to (x_i°, y_i°) defined as

$$\Omega_i \equiv \left\{m_i : m_i^{\min} \leq m_i \leq m_i^{\max}\right\} \tag{9.17}$$

The sets $\Omega(x_i^\circ, y_i^\circ)$ will play an important role in estimation below, because the posterior density of m_i (given (x_i°, y_i°) and a frontier estimate) is defined on this domain.

3.2 The likelihood function

Again, as in the previous chapters, the posterior analysis will be carried out on the basis of latent m_i variates which together with observations x_i°, y_i° uniquely determine the w_i terms. The conditional density of individual y_i° observations given a value of the latent variable m_i is thus determined as

$$\mathrm{d}_Y(y_i^\circ | \, x_i^\circ, m_i, \beta, \Sigma) = \prod_{s=1}^{2} \frac{\mathrm{y}_s^F(x_i^\circ, m_i)}{y_{is}^\circ(\mathrm{y}_s^F(x_i^\circ, m_i) - y_{is})} \, \mathrm{d}_W\Big(\mathrm{w}(x_i^\circ, y_i^\circ, m_i) | \, \beta, \Sigma\Big). \tag{9.18}$$

Because the w_i and m_i were assumed *iid* (identically and independently distributed) the same holds for the y_i° random vectors. Therefore the posterior density for the sample $y^\circ = \{y_i^\circ\}_{i=1}^{n_2}$ of output vectors conditional on input observations $x^\circ = \{x_i^\circ\}_{i=1}^{n_2}$ and latent output ratios $m = \{m_i\}_{i=1}^{n_2}$ is simply

$$[y^\circ | \, x^\circ, m, \beta, \Sigma] \sim \prod_{i=1}^{n_2} \{\mathrm{d}_Y(y_i^\circ | \, x_i^\circ, m_i, \beta, \Sigma)\}. \tag{9.19}$$

The marginal likelihood (in Non-Bayesian terms) of the observed data is derived from (9.19) by integrating out the latent variables (a summation in the present discrete case) leading to

$$\mathcal{L}(y^\circ | x^\circ, \beta, \Sigma, \alpha) = \prod_{i=1}^{n_2} \sum_{m_i \in \Omega_i} \mathrm{d}_Y(y_i^\circ | \, x_i^\circ, m_i, \beta, \Sigma) \, \mathrm{p}(m_i | \alpha) \tag{9.20}$$

Knowledge of this likelihood is necessary in some of the parameter updating steps to be described below. Note that it can be numerically evaluated, but it does not allow analytical derivation of maximum likelihood estimators mainly because the involved mapping $y_s^F(x_i^\circ, m_i)$ is not available in closed form.

3.3 Prior distributions

The following priors differ from those used so far, in particular because I switched onto the logit scale for target output-ratios, but also because I parameterized the bivariate Normal distribution of the logit efficiencies differently than before. In formulating these prior distributions for the parameters I will again make intensive use of the known posterior m_i-domains Ω_i and beyond that I try again to be as little informative as possible. Specifically I will assume the following priors (remember that the w_{is}-terms depend on $(x_i^\circ, y_i^\circ, m_i)$ via (9.13)):

$$\pi_{\alpha_1}(\alpha_1) = \mathcal{U}\left(\mathrm{E}_i[m_i^{\min}],\ \mathrm{E}_i[m_i^{\max}]\right) \tag{9.21}$$

$$\pi_{\alpha_2}(\alpha_2) = \mathcal{G}(\cdot\,,\cdot) \tag{9.22}$$

$$\pi_{\beta_1}(\beta_1) = \mathcal{U}\left(\mathrm{E}_i\left[\min_{m_g\in\Omega_i}[w_{i1}-w_{i2}]\right],\ \mathrm{E}_i\left[\max_{m_g\in\Omega_i}[w_{i1}-w_{i2}]\right]\right) \tag{9.23}$$

$$\pi_{\beta_2}(\beta_2) = \mathcal{U}\left(\mathrm{E}_i\left[\min_{m_g\in\Omega_i}\left(\frac{w_{i1}+w_{i2}}{2}\right)\right],\ \mathrm{E}_i\left[\max_{m_g\in\Omega_i}\left(\frac{w_{i1}-w_{i2}}{2}\right)\right]\right) \tag{9.24}$$

$$\pi_\Sigma(\Sigma^{-1}) = \mathcal{W}_2(\cdot\,,\cdot) \tag{9.25}$$

where $\mathcal{U}(a,b)$ denotes the Uniform distribution in the interval $[a,b]$, $\mathcal{G}(\cdot\,,\cdot)$ the Gamma distribution, $\mathcal{W}(\cdot\,,\cdot)$ a Wishart distribution (defined on the space of symmetric positive definite matrices) and $\mathrm{E}_i(\cdot)$ the expectation over all i. The priors for α_2 and Σ are improper (without specifying any hyperparameters and thus least informative), but they are conjugate to the distributions of the corresponding variables m_i resp. w_i and so the corresponding conditional posteriors are well defined. Conjugacy allows to sample from the posteriors directly and so I won't need the priors in updating. That is why they may be specified improperly. But also with regard to the other parameters the chosen uniform distributions convey extremely little information apart of course from the implied domain restrictions, which are based on reliable sample information.

4. Constructing the Markov chains

Unlike in the simulated settings from above I will work here with a mixture of Gibbs steps (i.e. direct draws from posterior distributions) and

Metropolis-Hastings steps (based on proposal distributions and calculations of acceptance probabilities based on numerical evaluation of the likelihood functions) to construct the Markov chains. As before I will separately update the individual latent m_i variables, the α_2 parameter and the block of Σ parameters, all based on the respective conditional posteriors, while I will use a so called random-walk Metropolis-Hastings (MH) step to update the parameter group $(\beta_1, \beta_2, \alpha_1)$.[6]

The required conditional posterior distributions can be derived from the definitions above. The unobserved logit target output ratios, confined a priori to the finite set $\mathbb{M}$ of possible values, are independent also in the posterior perspective with the following probabilities for feasible values

$$\mathrm{d}(m_i|x_i^\circ, y_i^\circ, \beta, \Sigma, \alpha) = \frac{\mathrm{d}(y_i^\circ|\, x_i^\circ, m_i, \beta, \Sigma)\ \mathrm{p}(m_i;\, \alpha)}{\sum\limits_{m_g \in \Omega_i} \mathrm{d}(y_i^\circ|\, x_i^\circ, m_g, \beta, \Sigma)\ \mathrm{p}(m_g;\, \alpha)} \tag{9.26}$$

Sampling from (9.26) via the cumulative distribution technique remains unchanged compared to the previous sections (note again that the posterior cumulative distribution of m_i given values for the involved parameters can be calculated exactly). Likewise updating the covariance matrix Σ is as before, again based on an exactly known conditional posterior distribution which by conjugacy is

$$[\Sigma^{-1}|\, x^\circ, y^\circ, m, \beta] \sim \mathcal{W}_2\Big(0.5 n_2,\ 0.5\,\mathrm{M}_C[\mathrm{w}(x_i^\circ, y_i^\circ, m_i), \beta]\Big) \tag{9.27}$$

where $\mathrm{M}_C[\cdot]$ as before indicates the second central moment operator, which in the present context is

$$\begin{aligned}\mathrm{M}_C[\mathrm{w}(x_i^\circ, y_i^\circ, m_i), \beta] \;&=\; \sum_{i=1}^{n_2} [w_{i1} - \beta_2 - 0.5\beta_1,\, w_{i2} - \beta_2 + 0.5\beta_1\,] \\ &\qquad \times\ [w_{i1} - \beta_2 - 0.5\beta_1,\, w_{i2} - \beta_2 + 0.5\beta_1\,]'\end{aligned}$$

with w_{is} as defined in (9.13). The conditional posterior distribution for parameter α_2 is only given approximately (due to discretizing m_i) by

---

[6] The MH step may appear as unnecessary complication in the present setup, because a conjugate analysis of parameters β_1, β_2 and α_1 would indeed be possible (in the case of α_1 at least approximately). But preliminary testing showed better mixing of the Markov chain with block-updating than with separate updating of β_1 and α_1 (between which the fundamental tradeoff in a likelihood perspective occurs).

conjugacy as

$$[\alpha_2|m, \alpha_1] \sim \mathcal{G}\Big(0.5n_2, 0.5\,\mathrm{M}_C(m_i, \alpha_1)\Big)\,, \tag{9.28}$$

where the moment here is to be evaluated relative to the mean α_1 of the scalar m_i-terms, i.e.

$$\mathrm{M}_C(m_i, \alpha_1) = \sum_{i=1}^{n_2} [m_i - \alpha_1]^2$$

Experimenting with a theoretically consistent updating procedure based on a Uniform prior for α_2 and using (9.28) as proposal lead to acceptance rates as high as 90% and had virtually no impact on the parameter estimates. This gave confidence in using (9.28) as proxy for this update step, which is far less time consuming than the otherwise necessary numerical evaluation of the likelihood.

So to update parameters Σ, α_2 and latent variables m_i I will draw new values at random directly from the above posterior distributions (or a proxy thereof in the case of α_2). To update parameters $(\beta_1, \beta_2, \alpha_1)$ I instead rely on a different strategy based on a proposal distribution. Denoting proposed new values of these variates as $(\tilde{\beta}_1, \tilde{\beta}_2, \tilde{\alpha}_1)$ I define this proposal distribution conditional on the old values as

$$[\tilde{\beta}_1, \tilde{\beta}_2, \tilde{\alpha}_1 \,|\, \beta_1, \beta_2, \alpha_1] \sim \mathcal{N}_3((\beta_1, \beta_2, \alpha_1), \Sigma_P) \tag{9.29}$$

This trivariate Normal proposal distribution with mean vector $(\beta_1, \beta_2, \alpha_1)$ and covariance matrix Σ_P is the core of the above mentioned random-walk Metropolis-Hastings updating technique. The update rule for proposed new parameter values according to this technique is thus:

Accept proposed parameters $(\tilde{\beta}_1, \tilde{\beta}_2, \tilde{\alpha}_1)$ drawn at random from (9.29) with probability

$$\frac{\mathcal{L}(\,y^\circ|x^\circ, \tilde{\beta}_1, \tilde{\beta}_2, \Sigma, \tilde{\alpha}_1, \alpha_2)\, \pi_{\beta_1}(\tilde{\beta}_1)\, \pi_{\beta_2}(\tilde{\beta}_2)\, \pi_{\alpha_1}(\tilde{\alpha}_1)}{\mathcal{L}(\,y^\circ|x^\circ, \beta_1, \beta_2, \Sigma, \alpha_1, \alpha_2)\, \pi_{\beta_1}(\beta_1)\, \pi_{\beta_2}(\beta_2)\, \pi_{\alpha_1}(\alpha_1)}. \tag{9.30}$$

It should be noted, that the proposed values may lie outside the prior domains of one or the other involved variates. In this case the acceptance probability would become zero due to the priors in the numerator. To effect the implied randomization I draw a [0,1]-uniform random variable and if its value is less than the above specified acceptance probability the proposed new values drawn from the proposal distribution are indeed accepted. If its value is larger, I use the old values instead.

Note also that sampling according to (9.30) is no longer dependent on m_i terms, i.e. we do not sample from the full conditional distribution but from a marginal distribution. It has been shown in Liu, 1994 (where this approach was labeled *collapsed sampling*) and illustrated for example in Chen et al., 2000 that it may often be beneficial to sample from such marginal distributions rather than the full fledged conditionals to improve convergence speed for highly correlated parameters. Preliminary testing based on the full conditionals proved this to be the case for the present application. The rational behind collapsed sampling is that such marginal posterior distributions may be far less peaked than the corresponding full conditional distributions and that therefore the parameter updates scan the respective prior domains much more rapidly.

Choosing the covariance matrix Σ_P for the proposal required some tuning to achieve a desired average acceptance probability for proper mixing. Roberts et al., 1994 and Gelman et al., 1995 have come up with an approximate range [0.15,0.5] for optimal acceptance rates in the general case. I based the variances used for the proposal on the Euclidian length of the domains of the respective variables and used a certain fraction thereof to construct the diagonal elements of Σ_P to achieve acceptance rates in the range of 35%.

The off-diagonal elements of Σ_P were chosen on posterior correlation considerations. Note again that for given y_i's a particular sample of m_i's (driving the α parameter estimates) uniquely determines the w_i-sample (driving the β parameter estimates). Therefore I know in particular that β_1 and α_1 must move in opposite directions in a posterior perspective to achieve similar plausibility (likelihood) for the sample observations. So I chose a correlation factor of -0.5 for these two parameters leading to $\Sigma_{P,[1,3]} = \Sigma_{P,[3,1]} = -0.5\sqrt{\Sigma_{P,[1,1]} * \Sigma_{P,[3,3]}}$. The case of β_2 is more tricky. It is easy to verify that moving β_1 from the lower to the upper end of its prior domain (accompanied by moving α_1 from the upper to the lower end) lets β_2 start with a high value which continuously decreases until it reaches a minimum somewhere in the interior of the β_1 and α_1 domains. From there on the most plausible β_2 values start to increase again until we reach the upper end of the β_1 domain (and the lower end of the α_1 domain). Because I don't know a priori whether the posterior mean of β_2 will lie in the downward or upward sloping part, I chose the correlation factor used in the proposal distribution as 0, leading to $\Sigma_{P,[1,2]} = \Sigma_{P,[2,1]} = \Sigma_{P,[2,3]} = \Sigma_{P,[3,2]} = 0$.

The start values for the parameters to be estimated were chosen as follows

$$\beta_1^{(0)} = 0, \quad \beta_2^{(0)} = \mathrm{E}_i[\ln(\varepsilon_i^*/(1-\varepsilon_i^*))]$$
$$\Sigma_{11}^{(0)} = \Sigma_{22}^{(0)} = \mathrm{VAR}[\ln(\varepsilon_i^*/(1-\varepsilon_i^*))]$$
$$\Sigma_{12}^{(0)} = \Sigma_{21}^{(0)} = 0.9\,\mathrm{VAR}[\ln(\varepsilon_i^*/(1-\varepsilon_i^*))]$$
$$\alpha_1^{(0)} = \mathrm{E}_i[\ln(\widetilde{m}_i^\circ/(1-\widetilde{m}_i^\circ))], \quad \alpha_2^{(0)} = 1/\mathrm{VAR}_i[\ln(\widetilde{m}_i^\circ/(1-\widetilde{m}_i^\circ))]$$

where $\widetilde{m}_i^\circ = y_{i1}^\circ/(y_{i1}^\circ + y_{i2}^\circ)$ for $i = 1 \ldots n_2$. So the startvalues are those associated with the radial DEA solutions, i.e. as if all efficiencies were perfectly correlated with equal means and target output-ratios equal to the observed ones. Theoretically the particular choice of startvalues should not influence the resulting estimates. This was confirmed in the present application by testing different random startvalues and finding no significant changes in the parameter estimates.

MC^2 estimation proper then starts by first drawing a sample of logit output-ratios from (9.26) for all $i = 1 \ldots n_2$ conditional on the starting values of the parameters. This sample shall be denoted $\{m_i^{(1)}\}_{i=1}^{n_2}$. Conditional on this sample a new covariance matrix $\Sigma^{(1)}$ is then drawn from (9.27) conditional on $\beta_1^{(0)}$, $\beta_1^{(0)}$. Then $\alpha_2^{(1)}$ is drawn according to posterior distribution (9.28) conditional on $\alpha_1^{(0)}$. And finally $\beta_1^{(1)}$, $\beta_2^{(1)}$ and $\alpha_1^{(1)}$ are drawn from (9.29) and accepted with probability (9.30) conditional on the latest sample of m_i-variates $\{m_i^{(1)}\}_{i=1}^{n_2}$ and the latest values $\Sigma^{(1)}$ resp. $\alpha_2^{(1)}$ of the remaining parameters.

The above sequence of steps (detailed only for the first round) is repeated T-times leading to a chain of vectors $\{m_1^{(t)} \ldots m_n^{(t)}, \beta_1^{(t)}, \beta_2^{(t)}, \Sigma^{(t)}, \alpha_1^{(t)}, \alpha_2^{(t)}\}_{t=1}^{T}$ whose limiting ($T \to \infty$) distribution is the joint posterior distribution of the parameters and the missing data conditional on the sample observations $\{x_i^\circ, y_i^\circ\}_{i=1}^{n_2}$. This distribution is the basis for the results reported below.

5. Data

The data to be analyzed here were published in the Financial Times (FT) on October 10th 2000. In fact this is a panel of data which has been published by the FT on a regular basis since 1992. The FT uses these data to generate what has become known as the FT-1000 league tables, in which 1000 UK secondary (private and non-private) schools are ranked according to average grades of graduating pupils. While the FT ranking is solely based on grades the intention here is to generate a ranking based on output-specific efficiencies, which requires modeling a schooling technology first. So an educational production process needs to be characterized where inputs are transformed into outputs, as is the case for every production function specified in economics. Reasonable input variables from the FT body of data include only tuition and boarding costs, so the present analysis will be necessarily restricted to a comparison amongst private schools.

The time frame for the secondary schooling process in the UK may be described graphically as follows:

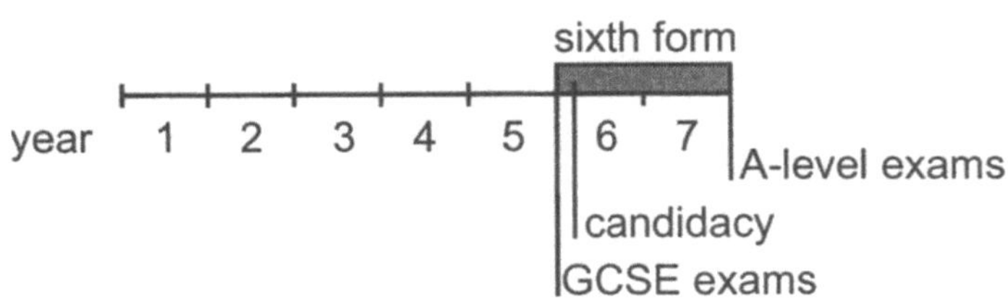

After five years of primary school (or roughly at age 11) pupils enter into secondary schools. Obligatory schooling ends with the General Certificate of Secondary Education (GCSE) in the fifth form. What is called the sixth form in the UK-schooling system actually consists of two additional years of secondary education, and is the prerequisite for entry into universities. Early on in the sixth form pupils apply for candidacy to take the ultimate A-level exams at the end of schooling year seven.

Tuition will be used as only input. Tuition is what all parents have to pay for the education of their children in private schools. Some parents consider the option of boarding their kids at the school location in which case they will pay additional attention to boarding fees. The primary reason for not including the latter into the input cost variable is that some parents necessarily have to incur such costs while others don't and consequently it would be unfair to assess school performance from a parental perspective based on such unequal ground. A further reason is that only 40% of kids are boarding in school offered facilities. And finally tuition and boarding fees are highly correlated (0.86), so that the tuition costs may be considered as roughly proportional to the sum of tuition plus boarding, the alternative input variable.

The first output of the present application is used to proxy quantity: Candidates/Pupils, i.e. the number of pupils taking the final exams in the 7th form relative to the total number of pupils in school. If all cohorts of pupils entering the 1st form were of equal size and if for no cohort there would be any dropout (or intake) during the curriculum, then this figure would be $1/7 \sim 14.3\%$. In fact the corresponding average (across all sample schools) figure is $\sim 13\%$. Thus the actual 13% relative to the ideal 14.3%, i.e. $\sim 91\%$, is sort of an ex ante probability of an average pupil to reach the final exams at all. So, unsurprisingly, the typical school in the sample has net-dropout, the size of which is roughly 9%. But the sample also contains 27 schools with probabilities higher than 20% and 22 schools with probabilities lower than 6%. This indicates considerable shift of pupils amongst schools during the curriculum. Some schools obviously have significant net-intake of pupils in later schooling years, possibly less performant pupils driven out of other, more selective schools. In any case this figure here is considered as indicative of the schools ability to provide quantities of educated pupils irrespective of their precise quality in terms of final grading, which is considered as separate output.

The second output used in modelling schooling technology is supposed to proxy quality: points per candidate (average grade). Correlation of this variable with an alternative quality variable, namely points per entry is 0.94 and using it instead of points/candidate does not change the results qualitatively. So I will only report results for the points/candidate figures as quality indices. In generating the FT-1000 league tables both of these alternative quality variables are used to construct a weighted performance index to rank private and non-private UK-secondary schools.

The schools in the sample may also be grouped in terms of faith, for each of which we will report average efficiencies below. Amongst these groups the 131 schools with Church of England faith is by far the largest. The others are 40 Interdenominational, 20 Roman Catholic, 17 Non Denominational, 22 Non Conformist and finally 1 Ecumenical school.

The DEA estimate of the efficiency frontier for this technology, transforming tuition input into a quality and a quantity output, is shown as input-isoquants for various input-levels in Figure 9.1.

Table 9.1. Data description

	Candidates	Total Pupils	%Male	%Boarding
MEAN	62	468	47	40
STD	40	222	34	28
MIN	10	101	0	0
MAX	208	1421	100	100

	Tuition	Quantity	Quality
MEAN	8513	0.130	20.55
STD	2095	0.053	4.29
MIN	3471	0.027	10.38
MAX	16455	0.283	32.76

Legend: Tuition = the single input, Quantity = Candidates/Pupils = output 1, Quality = Total A-level points per candidate (a grade A is counted 10 points, a grade B 8 points...) = output 2,

5.1 Using data information to define $\mathbb{M}$

I applied DEA to the input and output data as specified above, but used a rescaled quality variable with a mean of 1 for numerical stability. Based on the results from this first step I then determined the DMU specific posterior feasible range of $\widetilde{m}_i$-values. The joint set of these ranges, covering all DMU's, had $\widetilde{m}$-values between 0.020 and 0.330. Within these limits I constructed an equally spaced grid of a priori feasible target output-ratios $\widetilde{m}_g$ of size 100 and then translated it onto the logit scale to define set $\mathbb{M}$ (no longer equally spaced) with values ranging from -3.89 to -0.71.

Based on $\mathbb{M}$ the DMU-specific posterior feasible m_i-sets Ω_i were determined. The resulting number of elements in these Ω_i-sets ranged between 1 (for some very efficient school) and 88 (for some very inefficient school) with an average of 34. So for a typical school I considered 34 potential target output-ratios that might have led to the observed combination of quality and quantity output and thus the chosen $\mathbb{M}$ portrays the potential choices for the typical school with sufficiently fine granularity.

Figure 9.1. DEA Estimated Input-Isoquants for Schooling Technology

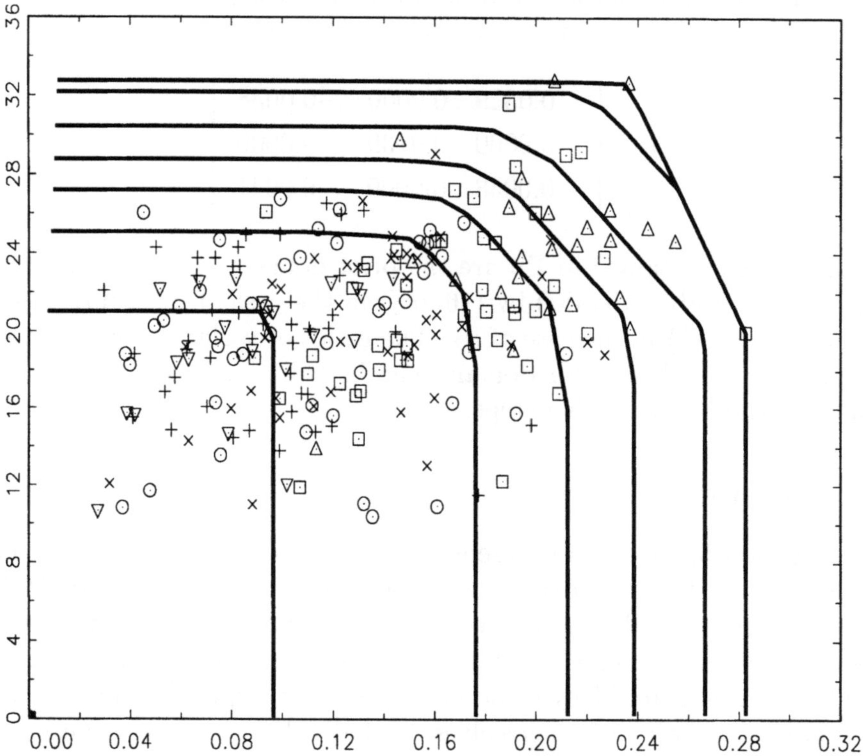

Horizontal axis: Quantity. Vertical axis: Quality. Input Isoquants are drawn for $x_{(1)}$, $x_{(0.1n)}$, $x_{(0.3n)}$, $x_{(0.5n)}$, $x_{(0.7n)}$, $x_{(0.9n)}$, $x_{(n)}$, where subscripts denotes the respective rank of the ascendingly ordered x_i and n denotes samplesize. Observations are shown as symbols: inverted triangles for $x_i \leq x_{(0.1n)}$, plus' for $x_{(0.1n)} \leq x_i \leq x_{(0.3n)}$, circles for $x_{(0.3n)} \leq x_i \leq x_{(0.5n)}$, stars for $x_{(0.5n)} \leq x_i \leq x_{(0.7n)}$, squares for $x_{(0.7n)} \leq x_i \leq x_{(0.9n)}$ and triangles for $x_i > x_{(0.9n)}$.

5.2 Using data information to define prior distributions

Knowledge of the Ω_i-sets in turn enabled to specify the prior distributions according to the general definitions (9.21) - (9.25) as follows:

$$\pi_{\alpha_1}(\alpha_1) = \mathcal{U}(-2.46, -1.48)$$

$$\pi_{\beta_1}(\beta_1) = \mathcal{U}(-4.78, 3.15)$$

$$\pi_{\beta_2}(\beta_2) = \mathcal{U}(1.03, 2.71)$$

with the improper priors for α_2 and Σ as before. Based on the resulting prior domain lengths of each of these parameters the proposal covariance matrix Σ_P for updating $(\beta_1, \beta_2, \alpha_1)$ was then specified as

$$\Sigma_P = \begin{bmatrix} 0.0329 & 0.0000 & -0.0058 \\ 0.0000 & 0.0139 & 0.0000 \\ -0.0058 & 0.0000 & 0.0041 \end{bmatrix}$$

The variances contained in Σ_P are the prior domain lengths of the corresponding variables divided by $(16\sqrt{n_2})$ in the case of β_1 and α_1 resp. divided by $(8\sqrt{n_2})$ in the case of β_2. The ratios of variances balanced in this manner based on prior domain lengths led to an acceptance ratio of 32% in the MH-updating steps.

6. Results

In subsection 6.1 some convergence information will be provided and results about estimates of the model parameters will be reported. Only in subsection 6.2 will I turn to efficiency measures proper in the form of sample means, which are functions of the estimated latent variables. The latter results are likely to be more useful for applied purposes than the parameter estimates themselves, so I divided the results into two subsections.

6.1 Parameter estimates and convergence information

Each MC^2 application requires a particular choice of the involved meta-parameters, like the number of overall iterations, of burn-in samples to discard or the degree of thinning of the original Markov chains to remove serial correlation. For general discussions of the involved issues the reader is referred to Raftery and Lewis, 1996, Gilks et al., 1996b or the survey of Cowles and Carlin, 1996.

I started with 50000 original iterations and discarded the first 10% thereof as burnin-iterations. To test for convergence of the remaining chain of length 45000 I followed the approach of Fernández et al., 2000 who constructed an approximate test statistic in the spirit of Geweke, 1992. This test statistic is the ratio of median differences (between the median of the first 10% of samples and the median of the last 50%)

and the interquartile range (a variation measure). This ratio is reported in the last row of Table (9.2) for each parameter. The maximum (in absolute terms) was found to be 0.047, indicative of convergence of the Markov chains towards the respective true posterior distributions.

Table 9.2. Convergence Information

	β_1	β_2	Σ_{11}	Σ_{22}	ρ	α_1	α_2
M10	-2.098	1.491	0.911	1.267	0.637	-1.652	0.088
M50	-2.079	1.484	0.911	1.257	0.642	-1.653	0.088
IQR	0.391	0.159	0.126	0.296	0.144	0.062	0.017
D/I	-0.047	0.044	0.002	0.035	-0.035	0.016	-0.008

Figures based on $T = 45000$ after burnin iterations. ρ: correlation between w_{i1} and w_{i2}, M10 resp. M50: medians of the first 10% resp. the last 50% iterations, IQR: the interquartile range and D/I= (M10-M50)/IQR.

To remedy the serial dependence problem only every fortieth of the remaining iterations was used (after investigation of the corresponding autocorrelation functions) to construct the final Markov-chains (one for each parameter). The latter therefore had length $T = 1125$ and in their AR representation only the first lag remained significant by the Box-Pierce teststatistic. Using this information about remaining serial correlation the numerical standard error (NSE) of the mean-estimator $\widehat{\mathrm{E}(\beta_1)} = \sum_{t=1}^{n} \beta_1^{(t)} / T$ for parameter β_1 (and analogous for all other parameters) was calculated following the time series approach of Geweke, 1992 and further details given in Chib, 1995 as:

$$\mathrm{NSE}\left(\widehat{\mathrm{E}(\beta_1)}\right) = T^{-1}\left[\mathrm{VAR}\left(\beta_1^{(t)}\right) + \mathrm{COV}\left(\beta_1^{(t)}, \beta_1^{(t-1)}\right)\right]^{0.5}.$$

Following the approach of Geweke, 1992 I also calculated the relative numerical efficiencies (RNE's) of the mean estimators relative to a true iid sample via

$$\mathrm{RNE}\left(\widehat{\mathrm{E}(\beta_1)}\right) = \mathrm{VAR}\left(\beta_1^{(t)}\right) T^{-1}\left[\mathrm{NSE}\left(\widehat{\mathrm{E}(\beta_1)}\right)\right]^{-2}.$$

From Table 9.3 it can be seen that the relative efficiency loss in estimating the means of the parameters from the MC^2-samples is at most around 14% (for parameter β_1) compared to a true iid sample of parameter values.

Table 9.3. Parameter Estimates

	β_1	β_2	Σ_{11}	Σ_{22}	ρ	α_1	α_2
Mean	-2.064	1.483	0.920	1.272	0.637	-1.659	0.089
Median	-2.076	1.480	0.913	1.256	0.647	-1.656	0.089
Min	-2.966	1.108	0.680	0.533	0.212	-1.931	0.048
Max	-0.683	1.942	1.382	2.398	0.877	-1.523	0.162
STD	0.293	0.119	0.096	0.231	0.108	0.047	0.013
NSE	0.009	0.004	0.003	0.007	0.003	0.002	0.000
RNE	0.864	0.886	1.030	1.000	0.953	0.898	1.010

Figures based on $T = 1125$ (after burnin and after thinning). ρ: correlation between w_{i1} and w_{i2}, STD: standarddeviation of sampled values, NSE: numerical standard error of mean estimator, RNE: relative numerical efficiency.

For practical purposes the parameter estimates as given in Table 9.3 are of little use, because they refer to the logit scaled variables. The only exception to this is the correlation coefficient ρ between the two logit-efficiency terms, because it also applies (approximately) to standard efficiency figures (which are constrained to the [0,1]-interval). This correlation was estimated to be around 0.64 with a minimum of 0.21 and a maximum of 0.88. It should be recalled from Chapter 8, that the performance of the correlation estimator is rather poor, so these figures should be interpreted very cautiously. So if anything, they tell that the provision of good quality grades comes along with provision of relatively high quantity of grades. This result does not support the often expressed view, that achievements in grading quality would come at the cost of quantity. Instead the correlation estimate of 0.64 provides at least tentative evidence, that schools tend to perform rather well in both respects or in neither of them. So the provision of quality resp. quantity of private secondary school graduates should not be seen as substitutes in a managerial perspective. But this does not imply, that private secondary schools on average cope equally well with quantity and quality tasks, as will become clear shortly.

6.2 Efficiencies and Rankings

The main finding (see Table 9.4) of this paper for practical purposes is, that average efficiency across schools of providing grading quality is far higher (0.89) than the average efficiency of providing grading quantity (0.59). In terms of targets this means that the typical UK private secondary school comes much closer to meet its quality target than its quantity target. The debate over secondary schooling issues in the UK lead to the critique that secondary schools would too willingly sacrifice quantity for quality in order to achieve higher ranks in the FT-1000 league tables which are solely based on quality variables. The presented findings gives clear support to this critique although the latter is usually targeting non-private schools, while here solely private schools are investigated. On the other hand the findings quantitatively substantiate the typical reputation of private schools of providing high grading quality rather than quantity. So the analysis of output-specific efficiencies sheds additional light on a controversial issue in the UK schooling debate in accordance with common judgement about the strength of private schools.

Table 9.4. Efficiencies

	RAD-EFF	O1-EFF	O2-EFF
MEAN	0.768	0.589	0.894
MEDIAN	0.779	0.587	0.896
STD	0.137	0.180	0.081
MIN	0.387	0.160	0.536
MAX	1.000	0.980	0.999

Table 9.5 displays the rank correlations between the various types of performance measures: The FT-1000 league scores (FT-SCORES), radial DEA efficiency scores (RAD-EFF), quantity specific (O1-EFF) and quality specific efficiency scores (O2-EFF). RAD-EFF is highly correlated (0.81) with FT-SCORES, despite the fact that the DEA estimated technology (unlike FT-SCORES) also takes inputs and a quantity output into account. As such the radial efficiencies do not provide much additional insight into systematic performance problems beyond the FT-

SCORES. The story with output-specific scores is different. In particular the correlation between ranks for quantity efficiency and the ranks for FT-Scores plums down to 0.53, clearly reflecting the lack of quantity considerations in the FT-Scores. The correlation of the ranks for FT-Scores with ranks for quality efficiency is unsurprisingly higher at 0.72, not too far from the corresponding figure 0.81 for radial efficiencies.

Table 9.5. Rank correlations

	RAD-EFF	O1-EFF	O2-EFF
FT-SCORES	0.813	0.535	0.716
RAD-EFF		0.735	0.911
O1-EFF			0.933

Detailed figures for data, estimated performance measures and associated ranks are given in tables 9.6 and 9.7 for some of the highest ranked schools according to one or the other performance measure. It highlights some marked differences in ranks depending on the type of measure used. For example the school ranked 8 acc. to the FT-1000 scores in the subsample of private schools falls back to rank 54 in a quantity efficiency perspective, mainly because it only provides about average grading quantity (0.15) at average costs (10050) and despite providing very good grading quality (27). Note that this deterioration in ranking applies also to the quality rank which is only 43. The reason for this latter result is that the likely (based on statistical plausibility) target output-ratios between quantity and quality of all schools were shifted towards more of quantity relative to the actually observed ratios. So this shift necessarily brings along improved quality efficiency for all schools (although to different degrees) leaving little room for school ranked 8 to improve its position relative to the other schools. An opposite argument applies to the school ranked 134 acc. to the FT-1000 scores in our subsample. It could dramatically improve its relative position to rank 9 according to the various efficiency measures, because it provides superior grading quantity (0.28) along with average grading quality (20) at average costs (10221).

Table 9.6. Results for selected schools

RO	R	TU	QN	QL	RR	ER	R1	EO1	R2	EO2
1	1	16.4	0.21	32.76	1	1.000	1	1.00	1	1.00
2	2	12.6	0.24	32.65	2	1.000	2	1.00	2	1.00
3	3	10.4	0.19	31.61	3	1.000	3	1.00	3	1.00
6	4	12.1	0.15	29.76	37	0.917	101	0.65	87	0.94
16	5	10.5	0.22	29.19	13	0.987	11	0.98	13	1.00
18	6	9.8	0.21	29.02	4	1.000	4	1.00	4	1.00
20	7	8.7	0.16	29.07	12	0.994	14	0.95	12	1.00
24	8	10.1	0.17	27.25	54	0.882	54	0.77	43	0.96
30	9	10.3	0.19	28.44	25	0.938	23	0.88	19	0.98
31	10	8.8	0.13	26.68	43	0.907	85	0.69	63	0.95
46	14	6.7	0.12	26.55	5	1.000	5	1.00	5	1.00
66	20	6.5	0.12	26.00	11	0.998	12	0.98	11	1.00
75	22	7.2	0.13	26.18	15	0.967	32	0.84	20	0.98

RO: Original rank in FT-1000 league table, R: rank acc. to FT-1000 scores within the subsample of private schools, TU: tuition (=Input) in thousand British pounds per year, QN: quantity (=Output 1), QL: quality (=Output 2), ER: radial efficiency score from output-oriented DEA with variable returns to scale, EO1: efficiency in producing quantity, EO2: efficiency in producing quality, RR, R1 resp. R2: ranks according to RE, O1E resp. O2E.

Regarding the relationship of performance scores with the proportion of boys or girls we see from Table 9.8 significantly higher average efficiency of pure boy schools vs. pure girl schools in achieving quantity and quality goals alike. Furthermore mixed schools perform worse than gender separated schools. Note that the most marked difference between pure boy and pure girl schools occurs in terms of quantity efficiency: 0.79 vs. 0.60, while difference in quality efficiency is rather small: 0.96 vs. 0.91. So primarily the quantity-efficiency accounts for the observed differences amongst these two groups of schools. Interpreting the quantity efficiency as reciprocal of selectivity I may thus state that it is much greater selectivity of pure girl schools which makes them appear inefficient from a quantity perspective. This story comes out even clearer if looking at the weighted average efficiencies, when the weights are the percentage of boys resp. girls of total pupils. Then the difference be-

Table 9.7. Results for selected schools (continued)

RO	R	TU	QN	QL	RR	ER	R1	EO1	R2	EO2
100	32	5.9	0.15	24.84	6	1.000	6	1.00	6	1.00
103	33	13.6	0.24	25.27	21	0.946	15	0.93	16	0.99
104	34	8.0	0.17	25.58	23	0.940	19	0.89	17	0.98
116	38	9.1	0.21	24.73	19	0.950	16	0.92	14	0.99
128	42	11.8	0.25	24.62	14	0.969	13	0.96	15	0.99
235	79	4.8	0.14	22.76	7	1.000	7	1.00	7	1.00
236	80	8.8	0.20	22.89	28	0.928	20	0.89	18	0.98
341	109	3.5	0.10	21.02	8	1.000	8	1.00	8	1.00
428	134	10.2	0.28	19.99	9	1.000	9	1.00	9	1.00
502	152	9.0	0.23	18.86	42	0.909	17	0.90	24	0.98
554	165	8.3	0.21	18.91	44	0.906	18	0.90	27	0.97
868	207	6.6	0.20	15.15	10	1.000	10	1.00	10	1.00

Legend see Table 9.6.

tween a typical boy school and a typical girl school is negligible in radial or quality-efficiency perspective, but considerable in magnitude (0.65 vs. 0.57) and significant from the quantity efficiency perspective. So this is another instance, where output-specific efficiencies tell more than the usual radial efficiency scores.

A common distinguishing criteria of observations in efficiency analysis is size of DMU's. Here I consider the total number of pupils per school as size indicator and look separately at the various performance scores of the group of schools with less than 400 pupils and the group with at least 400 pupils. As table 9.9 shows, all measures indicate a performance advantage of large schools versus small schools. But while the FT-scores, purely quality based performance measures, suggest that bigger schools perform 13% better on average in quality terms, a more detailed analysis accounting also for inputs and output quantity reveals a meager 4% advantage of bigger schools relative to smaller ones in terms of quality efficiency. On the other hand the output-specific efficiency analysis shows a 13% advantage of the bigger schools in terms of quantity efficiency. So once again we find: What primarily distinguishes schools is their ability

Table 9.8. Schools according to sex

	n	FTS	RE	O1E	O2E
boy schools	19	1.21	.89	.79	.96
mixed schools	168	0.99	.74	.59	.89
girl schools	50	1.13	.81	.60	.91
boy% weighted schools	-	1.02	.77	.65	.90
girl% weighted schools	-	1.05	.77	.57	.89

n=number of observations in each category, FTS: FT-1000 scores, RE: radial efficiency score from output-oriented DEA with variable returns to scale, O1E: efficiency in producing quantity, O2E: efficiency in producing quality.

to cope with the quantity issue rather than their ability of achieving high average grades for the GCSE. Obviously the different skills necessary to accomplish the second task vary much less across schools than the skills necessary to come up with efficient quantity figures.

Table 9.9. Schools according to size

	n	FTS	RE	O1E	O2E
total pupils < 400	106	0.969	.717	.564	.881
total pupils ≥ 400	131	1.097	.810	.643	.916
lead of schools ≥ 400	-	13.2%	13.0%	13.0%	4.0%

n=number of observations in each category, FTS: FT-1000 scores, RE: radial efficiency score from output-oriented DEA with variable returns to scale, O1E: efficiency in producing quantity, O2E: efficiency in producing quality.

A hot topic within the current debate in the UK is whether Church schools or Non Denominational schools perform better, an issue discussed recently for example in Dean, 2001. The Prime Minister and the Secretary of Education have proposed massive investments in Church schools based on the argument that church schools would typically perform better than other types of schools. The results from the present analysis, presented in table 9.10, do not support this argument.

While church of England schools have significantly higher average efficiencies than interdenominational and non-conformist schools,[7] they are in fact outperformed on average by non-denominational schools for all types of efficiency measures considered here. But also with respect to faith the performance differences between the various types of school is most pronounced for quantity-efficiency with averages varying between 52% and 66%, while in quality terms the differences appear much smaller in magnitude with per-type-averages lying in the narrow range between 87% and 92%.

Table 9.10. Schools according to faith

	n	FTS	RE	O1E	O2E
Church of England	131	1.07	.78	.64	.91
Interdenominational	40	0.96	.72	.54	.87
Roman Catholic	20	1.02	.78	.60	.90
Non-Denominational	17	1.07	.81	.66	.92
Non-Conformist	22	1.00	.73	.52	.87

n=number of observations in each category, FTS: FT-1000 scores, RE: radial efficiency score from output-oriented DEA with variable returns to scale, O1E: efficiency in producing quantity, O2E: efficiency in producing quality.

The relationship between the percentage of boarding pupils and school efficiency looks positive from all perspectives (see Table 9.11): Schools with higher percentages of boarding pupils tend to perform better than schools with lower percentages of boarding schools. But in magnitude only the quantity-efficiency differences seem noteworthy (0.66 for a typical boarding school vs. 0.57 for a typical non-boarding school), while neither FT-1000 performance scores nor radial efficiencies nor quality efficiencies are much affected by differences in the proportion of boarding pupils. This result is rather plausible when, as may be argued, private

[7] Significance levels are those achieved in non-parametric Wilcoxon-Mann-Whitney tests for equal means of distributions, which lie for this comparison between 90% and 99%.

schools feel more obliged to boarding pupils rather than non-boarding pupils because the former contribute much more than the latter to the economic well being of the school via boarding fees.

Table 9.11. Schools according to percentage of boarding pupils

	FTS	RE	O1E	O2E
boarding% weighted schools	1.06	.77	.66	.91
non-boarding% weighted schools	1.03	.77	.57	.89

FTS: FT-1000 scores, RE: radial efficiency score from output-oriented DEA with variable returns to scale, O1E: efficiency in producing quantity, O2E: efficiency in producing quality.

It should finally be noted that all the above comparisons amongst subgroups of the total population of private schools are based on the presumption of a common schooling technology. This is not the presumption underlying the concept of *system comparison* as applied in Brockett et al., 1998 or Cooper et al., 2000, p. 197-199, which actually comes down to the estimation of separate technologies for each subgroup.

6.3 A simple comparison based on observed output-ratios

In the following I will briefly compare the results with regard to target output-ratios from the present analysis to those from an intriguing simple consideration: In the perspective of the present analysis the actually achieved output ratios of Farrell-efficient schools are interpreted as being identical to their target output-ratios. So one might calculate the means of these output-ratios and use them as guideline for assessing systematic deficiencies of inefficient schools. In the present application this comes down to a comparison between two figures: The scalar mean of observed output-ratios $E_i(y_{i1}/(y_{i1}+y_{i2})]$ from efficient resp. inefficient schools.

Suppose we would find this mean of efficient schools to be higher than that of inefficient schools, i.e. the efficient schools were targeting and producing higher quantity to quality ratios than the inefficient schools. Taken for granted that the average target output-ratio of an efficient school was the same as that for an inefficient school, this would then imply, that lacking performance of inefficient schools was more due to missing the quantity target than missing the quality target. Otherwise their average observed output-ratio should have been higher than the one for efficient schools.

For the present two-output application output-ratios may be represented via the slopes of rays emanating from the origin in two-dimensional space as illustrated with Figure 9.2, which displays again the actually observed outputs along with the mean observed output ratios for efficient resp. inefficient schools and the estimated mean of target output-ratios for the inefficient schools.

Figure 9.2. Comparison of some mean output-ratios

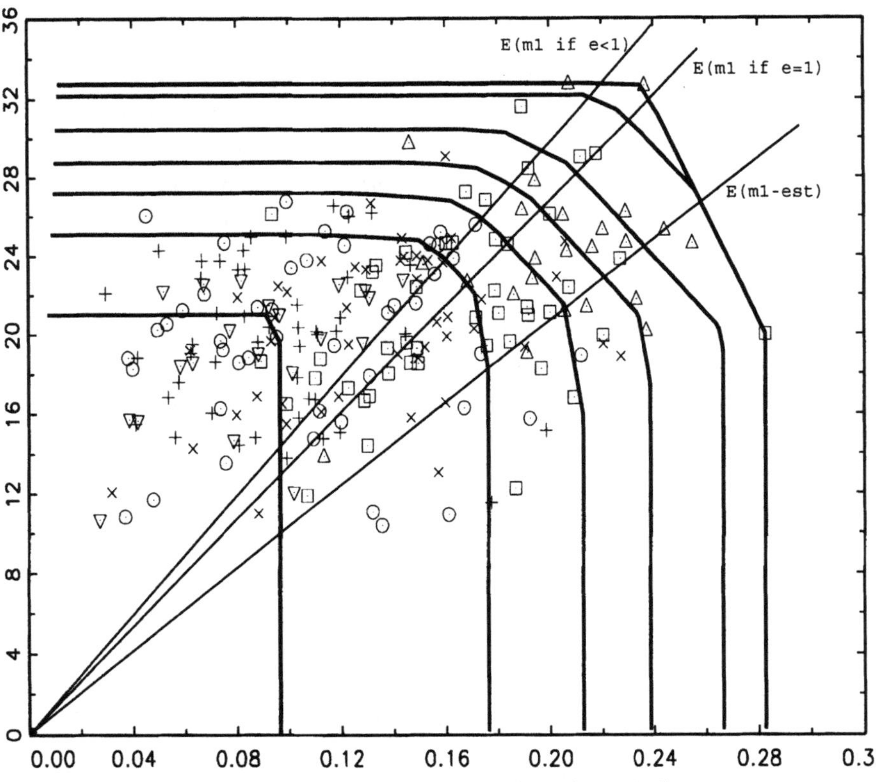

Legend as in Figure9.1 with additional lines, whose slopes indicate mean output-ratios: `E(m1 if e<1)` resp. `E(m1 if e=1)` refer to mean output-ratios of observed, inefficient resp. efficient schools, `E(m1-est)` refers to estimated mean of target output-ratios.

The actual figures for the schooling data set corresponding to the above considerations and Figure 9.2 are as follows: The mean of observed output ratios of inefficient schools is .0067, while the mean for efficient schools is .0075. So on average the efficient schools did produce higher quantity to quality ratios than there inefficient competitors. Guided by this difference we should then conclude, that the efficiency of meeting the quality target of inefficient schools is less on average than the mean radial DEA-efficiency score for this group. On the other hand their efficiency in meeting the quality target was higher than indicated by this mean radial efficiency score.

Now the estimated mean target output-ratio of inefficient firms from the preceding analysis is .0097, considerably higher than the 0.0075 mean of the efficient schools. So the simple comparison described above based on mean observed output-ratios of efficient and inefficient schools captures only about 27% of the effect as estimated by the proposed approach. But it points in the same direction and leads to the same qualitative conclusions with regard to output specific efficiencies and their likely deviation from radial efficiency scores on average. The real downside of the simple comparison is that it does not yield quantitative results for these output specific efficiencies because it does not translate in DMU specific measures for expected target output-ratios.

7. Conclusions from the application

It is interesting to see, that, based on this new type of methodology to investigate the two most important aspects of education, quantity and quality, the often claimed difference amongst schools in quality terms is by far less important than the difference in quantity terms. For this study I used average scores per pupil at A-level exams (the final exams of secondary schooling) as quality indicator and the ratio of candidates for these A-level exams to total pupils over all grades as quantity indicator. The only input considered here is tuition. Based on this specification it is shown that private secondary schools in the UK do pretty well (with little variability) in quality respects achieving on average 89% of what the best schools did achieve. But they performed rather poor (with high variability) with regard to quantity for which the corresponding figure is as low as 59%. As regards the ranking published in the Financial Times (the FT-1000 league table) the present application comes up with a completely different picture of where particular schools should be ranked.

On the other hand the often expressed idea that a school could either provide a high quantity or a high quality of A-level graduates seems misleading judged by the evidence from the presented analysis in a double sense: First I find that individual schools abilities to cope with these issues are strongly positively correlated. So schools basically either provide good quality graduates and also a high quantity of them or they perform bad in both these respects. It should be stressed that this does not contradict the main finding, that these basic abilities are obviously very differently developed and distributed. Secondly, because of the low average inefficiency of schools stated above, there seems to exist a lot of room for performance improvement and accordingly increasing education quantity could go a long way before it started to adversely affect education quality.

I also related the above efficiency results to certain school characteristics. With regard to religious orientation for example I find that non-denominational schools perform better than any other subgroup (including Church of England schools and Catholic Schools) with respect to both output categories, a finding which contrasts with the wisdom often expressed in the present UK secondary schooling debate. Also the revealed difference between boy and girl schools is interesting: I find evidence that boy schools are on average more efficiently managed when it comes to quantity than girl schools (while the difference in quality respect is comparably negligible). As my quantity variable could be interpreted as the reciprocal of a schools selectivity (driving pupils out of the curriculum before they become candidates to the final exams), this finding indicates much higher selectivity in girl schools than in boy schools. Finally I also find better performance in quality and quantity respects of large schools (with more than 400 pupils) than of small schools (less than 400), but again the big difference occurs in the quantity dimension, whereas in terms of graduates quality it is rather small.

The information about school performance that is regularly available to parents and pupils from league tables like the one published regularly by the Financial Times, is fairly limited. Looking additionally at the different dimensions of school performance as shown here (by using exactly the data which are published along with the FT-1000 league tables), parents and pupils can get a much more accurate picture of how any individual school may be giving value for money. While the present comparative analysis is restricted to private schools, a similar data analysis for State Sector Secondary schools could be illuminating. As can be verified from comparing the output-specific efficiencies with standard radial efficiency scores for specific schools listed in Table 9.7, the very ability to distinguish efficiencies on a per output basis does allow for much more informative rankings than are available from traditional efficiency estimation techniques.

Chapter 10

CONCLUDING REMARKS

1. Summary

The presented work provides a framework for estimating output-specific efficiencies, first simulation evidence about the performance of the corresponding estimators for a variety of settings and a first application highlighting the potential of this approach to reveal differences which otherwise would remain undetected. The presented approach should be considered as an extension of Data Envelopment Analysis (DEA), a widely used and thoroughly investigated efficiency frontier estimation technique. The proposed approach allows to address the question of systematic efficiency differences in a statistical sense across output categories, which can not be tackled by DEA itself. On the other hand it relies in fundamental ways on DEA capabilities of generating valuable information about technological possibilities (best practice) and about posterior feasible values of the unknown target output-ratios from the sample observations of input and output quantities.

In the introduction it has been argued, that it can be of considerable practical interest to learn about systematic efficiency differences in producing various output categories (as the application proves), because efforts to improve economic performance are costly. Thus these efforts should be directed towards products which promise the highest benefits in terms of efficiency improvements. Consider for example the medical care system as target of an efficiency analysis, with hospitals as the decision making units (DMU's) to be compared. If it turns out that intensive care (being one output) is provided with average efficiency of 0.98 across all hospitals and regular care (being another output) with average efficiency of 0.70, public authorities would not want to devote their resources in search of structural improvement potentials for intensive care, as the potential gains there are negligible.

The key elements in studying output-specific efficiencies are identified as target output-ratios. Once input and output quantities of a DMU are observed and given knowledge about the available technology, I measure output-specific efficiencies as related to these target output-ratios, which uniquely determine one amongst numerous best technological possibilities in a multi-output world. If the notion of output specific efficiencies is to have a meaning beyond an arbitrary comparison of observed and technologically feasible outputs, these efficiencies must be evaluated relative to this one point, as determined by the target output-ratios of that DMU.

It is noteworthy that in this conceptual framework eventually formulated target outputs of DMU's may be inefficient in the first place and that this does not invalidate the approach, because it is not based on absolute targets, but quantity ratios thereof. This is a valuable modelling feature from a principal-agent perspective, because agents may choose lower targets than would be efficient, as they are easier to reach. This argument also applies to infeasible target output quantities, although it appears hard to find an economic rationale for such behavior apart from lacking knowledge about technological possibilities. Furthermore the target output-ratio idea also has an appealing dual interpretation in price space: Assuming a prior distribution on target output-ratios implies a distribution of DMU-specific relevant price-ratios, which captures the spirit of market power in a very general sense. Furthermore working with target output-ratios (rather than target outputs) enables a formulation of the data generation process where the distribution of DMU's targets (the output-ratios) and of output-specific efficiencies are a priori independent.

The proposed estimation technique in practice will be based on a separately estimated technology. It is shown how DEA can serve this preparatory role of providing a flexible and consistent frontier estimate for later output specific efficiency estimation. To correct for the inherent bias of DEA the use of a bootstrapping enhanced version of DEA is proposed. But the latter needs to be carefully adapted to the case of output-specific efficiencies for consistency to hold. A simple proposal for such an adaptation is given.

Looking at radial DEA efficiency scores raises interesting questions with regard to the relation to output-specific efficiencies. In particular whether it is possible to infer from observable radial efficiencies conditioned on observed output ratios to unobserved output-specific efficiencies. If so then one could for example, along the lines of other two-step procedures, which subject the DEA estimated efficiency scores to additional analysis, regress these radial scores on the observed output-ratios. If systematic output specific efficiency differences indeed characterize the sample observations, one may find this reflected in significantly different coefficients of the corresponding regression equation. In Chapter 3 this issue is investigated based on the conjecture, that for certain statistical structures the output-specific efficiency distributions may be nothing but the limits of the output-dependent radial efficiency distributions as the relevant output-ratio approaches 1. While for the case of independent and perfectly correlated output-specific efficiencies this may hold indeed, a potential generalization of this finding is rejected after analysis of a counterexample.

To estimate output-specific efficiencies data-augmented Markov Chain Monte Carlo (MC^2) analysis in a Bayesian setup is proposed, a technique which has been widely applied in other areas so detailed consideration was only given with respect to the specifics of the present purpose. Treating the output-ratios as unobserved variables enables consistent estimation of the parameters of the assumed parametric distributions of target output-ratios and output-specific efficiencies. Due to the involved structure of the associated likelihood function of this model and the necessary permanent recourse to non-functional representations of the underlying technology MC^2 appears as particularly suitable estimation technique here. Specific features of the estimation setup include a discrete but arbitrarily large set of possible target output-ratios and a data generating process formulated in terms of logit transformed efficiencies. Both of these features are shown to greatly facilitate the necessary sampling process.

Discussing the potential of parameter identification from a likelihood perspective a basic tradeoff is noted: By increasing the mean target ratio of some specific output to total output, lowering the mean efficiency in producing this specific output and increasing the mean efficiencies in producing the other outputs appropriately the expected value of any particular output observation will remain unchanged. So for identification of the involved mean parameters, the focal point of the present work, the assumed distributions are of crucial importance. Without any prior specification of these distributions (which would clearly be more in the spirit of DEA) output specific efficiencies can simply not be estimated unless alternative assumptions enter the stage. Given the framework of parametric distributions it is then explained how a sample of observations on the posterior feasible domains of output-ratios and output-specific efficiencies principally drives the identification process.

To get a rough idea of potential estimation problems the likelihood surfaces arising from this model for various parameter combinations based on a Monte Carlo data set are analyzed in section 3 of Chapter 6. It is shown that these surfaces are generally non-regular with little similarity to the usually desired bump-shapes. This is interpreted as warning about potentially bad convergence of the estimation process towards the true posterior distribution and makes the search for better parameterizations and/or scalings of the underlying distributions worthwhile. Only one such reparameterization is actually found. It leads to a more regularly shaped likelihood surface with respect to the two involved parameters and is shown to be suited for application of prior restrictions on parameter domains arising from the data. From the perspective of the correlation parameter of the output-specific efficiency distribution the likelihood surface appears extremely flat giving little hope for a reasonably accurate correlation estimator. Variance components of the model in general seem to play ambiguous roles.

It is proposed to base the data generating process on logit-transformed efficiencies, because this allows for a straightforward and very general account of possible covariance structures. After all I have no experience to date with correlations amongst the efficiencies of various lines of production because no techniques to estimate them were available so far. On the other hand it is unlikely that we will ever be able to come up with a generally valid theory for such correlations as the organization of multi-output production varies from firm to firm. So presumably it will be necessary to estimate such correlations on a case by case basis. An additional benefit from the logit-transformation will be shown to be an easily tractable conjugate structure with regard to the parameters of the efficiency distribution. This facilitates the necessary sampling, a key consideration in any MC^2 application, significantly.

With regard to the distribution of target output-ratios this sampling issue is addressed by restricting the feasible set of such output-ratios to a finite grid of points. This enables direct sampling from the posterior distribution of target output-ratios even when a conjugate prior distribution for the involved density parameters is missing, a likely case to arise in practice. It is argued that the restriction to a finite grid of feasible output-ratios is actually rather soft given the fact, that this grid may be chosen arbitrarily fine. Working instead with continuous target output-ratios is basically possible but the convergence properties of such an approach are less clearly understood, while geometric convergence was proven elsewhere for discrete variables.

Evidence from large scale Monte Carlo simulations about the performance of the proposed approach is finally presented, as this is the only way to assess the practical usefulness of the presented approach, while consistency per se is of little practical use. The samples generated for these simulations are all from a two output technology with different degrees of transformation elasticity ranging from full substitutability (between outputs!) to a Leontief type of technology. When starting this work I conjectured for several reasons that output-specific efficiency estimation would be easier for highly curved (low substitutability) technologies. Validity of this conjecture is investigated by varying the degree of substitutability.

To get an idea about convergence of the approach sample sizes between 30 and 300 are generated for the simulations. As is argued these sample sizes are meant to cover typical ranges of sample information arising in applied efficiency analysis relative to the dimensionality of the respective problems. The mean efficiencies of the two lines of production were chosen with 70% and 93% respectively. Clearly the capability of the proposed approach to estimate eventual differences in such means is positively related to the size of this difference: Less distinct mean efficiencies for different lines of production will in general be harder to estimate but also give less reason for output-specific efficiency estimation in the first place. In this sense the chosen difference may be considered large enough to justify this tedious sort of estimation and small enough to make this task non-trivial.

The results for the estimators of mean output-specific efficiencies are of primary interest, as they essentially tell the story of systematic efficiency differences across various lines of production. The general finding in this respect is significant bias in statistical terms but nevertheless very useful figures for applied work. Bias in the worst cases is roughly 10% of target values coming down to approximately 4% with larger samples. Taking into account the observed variability of the estimators we may safely conclude a great potential of the proposed technique to identify more and less efficient lines of production reliably. This holds for all but the full substitutability cases with very small samples.

A comparison with simulation results based on a known (rather than DEA estimated) technology in section 3 of Chapter 8 allows to attribute roughly two thirds of the observed bias to the DEA-step involved, while estimator variance is of similar magnitude in both scenarios. So the estimation problems are not confined to the empirically relevant case of an unknown frontier but show up as well in the apparently much simpler case of a known frontier.

The performance of the estimators for the two output-specific variance components of the efficiency distribution are less satisfying, an outcome already suspected when analyzing the likelihood surfaces. But again: For most applied purposes the result indicate usefulness of the approach also with respect to variance estimation. The influence of the substitution elasticity of the underlying model on the quality of the results now is of reverse sign compared to the mean estimators.

The results for the correlation estimator are little more than frustrating. Obviously it is extremely difficult to identify any underlying correlation amongst efficiencies. In comparison with standard efficiency estimates particularly one result is of interest: For the smaller sample sizes this estimator of correlation is consistently biased towards 1 (perfect correlation). So we should not expect results from MC^2-estimation to be much different from the simple type of regression analysis discussed above for smaller sample sizes. Furthermore this finding does not allow to confidently reject the perfect correlation hypothesis (on which standard radial DEA efficiency scores are based) even if it is as far from the truth as in our setting.

The observed convergence of the estimators in general is slow which is definitely owed to the poor convergence rates of the underlying frontier estimation technique DEA. Convergence also is sometimes nonmonotone, a fact which can be attributed to the bias correction used in deriving the DEA estimates. Without such bias correction this result would be rather surprising as DEA yields gradually and monotonically improving frontier estimates for increasing sample size. The latter feature of DEA of course does not necessarily hold with bias correction.

To show the potential of the proposed approach it was applied to a data set describing characteristics of 237 UK private secondary schools. The idea was to estimate the efficiency from a parental perspective, using tuition as single input and quality resp. quantity of graduates as output variables. This 1-input, 2-output model conforms on one hand to the setting analyzed in the preceding Monte-Carlo simulations and on the other hand nicely reflects the ongoing debate in the UK about the inevitable respectively desired tradeoff between quality and quantity of secondary education.

Along with illustrating basic implementation issues, this application also indicated the versatility of the proposed approach, because it was based on different parameterizations and different prior assumptions about the distributions of the involved random variables and involved a more general type of updating procedure than was used in the simulation setting. The application was also considered as proper place to take a closer look at serial dependence amongst estimates and convergence issues from an applied viewpoint. This included the calculation of corresponding test statistics to check for convergence and a thinning of the original Markov Chains based on sample autocorrelation coefficients to come up with an as-if iid sample.

The results from output-specific efficiency estimation for these schools give a striking example of the usefulness of the approach: It turns out that average performance of these schools as regards the provision quality of graduates is much higher (89%) than there average performance with regard to quantity of graduates (59%), while the average radial efficiency score for this dataset is 77%. These results highlight the practical relevance of the issues raised in the introduction to this book: That we may find systematic efficiency differences across outputs which would go undetected by radial efficiency measures and that these differences may be worthwhile (large enough) to be evaluated.

Furthermore the results for UK schools are in line with the common perception of private schools as being specialized in providing quality (the deviations of individual schools from the best possibilities are small in magnitude and variability) while they have no particularly good reputation in providing education quantity (with deviations being large in both respects). On the other hand it is found that the correlation coefficient between the two output-specific efficiencies is as high as 0.66, indicating that schools by and large are either performing efficiently in both respects (quantity and quality) or in neither of them (given the above qualifications about the likely quality of the correlation estimate). Based on this figure, one should therefore reject the hypotheses, that, in a school managements perspective, providing higher quantity necessarily goes along with lower quality, as has sometimes been claimed in the debate.

2. Routes for future research

The present work is a first attempt to deal with the statistical problem of output-specific efficiencies and accordingly offers a lot of improvement potentials. As illustrated in this book with a stylized example and in the application, one of the very promising routes for further research is to check alternative parameterizations leading to more regular types of likelihood surfaces. Alternative parameterizations could also take into account the extremely unbalanced variances amongst the variates, a deficiency found to lead to poor estimators of some parameters.

Another route is the search for alternative sampling strategies like collapsed sampling (used in the above simulations for a single set of variables already) or block-updating (used in the application), which may generally be better suited to the present type of problem. As is well investigated in the MC^2 literature such strategies might help to overcome slow mixing, for example in cases where parameters are highly correlated a posteriori. This, as has been discussed, is the case here in particular for means of output-specific efficiencies on one hand and means of target output-ratios on the other.

One might also consider different prior parameter distributions. The ones underlying the present Monte Carlo simulations were non-informative to the largest conceivable degree, while in practice available data might tell more about them then can be assumed in general. Vague information about the range of observed price ratios for example would already justify the use of a much more informed type of target output-ratio distribution. The general role of possible domain restrictions in this respect was discussed on several occasions in the text.

As has been indicated, there are no principle obstacles to extending the presented ideas to multi-output cases. But early simulation results for settings with more than two-outputs clearly indicate the need for a better understanding of how to improve estimator convergence for this general type of problems. Only if these efforts have led to better convergence in the 2-output case does it seem worthwhile from a practical viewpoint to contemplate on specific adaptations of the sampling strategy, distributional parameterizations and related matters for settings with more than 2 outputs.

Another issue for future research might be an adaptation of the sampling algorithm to the case of continuous target output-ratios. This was not attempted in the present book for time considerations. But with ever increasing computing power it should be possible to do large scale simulations also for this case.

To implement size dependent target output ratios into the parameterization of the estimation model seems particularly worth further investigations. The present books limitation to size-independent target output-ratio distributions was, like the restriction to the 2-output case, primarily owed to the convergence problems found for the simpler settings. So with improved sampling strategies this limitation might become superfluous, although the introduction of size-dependent target output-ratio distributions will necessitate to raise the identification question anew.

In the light of such not yet exploited improvement and extension possibilities the presented results about the performance of the estimator for output specific efficiencies should be considered as a very cautious guess about the future prospects of the technique as such. Nevertheless the early simulation results contained in this book and the application to a real world data set already indicate the huge potential of the approach along with some potential pitfalls lurking on the way to output specific efficiency estimates. Overall it seems clear that the data usually available to the analyst contain more information about systematic efficiency differences across lines of production than hitherto has been used for efficiency evaluation. And given the rapid integration of other theoretical developments in this field (already including resampling techniques like bootstrapping) into commercial efficiency evaluation packages, we may be able to find output-specific efficiencies at a mouse click rather soon.

References

Aigner, D., Lovell, C., and Schmidt, P. (1977). Formulation and estimation of frontier production function models. *Journal of Econometrics*, 6:21–37.

Ali, A. I. and Seiford, L. M. (1990). Translation invariance in Data Envelopment Analysis. *Operations Research Letters*, 9(5):403–405.

Ali, A. I. and Seiford, L. M. (1993). The mathematical programming approach to efficiency analysis. In Fried, H. O., Lovell, C., and Schmidt, S. S., editors, *The Measurement of Productive Efficiency*, pages 120–159. Oxford University Press, Oxford.

Authella M. Bessent, E. Wailand Bessent, J. E. and Long, D. (1984). Educational productivity council employs management science methods to improve educational quality. *Interfaces*, 14(6):1–8.

Authella M. Bessent, E. Wailand Bessent, J. K. and Reagan, B. (1982). An application of mathematical programming to assess productivity in the Houston independent school district. *Management Science*, 28(12):1355–1367.

Banker, R. D. (1993). Maximum likelihood, consistency and Data Envelopment Analysis. *Management Science*, 39(10):1265–1273.

Banker, R. D., Charnes, A., and Cooper, W. (1984). Some models for estimating technical and scale efficiencies in Data Envelopment Analysis. *Management Science*, 30(9):1078–1092.

Banker, R. D. and Maindiratta, A. (1988). Nonparametric analysis of technical and allocative efficiencies in production. *Econometrica*, 56(6):1315–1332.

Beattie, B. R. and Taylor, C. R. (1985). *The Economics of Production*. John Wiley & Sons, Inc., New York.

Beck, M. (1991). Empirical applications of frontier functions. A bibliography. Unpublished manuscript, Bundesamt fuer Statistik, Wiesbaden, Germany.

Behrman, J. R. and Birdsall, N. (1983). The quality of schooling: Quantity alone is misleading. *The American Economic Review*, 73(5):928–946.

Bernardo, J. M. and Smith, A. F. (1994). *Bayesian Theory.* Wiley series in probability and mathematical statistics. John Wiley and Sons, Ltd., Chichester.

Bessent, A. M. and Bessent, E. W. (1980). Determining the comparative efficiency of schools through data envelopment analysis. *Educational Administration Quarterly*, 16(2):57–75.

Brockett, P. L., Cooper, W. W., Rosseau, J., and Wang, Y. (1998). DEA evaluations of the efficiency of organizational forms and distribution systems in the U.S. property and liability insurance industry. *International Journal of System Science*, 29:1235–1247.

Chalos, P. (1997). An examination of budgetary inefficiency in education using Data Envelopment Analysis. *Financial Accountability and Management*, 13(1):55–69.

Charnes, A., Cooper, W. W., Golany, B., Seiford, L. M., and Stutz, J. (1985). Foundations of Data Envelopment Analysis for Pareto-Koopmans efficient empirical production functions. *Journal of Econometrics*, 30(1/2):91–107.

Charnes, A., Cooper, W. W., Lewin, A. Y., and Seiford, L. M., editors (1994). *Data Envelopment Analysis: Theory, Methodology and Application.* Kluwer Academic Publishers.

Charnes, A., Cooper, W. W., and Rhodes, E. (1978). Measuring the efficiency of decision making units. *European Journal of Operational Research*, 2(6):429–444.

Charnes, A., Cooper, W. W., and Rhodes, E. (1981). Evaluating program and managerial efficiency: An application of Data Envelopment Analysis to program follow through. *Management Science*, 27(6):668–697.

Charnes, A., Cooper, W. W., Rousseau, J. J., and Semple, J. (1987). Data Envelopment Analysis and axiomatic notions of efficiency and reference sets. Research report ccs 558, University of Texas at Austin, Center for Cybernetic Studies.

Chen, M.-H., Shao, Q.-M., and Ibrahim, J. G. (2000). *Monte Carlo Methods in Bayesian Computation.* Springer Series in Statistics. Springer Verlag, New York.

Chib, S. (1995). Marginal likelihood from the Gibbs output. *Journal of the American Statistical Association*, 90(432):1313–1321.

Chib, S. and Greenberg, E. (1996). Markov chain Monte Carlo simulation methods in econometrics. *Econometric Theory*, 12:409–431.

Coelli, T. (1998). A multi-stage methodology for the solution of oriented DEA models. *Operations Research Letters*, 22:143–149.

Coelli, T. and Perelman, S. (1996). A comparison of parametric and non-parametric distance functions: With application to european railways. CREPP Discussion Paper 96/11, University of Liege, Belgium.

Coelli, T., Rao, D. P., and Battese, G. E. (1998). *An introduction to Efficiency and Productivity Analysis.* Kluwer Academic Publishers.

Collins, A. and Snell, M. C. (2000). Parental preferences and choice of school. *Applied Economics*, 32(7):803–813.

Cooper, W. W., Seiford, L. M., and Tone, K., editors (2000). *Data Envelopment Analysis: A Comprehensive Text with Models, Applications References and DEA-solver software*. Kluwer Academic Publishers.

Cowles, M. and Carlin, B. (1996). Markov chain Monte Carlo convergence diagnostics: A comparative review. *Journal of the American Statistical Association*, 91:883–904.

Dean, C. (2001). Backlash against church schools drive. *The Times Educational Supplement, February 23*, page 3.

Debreu, G. (1951). The coefficient of ressource utilization. *Econometrica*, 19(3):273–292.

Desai, A., Ratick, S. J., and Schinnar, A. P. (1994). Data Envelopment Analysis with stochastic variations in data. Working Paper 94-51, Ohio State University, Max M. Fisher College of Business,.

Diaconis, P. and Ylvisaker, D. (1979). Conjugate priors for exponential families. *Annals of Statistics*, 7:269–281.

Dogramaci, A. and Färe, R. (1988). *Applications of Modern Production Theory: Efficiency and Productivity*. Kluwer Academic Publishers.

Efron, B. (1979). Bootstrap methods: Another look at the Jackknife. *Annals of Statistics*, 7:1–26.

Efron, B. and Tibshirani, R. J. (1993). *An Introduction to the Bootstrap*. Monographs on Statistics and Applied Probability 57. Chapman and Hall.

Engert, F. (1996). The reporting of school district efficiency: The adequacy of ratio measures. *Public Budgeting and Financial Management*, 8(2):247–271.

Färe, R. and Grosskopf, S. (1996). *Intertemporal Production Frontiers: With dynamic DEA*. Kluwer Academic Publishers.

Färe, R., Grosskopf, S., and Lovell, C. K. (1985). *The Measurement of Efficiency of Production*. Kluwer-Nijhoff Publishing.

Färe, R., Grosskopf, S., and Weber, W. L. (1989). Measuring school district performance. *Public Finance Quarterly*, 17(4):409–428.

Färe, R. and Primont, D. (1995). *Multi-Output Production and Duality: Theory and Applications*. Kluwer Academic Publishers.

Farrell, M. (1957). The measurement of productive efficiency. *Journal of the Royal Statistical Society, Series A*, 120:253–281.

Fernández, C., Koop, G., and Steel, M. F. (2000). A Bayesian analysis of multiple-output production frontiers. *Journal of Econometrics*, 98:47–79.

Fernández, C., Osiewalski, J., and Steel, M. F. (1997). On the use of pnael data in stochastic frontier models with improper priors. *Journal of Econometrics*, 79:169–193.

Ferrier, G. and Hirschberg, J. G. (1997). Bootstrapping confidence intervals for linear programming efficiency scores: With an illustration using Italian banking data. *Journal of Productivity Analysis*, 8(1):19–33.

Ferrier, G. and Hirschberg, J. G. (1999). Can we bootstrap DEA scores. *Journal of Productivity Analysis*, 11(1):81–92.

Försund, F. R. and Sarafoglou, N. (2000). On the origins of Data Envelopment Analysis. Memorandum no 24/2000, Department of Economics, University of Oslo.

Fox, K. J. and Hill, R. J. (2000). Identifying outliers in multi-output models. Technical report, School of Economics, University of New South Wales, Sydney, Australia, April 17, 2000.

Fried, H. O., Lovell, C. K., and Schmidt, S. S., editors (1993). *The Measurement of Productive Efficiency*. Oxford University Press.

Gamerman, D. (1997). *Markov chain Monte Carlo: Stochastic simulation for Bayesian inference*. Chapman & Hall, London.

Ganley, J. A. and Cubbin, J. S. (1992). *Public Sector Efficiency Measurement: Applications of Data Envelopment Analysis*. North Holland.

Gelfand, A. and Smith, S. (1990). Sampling-based approaches to calculating marginal densities. *Journal of the American Statistical Association*, 85:398–409.

Gelman, A., Roberts, G. O., and Gilks, W. R. (1995). Efficient Metropolis jumping rules. In Bernardo, J. M., Berger, J. O., Dawid, A. P., and Smith, A. F. M., editors, *Bayesian Statistics 5*. Oxford University Press, Oxford.

Gelman, A. and Rubin, D. (1992). Inference from iterative simulation using multiple sequences. *Statistical Science*, 7(4):457–511.

Geman, S. and Geman, D. (1984). Stochastic relaxation, Gibbs distributions and the Bayesian restoration of images. *IEEE Trans. Pattn. Anal. Mach. Intel.*, 6:721–741.

Geweke, J. (1992). Evaluating the accuracy of sampling-based approaches to the calculation of posterior moments. In Bernardo, J. M., Berger, J. O., Dawid, A. P., and Smith, A. F. M., editors, *Bayesian Statistics 4*, pages 169–193. Oxford University Press, Oxford.

Geyer, C. J. (1992). Practical markov chain monte carlo. *Statistical Science*, 7(4):473–511.

Geyer, C. J. and Tierney, L. (1996). Convergence of monte carlo approximations to the posterior density. In Berry, D. A., Chaloner, K. M., and Geweke, J. K., editors, *Bayesian Analysis in Statistics and Econometrics*. Wiley.

Gilks, W., Richardson, S., and Spiegelhalter, D. (1996a). Introducing Markov chain Monte Carlo. In Gilks, W., Richardson, S., and Spiegelhalter, D., editors, *Markov Chain Monte Carlo in Practice*. Chapman & Hall, London.

Gilks, W., Richardson, S., and Spiegelhalter, D. (1996b). *Markov Chain Monte Carlo in Practice*. Chapman and Hall, London.

Green, P. J. (1999). A primer on Markov Chain Monte Carlo. To be found at `http://www.stats.bris.ac.uk/~peter/papers/semstat2.ps`, University of Bristol, Department of Statistics.

Grosskopf, S. (1996). Statistical inference and nonparametric efficiency: A selective survey. *Journal of Productivity Analysis*, 7(2/3):161–176.

Grosskopf, S. and Hayes, K. J. (1993). Local public sector bureaucrats and their input choices. *Journal of Urban Economics*, 33:151–166.

Gstach, D. (1995). Comparing structural efficiency of unbalanced subsamples: A resampling adaptation of Data Envelopment Analysis. *Empirical Economics*, 20:531–542.

Gstach, D. (1998). Another approach to Data Envelopment Analysis in noisy environments: DEA+. *Journal of Productivity Analysis*, 9:161–176.

Gstach, D. (1999a). Recent advances in efficiency estimation. In Dahiya, S. B., editor, *The Current State of Economic Science, Vol. 2*, pages 827–844. Spellbound Publications, Rohtak, India.

Gstach, D. (1999b). Technical efficiency in noisy multi-output settings. *Central European Journal of Operations Research*, 7(2):827–844.

Halme, M., Joro, T., Korhonen, P., Salo, S., and Wallenius, J. (1999). Value efficiency analysis for incorporating preference informationin Data Envelopment Analysis. *Management Science*, 45(1):103–115.

Hanushek, E. A. (1986). The economics of schooling: Production and efficiency in public schools. *Journal of Economic Literature*, 24(3):1141–1177.

Johnson, M. E. (1987). *Multivariate Statistical Simulation.* Wiley series in probability and statistics. John Wiley and Sons, Chichester.

Kneip, A., Park, B. U., and Simar, L. (1998). A note on the convergence of nonparametric DEA estimators for production efficiency scores. *Econometric Theory*, 14:783–793.

Kneip, A. and Simar, L. (1996). A general framework for frontier estimation with panel data. *Journal of Productivity Analysis*, 7(2/3):187–212.

Koop, G., Osiewalski, J., and Steel, M. F. (1994). Bayesian efficiency analysis with a flexible cost function. *Journal of Business and Economic Statistics*, 12:93–106.

Koop, G., Osiewalski, J., and Steel, M. F. (1997). Bayesian efficiency analysis through individual effects. *Journal of Econometrics*, 76:77–105.

Koop, G., Steel, M. F., and Osiewalski, J. (1995). Posterior analysis of stochastic frontier models using Gibbs sampling. *Computational Statistics*, 10:353–373.

Koopmans, T. (1951). *Activity Analysis of Production and Allocation.* John Wiley and Sons, New York.

Korostelev, A., Simar, L., and Tsybakov, A. (1995a). Efficient estimation of monotone boundaries. *The Annals of Statistics*, 23:476–489.

Korostelev, A., Simar, L., and Tsybakov, A. (1995b). On the estimation of monotone and convex boundaries. *Publications de l'Institut de Statistique de l'Université de Paris*, 39(1):3–18.

Kumbhakar, S. C. (1996). Efficiency measurement with multiple outputs and multiple inputs. *Journal of Productivity Analysis*, 7(2/3):225–255.

Kumbhakar, S. C. and Lovell, C. A. K. (2000). *Stochastic Frontier Analysis*. Cambridge University Press.

Kurkalova, L. A. and Carriquiry, A. (2000). Bayesian estimation of technical efficiency of a single input. Discussion paper, Center for Agricultural and Rural Development, Iowa State University.

Land, K., Lovell, C., and Thore, S. (1993). Chance constrained Data Envelopment Analysis. *Managerial and Decision Economics*, 14(6):541–554.

Leibenstein, H. (1966). Allocative efficiency vs. *x-efficiency. American Economic Review*, 56(3):392–415.

Liu, J. (1994). The collapsed Gibbs sampler in Bayesian computations with applications to a gene regulation problem. *Journal of the American Statistical Association*, 89:958–966.

Löthgren, M. (1997). Generalized stochastic frontier production models. *Economics Letters*, 57:255–259.

Lovell, C. A. K., Walters, L. C., and Wood, L. L. (1994). Stratified models of education production using modified DEA and regression analysis. In Abraham Charnes, William W. Cooper, A. Y. L. and Seiford, L., editors, *Data Envelopment Analysis: Theory, Methodology, and Application*, pages 329–351. Kluwer Academic Publishers, Boston/Dordrecht/London.

Lovell, C. K. and Pastor, J. T. (1997). Target setting: An application to a bank branch network. *European Journal of Operational Research*, 98(2):290–299.

Mancebon, M. and Moliero, C. M. (2000). Performance in primary schools. *Journal of the Operational Research Society*, 51(7):843–854.

Mayston, D. and Jesson, D. (1988). Developing models of educational accountability. *Oxford Review of Education*, 14(3):321–339.

McCarthy, T. A. and Yaisawarng, S. (1993). Technical efficiency in new jersey school districts. In Fried, H. O., Lovell, C. A. K., and Schmidt, S. S., editors, *The Measurement of Productive Efficiency, Techniques and Applications*, pages 271–287. Oxford University Press, New York, Oxford.

Meeusen, W. and van den Broeck, J. (1977). Efficiency estimation from Cobb-Douglas production functions with composed error. *International Economic Review*, 18:435–444.

Mengersen, K. and Tweedie, R. (1993). Rates of convergence of the Hastings and Metropolis algorithms. Unpublished manuscript, Colorado State University.

Meyn, S. and Tweedie, R. (1993). *Markov Chains and Stochastic Stability.* Springer-Verlag, New York.

Mincer, J. (1974). Schooling, experience and earnings. *Applied Economics.*

Mood, A. M., Graybill, F. A., and Boes, D. C. (1974). *Introduction to the Theory of Statistics.* McGraw-Hill Series in Probability and Statistics. McGraw-Hill, New York.

Noulas, A. G. and Ketkar, K. W. (1998). Efficient utilization of resources in public schools: a case study of new jersey. *Applied Economics*, 30(10):1299–1306.

Olesen, O. B. and Petersen, N. C. (1989). Chance-constrained efficiency evaluation. Working Paper 9, Odense University, Department of Management.

Pareto, V. (1971). *Manual of Political Economy.* Macmillan, London. Translated by Ann S. Schwier from French edition of 1927, edited by Ann S. Schwier and Alfred N. Page.

Pastor, J. T. (1996). Translation invariance in DEA: A generalization. *Annals of Operations Research*, 66:93–102.

Raftery, A. E. and Lewis, S. M. (1996). Implementing MCMC. In Gilks, W., Richardson, S., and Spiegelhalter, D., editors, *Markov Chain Monte Carlo in Practice.* Chapman & Hall, London.

Ray, S. C. and Mukherjee, K. (1998). Quantity, quality, and efficiency for a partially super-additive cost function: Connecticut public schools revisited. *Journal of Productivity Analysis*, 10(1):47–62.

Read, L. E. and Thanassoulis, E. (1996). A comparison of Data Envelopment Analysis (DEA) and Stochastic Frontiers (SF) under variation of fit. Research paper no. 234, Warwick Business School, UK.

Reinhard, S., Lovell, C., and Thijssen, G. (1999). Econometric estimation of technical and environmental efficiency: An application to Dutch dairy farms. *American Journal of Agricultural Economics*, 81:44–60.

Robert, C. P. (1994). *The Bayesian Choice. A Decision-Theoretic Motivation.* Springer Texts in Statistics. Springer, New York.

Roberts, G. O., Gelman, A., and Gilks, W. R. (1994). Weak convergence and the optimal scaling of random walk Metropolis algorithms. Research Report 94/16, Statistical Laboratory, University of Cambridge, UK.

Roberts, G. O. and Tweedie, R. L. (1994). Geometric convergence and central limit theorems for multidimensional Hastings and Metropolis algorithms. Research Report 94/9, Statistical Laboratory, University of Cambridge, UK.

Ruggiero, J. (1999). Nonparametric analysis of educational costs. *European Journal of Operational Research*, 119(3):605–612.

Ruggiero, J. and Vitalino, D. F. (1999). Assessing the efficiency of public schools using Data Envelopment Analysis and frontier regression. *Contemporary Economic Policy*, 17(3):321–331.

Seiford, L. M. (1994). A DEA bibliography (1978-1992). In Charnes, A., Cooper, W., Lewin, A. Y., and Seiford, L., editors, *Data Envelopment Analysis. Theory, Methodology and Applications*, pages 437–470. Kluwer Academic Publishers.

Sengupta, J. K. (1987). Data Envelopment Analysis for efficiency measurement in the stochastic case. *Computers and Operations Research*, 14(2):117–129.

Sengupta, J. K. (1989). *Efficiency Analysis by Production Frontiers. The Nonparametric Approach.* Kluwer Academic Publishers.

Sengupta, J. K. (1995). *Dynamics of Data Envelopment Analysis. Theory of Systems Efficiency.* Kluwer Academic Publishers.

Simar, L. (1996). Aspects of statistical analysis in DEA-type frontier models. *Journal of Productivity Analysis*, 7(2/3):177–186.

Simar, L. and Wilson, P. W. (1995). Sensitivity analysis of efficiency scores: How to boostrap in nonparametric frontier models. Discussion paper 9543, CORE, Belgium.

Tanner, M. and Wong, W. (1987). The calculation of posterior distributions by data augmentation. *J. Am. Statist. Ass.*, 82:528–550.

Thanassoulis, E. (1996a). Altering the bias in differential school effectiveness using Data Envelopment Analysis. *Journal of the Operational Research Society*, 47(7):882–894.

Thanassoulis, E. (1996b). Assessing the effectiveness of schools with pupils of different ability using Data Envelopment Analysis. *Journal of the Operational Research Society*, 47(1):84–97.

Thanassoulis, E. (1999). Setting achievement targets for school children. *Education Economics*, 7(2):101–119.

Thanassoulis, E. and Dunstan, P. (1994). Guiding schools to improved performance using Data Envelopment Analysis: An illustration with data from local education authority. *Journal of the Operational Research Society*, 45(11):1247–1262.

Tierney, L. (1994). Markov chains for exploring posterior distributions. *The Annals of Statistics*, 22:1701–1762.

Tone, K. (2001). A slacks-based measure of efficiency in Data Envelopment Analysis. *European Journal of Operational Research*, 130(3):498–509.

van den Broeck, J., Koop, G., Osiewalski, J., and Steel, M. F. (1997). Stochastic frontier models: A Bayesian perspective. *Journal of Econometrics*, 76:77–105.

Wenger, J. W. (2000). What do schools produce? implications of multiple outputs in education. *Contemporary Economic Policy*, 18(1):27–36.

Wilson, P. W. (1994). A bootstrap methodology for nonparametric efficiency estimates. Paper presented at the inaugural productivity workshop, University of Georgia, Athens.

Xue, M. and Harker, P. T. (1999). Overcoming the inherent dependency of DEA efficiency scores: A bootstrap approach. Manuscript, University of Pennsylvania.

Applied Optimization

1. D.-Z. Du and D.F. Hsu (eds.): *Combinatorial Network Theory.* 1996 ISBN 0-7923-3777-8
2. M.J. Panik: *Linear Programming: Mathematics, Theory and Algorithms.* 1996 ISBN 0-7923-3782-4
3. R.B. Kearfott and V. Kreinovich (eds.): *Applications of Interval Computations.* 1996 ISBN 0-7923-3847-2
4. N. Hritonenko and Y. Yatsenko: *Modeling and Optimimization of the Lifetime of Technology.* 1996 ISBN 0-7923-4014-0
5. T. Terlaky (ed.): *Interior Point Methods of Mathematical Programming.* 1996 ISBN 0-7923-4201-1
6. B. Jansen: *Interior Point Techniques in Optimization.* Complementarity, Sensitivity and Algorithms. 1997 ISBN 0-7923-4430-8
7. A. Migdalas, P.M. Pardalos and S. Storøy (eds.): *Parallel Computing in Optimization.* 1997 ISBN 0-7923-4583-5
8. F.A. Lootsma: *Fuzzy Logic for Planning and Decision Making.* 1997 ISBN 0-7923-4681-5
9. J.A. dos Santos Gromicho: *Quasiconvex Optimization and Location Theory.* 1998 ISBN 0-7923-4694-7
10. V. Kreinovich, A. Lakeyev, J. Rohn and P. Kahl: *Computational Complexity and Feasibility of Data Processing and Interval Computations.* 1998 ISBN 0-7923-4865-6
11. J. Gil-Aluja: *The Interactive Management of Human Resources in Uncertainty.* 1998 ISBN 0-7923-4886-9
12. C. Zopounidis and A.I. Dimitras: *Multicriteria Decision Aid Methods for the Prediction of Business Failure.* 1998 ISBN 0-7923-4900-8
13. F. Giannessi, S. Komlósi and T. Rapcsák (eds.): *New Trends in Mathematical Programming.* Homage to Steven Vajda. 1998 ISBN 0-7923-5036-7
14. Ya-xiang Yuan (ed.): *Advances in Nonlinear Programming.* Proceedings of the '96 International Conference on Nonlinear Programming. 1998 ISBN 0-7923-5053-7
15. W.W. Hager and P.M. Pardalos: *Optimal Control.* Theory, Algorithms, and Applications. 1998 ISBN 0-7923-5067-7
16. Gang Yu (ed.): *Industrial Applications of Combinatorial Optimization.* 1998 ISBN 0-7923-5073-1
17. D. Braha and O. Maimon (eds.): *A Mathematical Theory of Design: Foundations, Algorithms and Applications.* 1998 ISBN 0-7923-5079-0

Applied Optimization

18. O. Maimon, E. Khmelnitsky and K. Kogan: *Optimal Flow Control in Manufacturing.* Production Planning and Scheduling. 1998 ISBN 0-7923-5106-1
19. C. Zopounidis and P.M. Pardalos (eds.): *Managing in Uncertainty: Theory and Practice.* 1998 ISBN 0-7923-5110-X
20. A.S. Belenky: *Operations Research in Transportation Systems:* Ideas and Schemes of Optimization Methods for Strategic Planning and Operations Management. 1998 ISBN 0-7923-5157-6
21. J. Gil-Aluja: *Investment in Uncertainty.* 1999 ISBN 0-7923-5296-3
22. M. Fukushima and L. Qi (eds.): *Reformulation: Nonsmooth, Piecewise Smooth, Semismooth and Smooting Methods.* 1999 ISBN 0-7923-5320-X
23. M. Patriksson: *Nonlinear Programming and Variational Inequality Problems.* A Unified Approach. 1999 ISBN 0-7923-5455-9
24. R. De Leone, A. Murli, P.M. Pardalos and G. Toraldo (eds.): *High Performance Algorithms and Software in Nonlinear Optimization.* 1999 ISBN 0-7923-5483-4
25. A. Schöbel: *Locating Lines and Hyperplanes.* Theory and Algorithms. 1999 ISBN 0-7923-5559-8
26. R.B. Statnikov: *Multicriteria Design.* Optimization and Identification. 1999 ISBN 0-7923-5560-1
27. V. Tsurkov and A. Mironov: *Minimax under Transportation Constrains.* 1999 ISBN 0-7923-5609-8
28. V.I. Ivanov: *Model Development and Optimization.* 1999 ISBN 0-7923-5610-1
29. F.A. Lootsma: *Multi-Criteria Decision Analysis via Ratio and Difference Judgement.* 1999 ISBN 0-7923-5669-1
30. A. Eberhard, R. Hill, D. Ralph and B.M. Glover (eds.): *Progress in Optimization.* Contributions from Australasia. 1999 ISBN 0-7923-5733-7
31. T. Hürlimann: *Mathematical Modeling and Optimization.* An Essay for the Design of Computer-Based Modeling Tools. 1999 ISBN 0-7923-5927-5
32. J. Gil-Aluja: *Elements for a Theory of Decision in Uncertainty.* 1999 ISBN 0-7923-5987-9
33. H. Frenk, K. Roos, T. Terlaky and S. Zhang (eds.): *High Performance Optimization.* 1999 ISBN 0-7923-6013-3
34. N. Hritonenko and Y. Yatsenko: *Mathematical Modeling in Economics, Ecology and the Environment.* 1999 ISBN 0-7923-6015-X
35. J. Virant: *Design Considerations of Time in Fuzzy Systems.* 2000 ISBN 0-7923-6100-8

Applied Optimization

36. G. Di Pillo and F. Giannessi (eds.): *Nonlinear Optimization and Related Topics.* 2000 ISBN 0-7923-6109-1
37. V. Tsurkov: *Hierarchical Optimization and Mathematical Physics.* 2000 ISBN 0-7923-6175-X
38. C. Zopounidis and M. Doumpos: *Intelligent Decision Aiding Systems Based on Multiple Criteria for Financial Engineering.* 2000 ISBN 0-7923-6273-X
39. X. Yang, A.I. Mees, M. Fisher and L.Jennings (eds.): *Progress in Optimization.* Contributions from Australasia. 2000 ISBN 0-7923-6286-1
40. D. Butnariu and A.N. Iusem: *Totally Convex Functions for Fixed Points Computation and Infinite Dimensional Optimization.* 2000 ISBN 0-7923-6287-X
41. J. Mockus: *A Set of Examples of Global and Discrete Optimization.* Applications of Bayesian Heuristic Approach. 2000 ISBN 0-7923-6359-0
42. H. Neunzert and A.H. Siddiqi: *Topics in Industrial Mathematics.* Case Studies and Related Mathematical Methods. 2000 ISBN 0-7923-6417-1
43. K. Kogan and E. Khmelnitsky: *Scheduling: Control-Based Theory and Polynomial-Time Algorithms.* 2000 ISBN 0-7923-6486-4
44. E. Triantaphyllou: *Multi-Criteria Decision Making Methods.* A Comparative Study. 2000 ISBN 0-7923-6607-7
45. S.H. Zanakis, G. Doukidis and C. Zopounidis (eds.): *Decision Making: Recent Developments and Worldwide Applications.* 2000 ISBN 0-7923-6621-2
46. G.E. Stavroulakis: *Inverse and Crack Identification Problems in Engineering Mechanics.* 2000 ISBN 0-7923-6690-5
47. A. Rubinov and B. Glover (eds.): *Optimization and Related Topics.* 2001 ISBN 0-7923-6732-4
48. M. Pursula and J. Niittymäki (eds.): *Mathematical Methods on Optimization in Transportation Systems.* 2000 ISBN 0-7923-6774-X
49. E. Cascetta: *Transportation Systems Engineering: Theory and Methods.* 2001 ISBN 0-7923-6792-8
50. M.C. Ferris, O.L. Mangasarian and J.-S. Pang (eds.): *Complementarity: Applications, Algorithms and Extensions.* 2001 ISBN 0-7923-6816-9
51. V. Tsurkov: *Large-scale Optimization – Problems and Methods.* 2001 ISBN 0-7923-6817-7
52. X. Yang, K.L. Teo and L. Caccetta (eds.): *Optimization Methods and Applications.* 2001 ISBN 0-7923-6866-5
53. S.M. Stefanov: *Separable Programming Theory and Methods.* 2001 ISBN 0-7923-6882-7

Applied Optimization

54. S.P. Uryasev and P.M. Pardalos (eds.): *Stochastic Optimization: Algorithms and Applications.* 2001 ISBN 0-7923-6951-3
55. J. Gil-Aluja (ed.): *Handbook of Management under Uncertainty.* 2001 ISBN 0-7923-7025-2
56. B.-N. Vo, A. Cantoni and K.L. Teo: *Filter Design with Time Domain Mask Constraints: Theory and Applications.* 2001 ISBN 0-7923-7138-0
57. S. Zlobec: *Stable Parametric Programming.* 2001 ISBN 0-7923-7139-9
58. M.G. Nicholls, S. Clarke and B. Lehaney (eds.): *Mixed-Mode Modelling: Mixing Methodologies for Organisational Intervention.* 2001 ISBN 0-7923-7151-8
59. F. Giannessi, P.M. Pardalos and T. Rapcsák (eds.): *Optimization Theory. Recent Developments from Mátraháza.* 2001 ISBN 1-4020-0009-X
60. K.M. Hangos, R. Lakner and M. Gerzson: *Intelligent Control Systems.* An Introduction with Examples. 2001 ISBN 1-4020-0134-7
61. D. Gstach: *Estimating Output-Specific Efficiencies.* 2002 ISBN 1-4020-0483-4

KLUWER ACADEMIC PUBLISHERS – DORDRECHT / BOSTON / LONDON

MIX
Papier aus verantwortungsvollen Quellen
Paper from responsible sources
FSC® C105338

If you have any concerns about our products,
you can contact us on
ProductSafety@springernature.com

In case Publisher is established outside the EU,
the EU authorized representative is:
Springer Nature Customer Service Center GmbH
Europaplatz 3, 69115 Heidelberg, Germany

Printed by Libri Plureos GmbH
in Hamburg, Germany